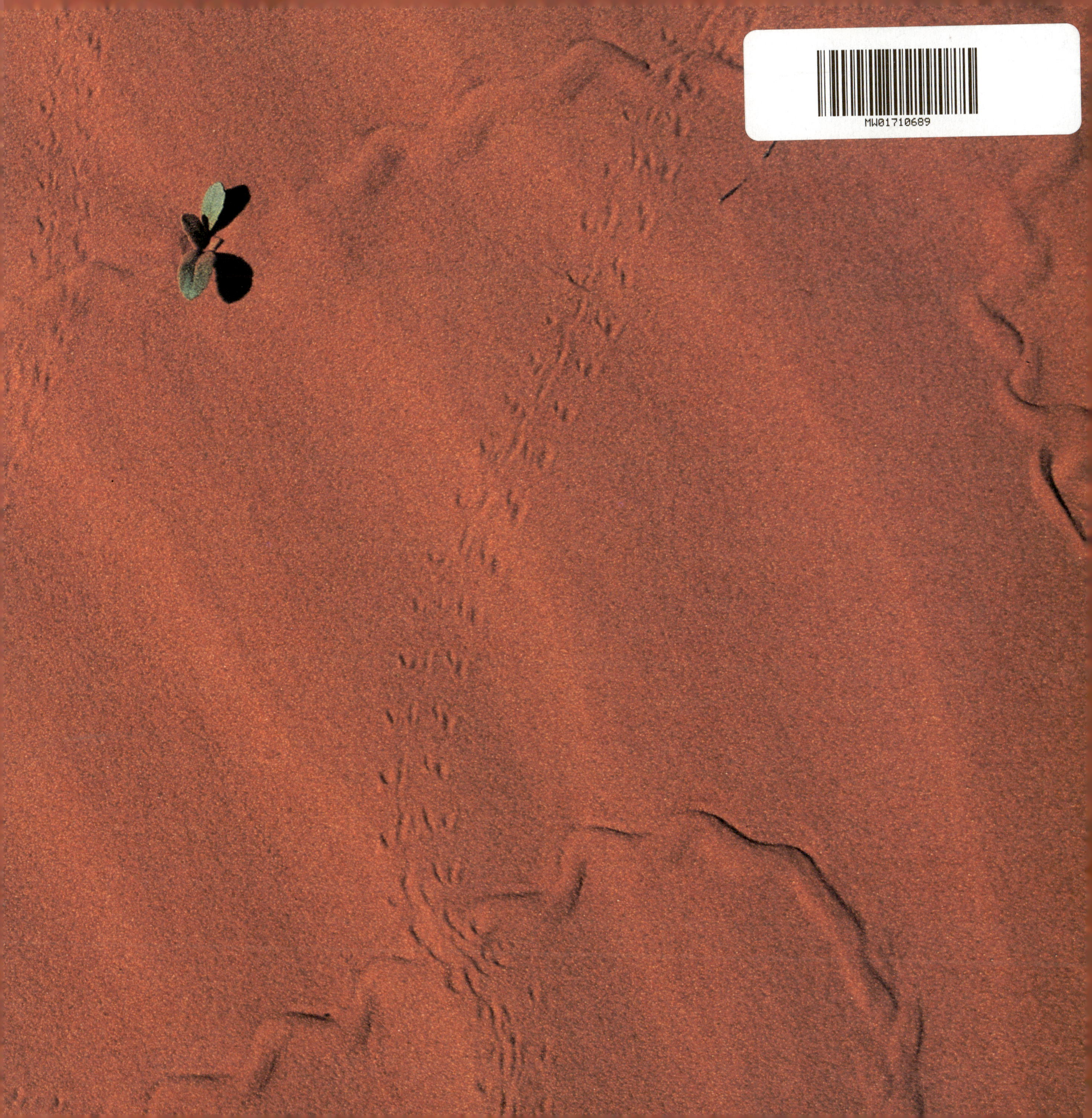

Scenic
AUSTRALIA

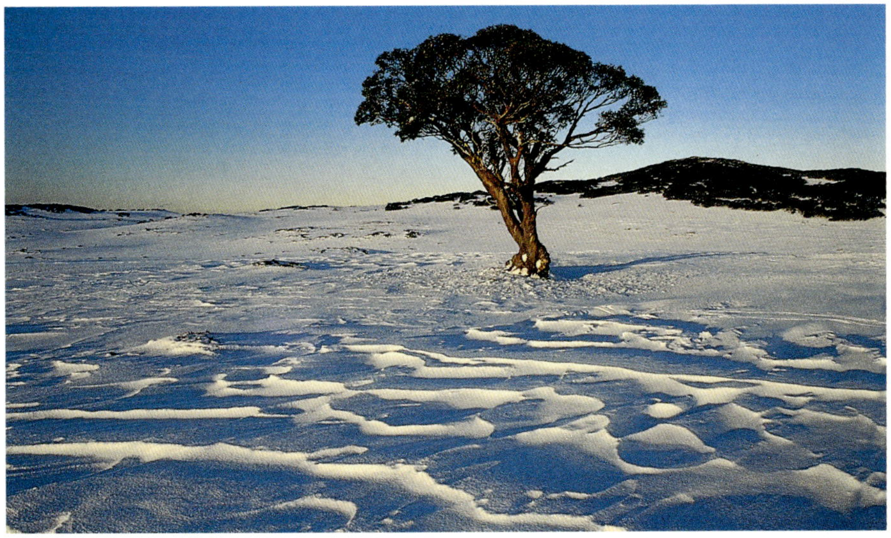

Anne Matthews

NEW HOLLAND

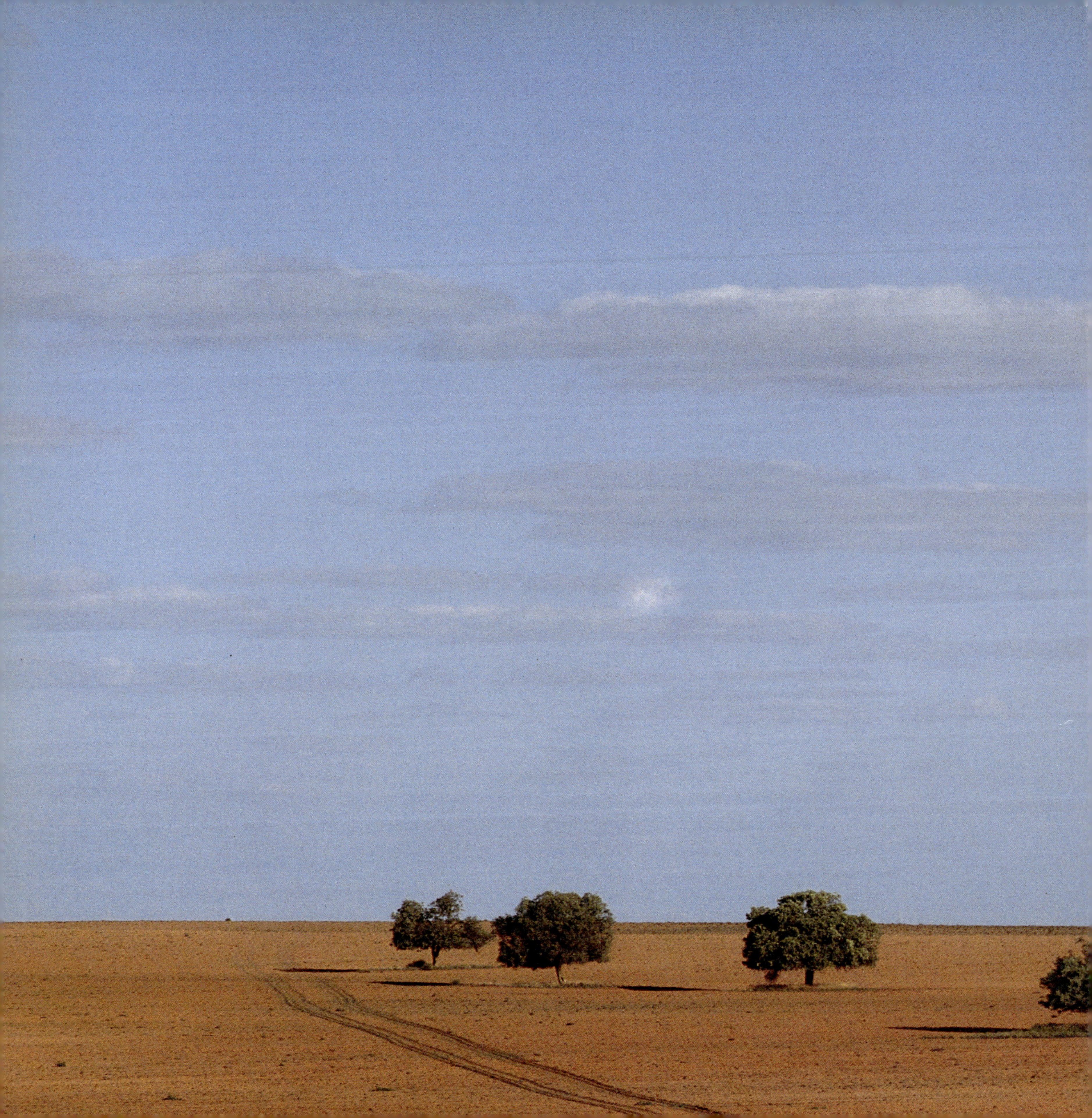

CONTENTS

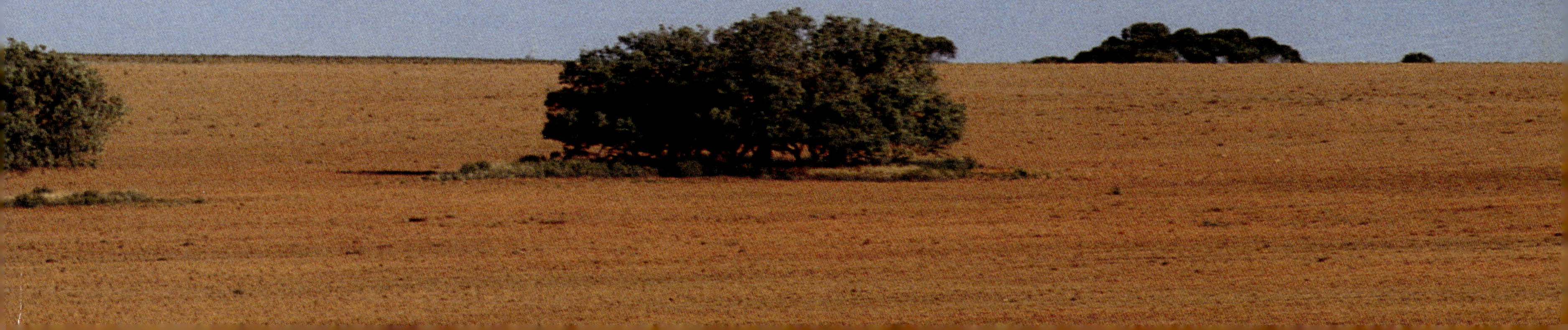

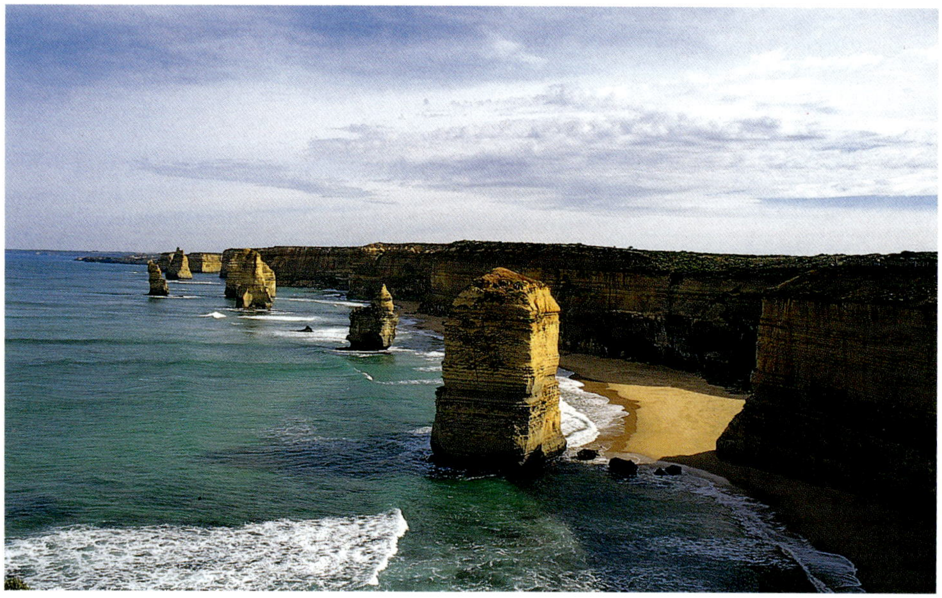

ABOVE: The Twelve Apostles are spectacular cliffs fringed by golden sands on the windswept southern Victorian coast. They are just one of an incredible range of scenery that provides majestic colour to Australia's coastal landscapes.

BELOW: Queensland's gulf country illustrates the force of the continent's vast, arid interior. It is a terrain of rust-coloured earth with clear blue skies, wide open spaces and sparse vegetation, intense light and heat, and an horizon that appears endless.

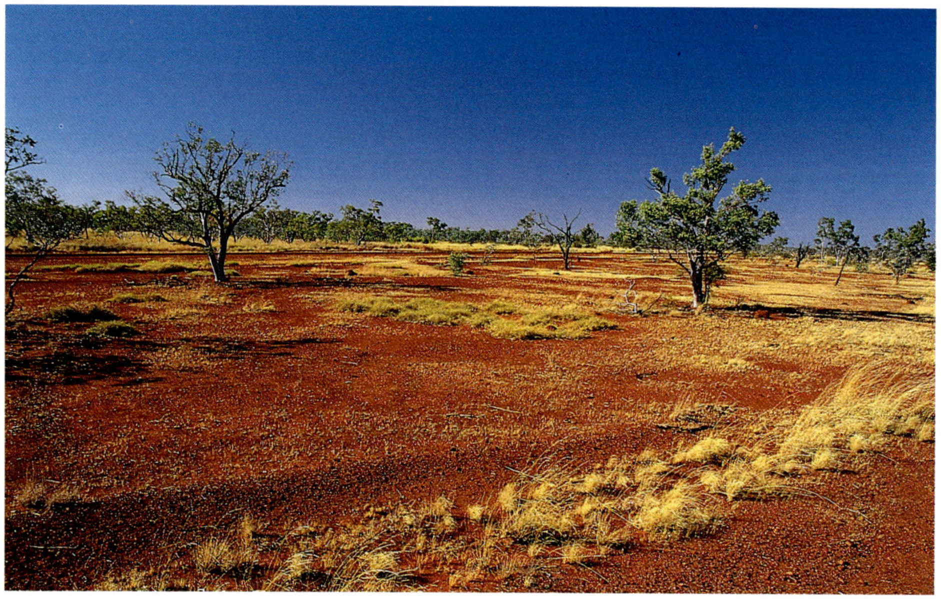

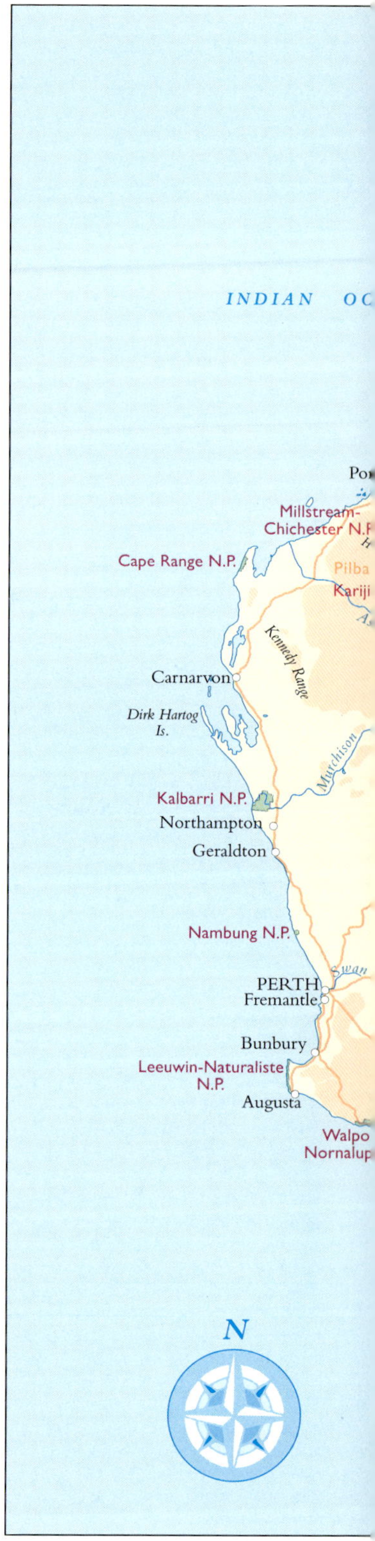

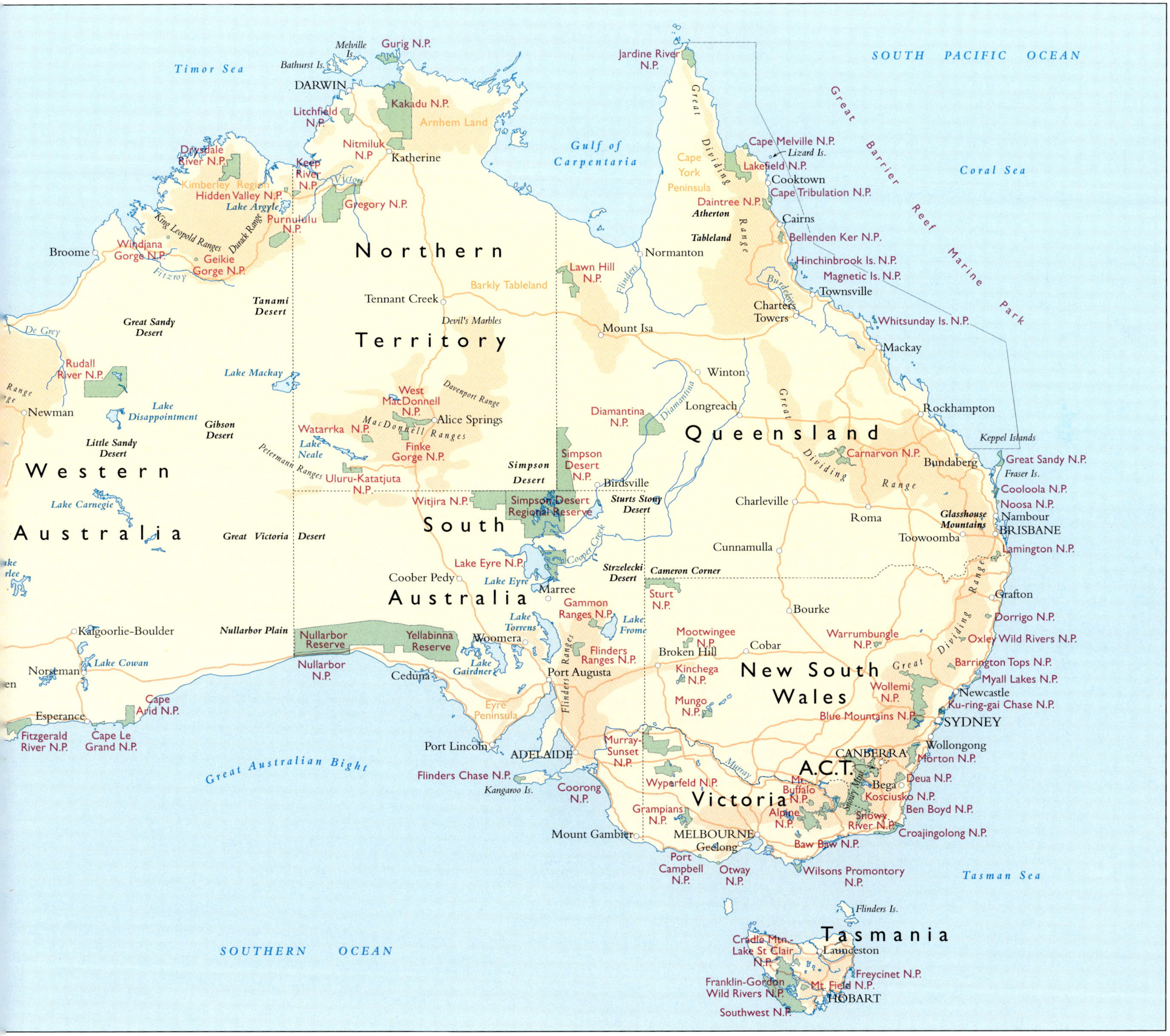
Timor Sea
Melville Is.
Bathurst Is.
Gurig N.P.
DARWIN
Litchfield N.P.
Kakadu N.P.
Arnhem Land
Nitmiluk N.P.
Katherine
Drysdale River N.P.
Keep River N.P.
Victoria
Kimberley Region
Hidden Valley N.P.
Lake Argyle
Gregory N.P.
King Leopold Ranges
Durack Range
Purnululu N.P.
Broome
Windjana Gorge N.P.
Geikie Gorge N.P.
Fitzroy
Northern Territory
Tanami Desert
Tennant Creek
Barkly Tableland
Devil's Marbles
Great Sandy Desert
De Grey
Rudall River N.P.
Lake Mackay
Newman
Lake Disappointment
Gibson Desert
Little Sandy Desert
West MacDonnell N.P.
Davenport Range
Alice Springs
MacDonnell Ranges
Watarrka N.P.
Lake Neale
Finke Gorge N.P.
Petermann Ranges
Uluru-Kata Tjuta N.P.
Western Australia
Lake Carnegie
Great Victoria Desert
Simpson Desert
Simpson Desert N.P.
Witjira N.P.
Simpson Desert Regional Reserve
Birdsville
Sturts Stony Desert
South Australia
Lake Eyre N.P.
Lake Eyre
Coober Pedy
Marree
Cooper Creek
Strzelecki Desert
Cameron Corner
Gammon Ranges N.P.
Lake Torrens
Lake Frome
Kalgoorlie-Boulder
Nullarbor Plain
Nullarbor Reserve
Yellabinna Reserve
Woomera
Flinders Ranges N.P.
Lake Cowan
Norseman
Nullarbor N.P.
Lake Gairdner
Ceduna
Port Augusta
Flinders Ranges
Cape Arid N.P.
Esperance
Eyre Peninsula
Fitzgerald River N.P.
Cape Le Grand N.P.
Great Australian Bight
Port Lincoln
ADELAIDE
Flinders Chase N.P.
Kangaroo Is.
Coorong N.P.
Mount Gambier
SOUTHERN OCEAN
Gulf of Carpentaria
Jardine River N.P.
Great Dividing Range
Cape York Peninsula
Cape Melville N.P.
Lizard Is.
Lakefield N.P.
Cooktown
Cape Tribulation N.P.
Daintree N.P.
Atherton Tableland
Cairns
Bellenden Ker N.P.
Normanton
Lawn Hill N.P.
Flinders
Hinchinbrook Is. N.P.
Magnetic Is. N.P.
Burdekin
Townsville
Charters Towers
Mount Isa
Whitsunday Is. N.P.
Mackay
Winton
Diamantina
Longreach
Diamantina N.P.
Rockhampton
Keppel Islands
Queensland
Carnarvon N.P.
Bundaberg
Great Sandy N.P.
Fraser Is.
Cooloola N.P.
Noosa N.P.
Nambour
BRISBANE
Glasshouse Mountains
Charleville
Roma
Toowoomba
Cunnamulla
Lamington N.P.
Grafton
Dorrigo N.P.
Oxley Wild Rivers N.P.
Sturt N.P.
Bourke
Mootwingee N.P.
Warrumbungle N.P.
Cobar
Broken Hill
Kinchega N.P.
New South Wales
Barrington Tops N.P.
Myall Lakes N.P.
Newcastle
Ku-ring-gai Chase N.P.
Wollemi N.P.
Blue Mountains N.P.
SYDNEY
Mungo N.P.
Murray-Sunset N.P.
Murray
Wollongong
Morton N.P.
CANBERRA
A.C.T.
Wyperfeld N.P.
Mt. Buffalo N.P.
Bega
Deua N.P.
Kosciusko N.P.
Victoria
Grampians N.P.
Alpine N.P.
Snowy Mtns
Snowy River N.P.
Ben Boyd N.P.
MELBOURNE
Geelong
Croajingolong N.P.
Baw Baw N.P.
Port Campbell N.P.
Otway N.P.
Wilsons Promontory N.P.
SOUTH PACIFIC OCEAN
Great Barrier Reef Marine Park
Coral Sea
Tasman Sea
Flinders Is.
Tasmania
Cradle Mtn.-Lake St Clair N.P.
Launceston
Freycinet N.P.
Franklin-Gordon Wild Rivers N.P.
Mt. Field N.P.
HOBART
Southwest N.P.

INTRODUCTION

Australia, the world's flattest continent and largest island, is a unique country of extreme contrasts. The landscape seems to encompass everything. There is the scorched and predominantly flat outback, along with thickly-forested coastal hills and valleys. There are mountains made of 3000-million-year-old rocks, and there are more recently-formed cliffs, reefs and sandy beaches which form 36 700 kilometres of coastline.

The climate of this island continent is equally diverse, with high temperatures bearing down on the interior as the thermometer drops to below-freezing, causing snow, in the highland region of the south east of the country. Lush tropical rainforests and brittle, drought-resistant scrubs illustrate how the continent's vegetation has adapted to these fluctuating weather patterns.

All these ingredients create varied and exciting panoramas displayed in an equally amazing array of colours. Extravagant primary hues prevail, but far more subtle tones—among them, refreshing greens, soft mauves, cool greys and many tones of brown—are also embraced within nature's superb palette. And within each colour there are shades of richness: the blue of the seas can range from pale turquoise to deep sapphire and is often presided over by a strong, intense, azure sky. The glorious colour spectrum is unlimited in scope.

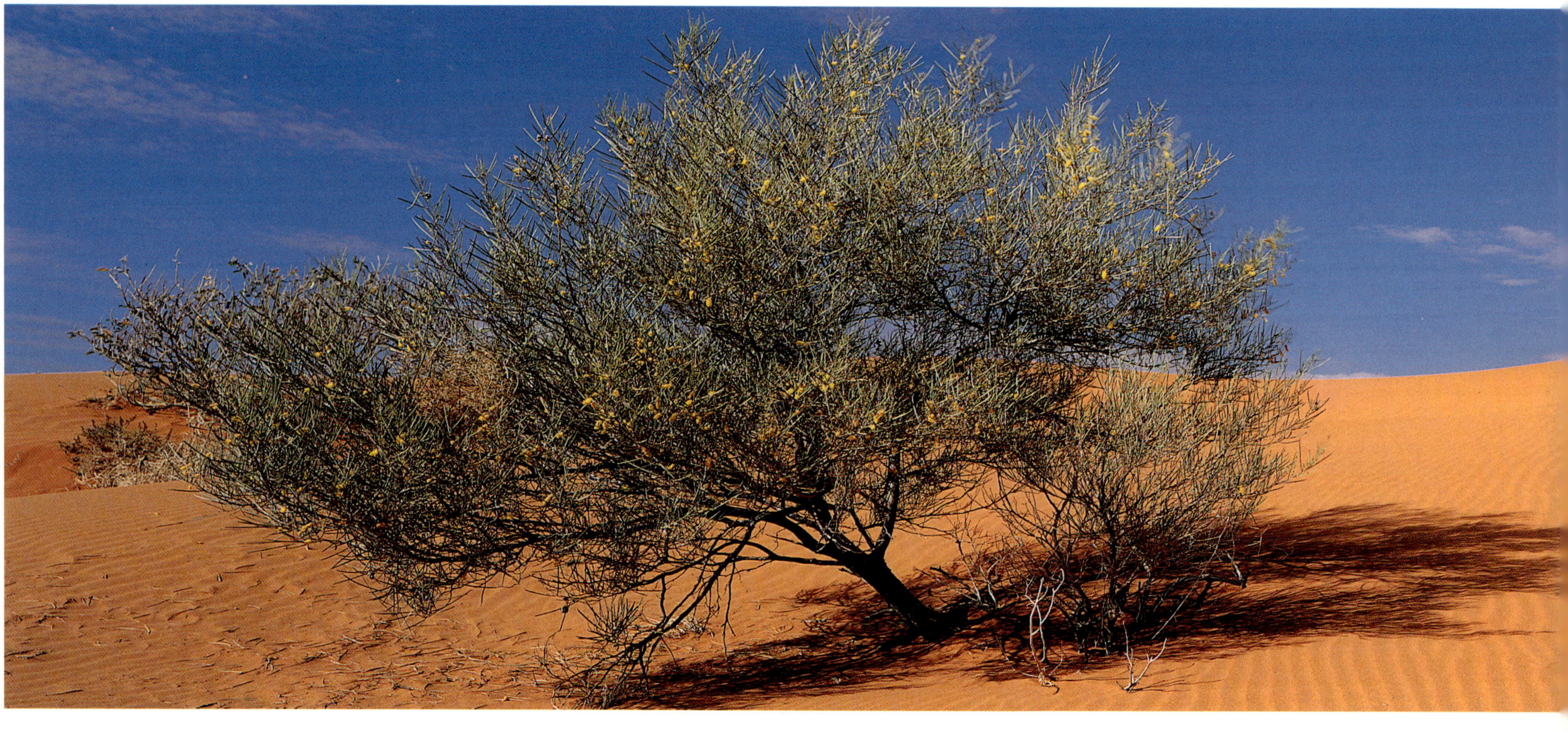

Warm and cool variations of a colour can very often overlap, or complement and contrast with other shades. Deep reds may dominate the dry centre, but rich terracotta, rust and tawny tints, symbolising the same energy and power, are also found in craggy rocks hemming the ocean. Opulent tones of orange very often shoulder a dazzling horizon of hazed light and create an even greater appearance of an almost limitless sense of space. Tall, yellow grass can be seen leaning against soft grey, pink or rough brown tree trunks, which in turn reach up to verdant foliage in many light and dark shades.

These are the magic spells woven all over the continent by nature's vibrant dyes. On the coastline rolling tints of blue, turquoise, gold and white blend together. The power and warmth of the strong southern sun is reflected in the yellows and oranges of ochre sands and pale gold wheatfields. The rugged highlands of the south and east throw restful greys, browns and greens together with the cool blues and whites of frolicking mountain streams. The lush green of emerald rainforests softens into lighter hues in crops that sweep vast and undulating plains.

The country has been immortalised as a sweeping landscape. This timeless land alternately energises, soothes and inspires all who experience it, and over the centuries many artists have taken up pen, paint and camera to capture its endless variations. It is these tones, tints and tinges that create a very *Scenic Australia*.

BELOW: Australia's landscape can be brash, bold and dazzling. In the aptly-named red centre, plants struggle for life under an outrageously blue skies and the ubiquitous terracotta earth, rocks and sand.

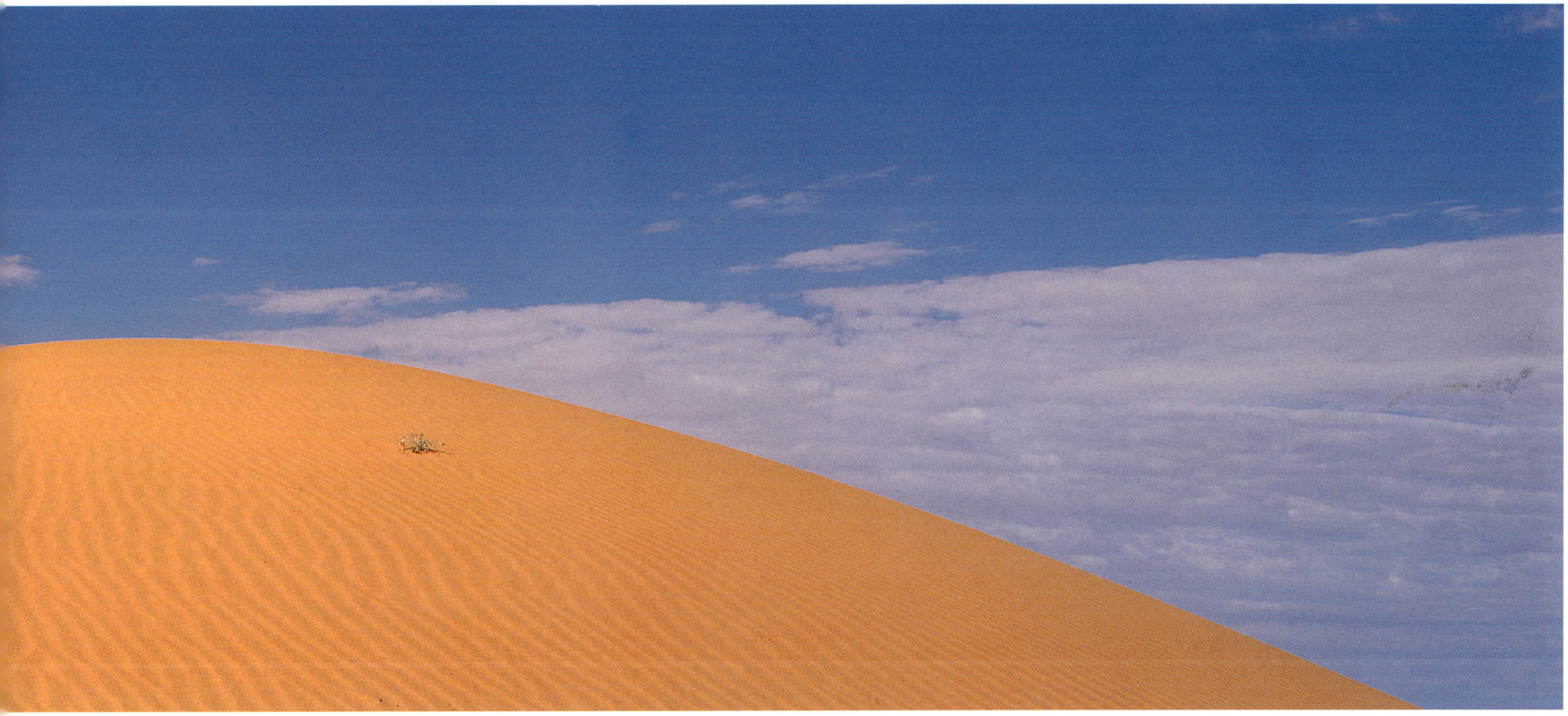

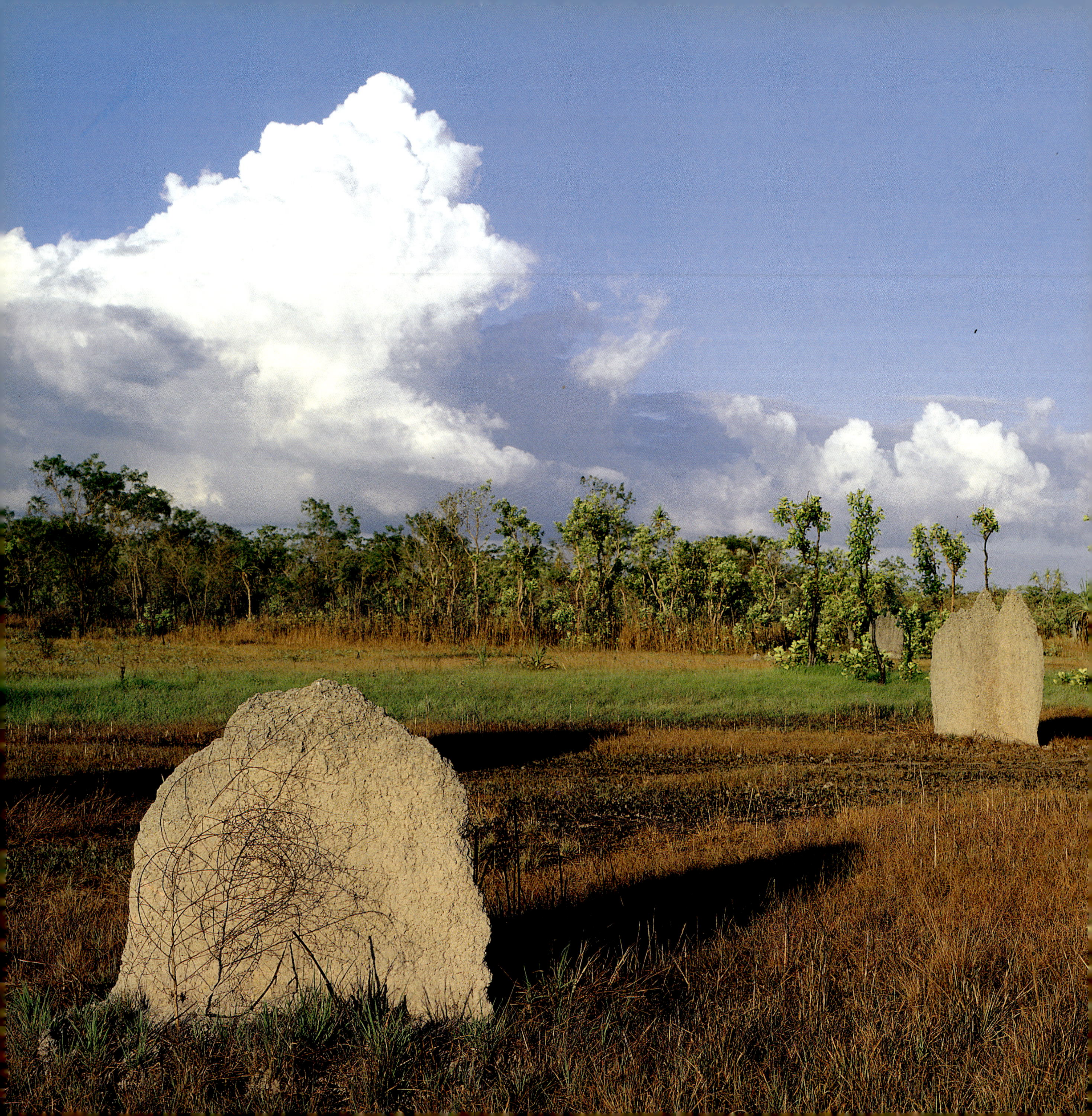

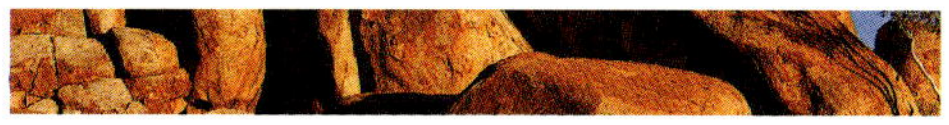

RED DIRT AND THE WILD BLUE YONDER

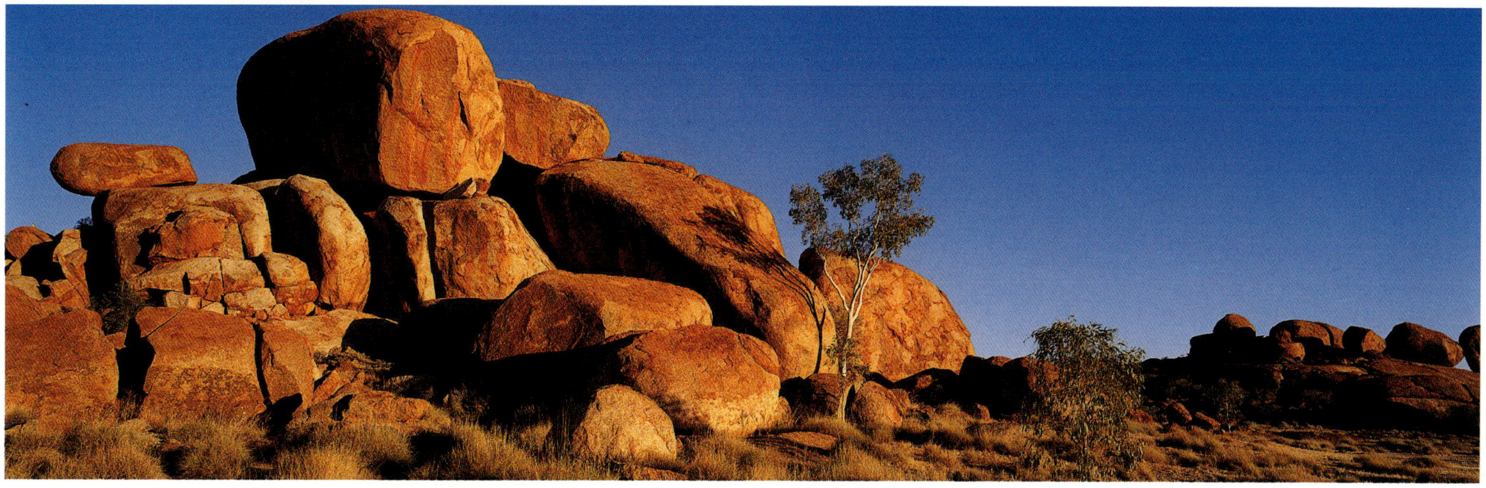

OPPOSITE: Stone-coloured termite mounds, a common sight in the north, can reach to over two metres in height.
ABOVE: The Devils Marbles, a collection of smoothly-rounded boulders in the Northern Territory, are composed of granite but glow vivid in the harsh sunlight, becoming more subtle at sunrise and dusk.

Australia is an ancient and sparsely populated land. The most famous image it invokes in people's mind is that of red dirt, broad horizons, bold colours and the seemingly endless wild blue yonder of the continent's interior.

The interior, known as the red centre, the dead heart or simply the outback, is a harsh, forbidding, yet ruggedly beautiful landscape. The heat in this arid region is intense, with blazing bushfires common in summer, but the temperature can also plummet dramatically at night in the colder months. Most of the vegetation is dry and pale, and long periods of drought are a regular feature. When the rains finally arrive they can create havoc, but they also have the ability to transform the deserts into wildflower gardens in a profusion of colour.

This extraordinary land appears very flat and featureless, yet rocky outcrops like Uluru and Katatjuta will suddenly arise abruptly out of an endless plains. Many of these peaks and mountains are composed of sandstone, which has eroded over many thousands of years to their present strange shapes. They appear terracotta because of the layers of mineral-rich sands that have clung to their sides over the centuries. It is this mixture of composition, the atmospheric conditions and the position of the sun that changes their colour over the course of a day.

These quintessential Australian scenes are looked upon by a fierce sun, set in skies that are impossibly blue, which help create the wide, open horizon and often awe-inspiring sense of space. Mingled with these vibrant reds and blues are soft sages, greys, and even white of drought-resistant vegetation. Softer tones of limestone and granite also take their place in nature's etchings, often surrounded by well-watered tropical plants that feature lush green foliage. The sunrises and sunsets cast the rugged land with gentler shades, spreading pale golds, oranges, pinks and lilacs across the red dirt and wild blue yonder.

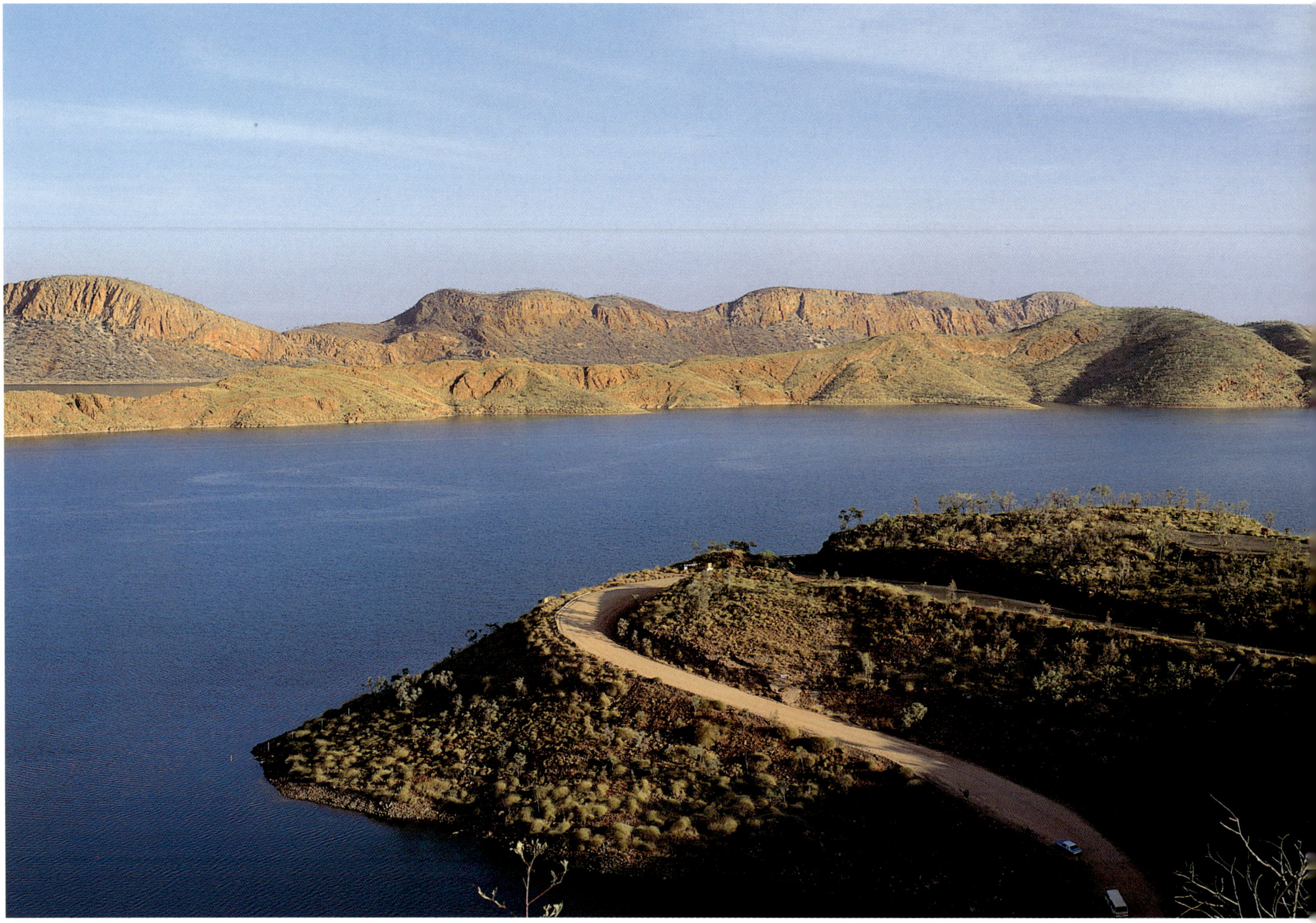

Above: The vast, sapphire Lake Argyle in north Western Australia absorbs softer tones from the sky and provides a striking contrast to the terrain's ancient reddish-brown rocks and motley vegetation.

Opposite top: This thin, almost straight, line of a bitumen highway cuts through the Kalbarri's flat, wide open spaces of ochre earth, green shrubs and yellow wildflowers.

Opposite bottom: At dusk the Devils Marbles silhouette against a softer light of golds, pinks and purples, while the moon begins to carve its own space in the evening sky.

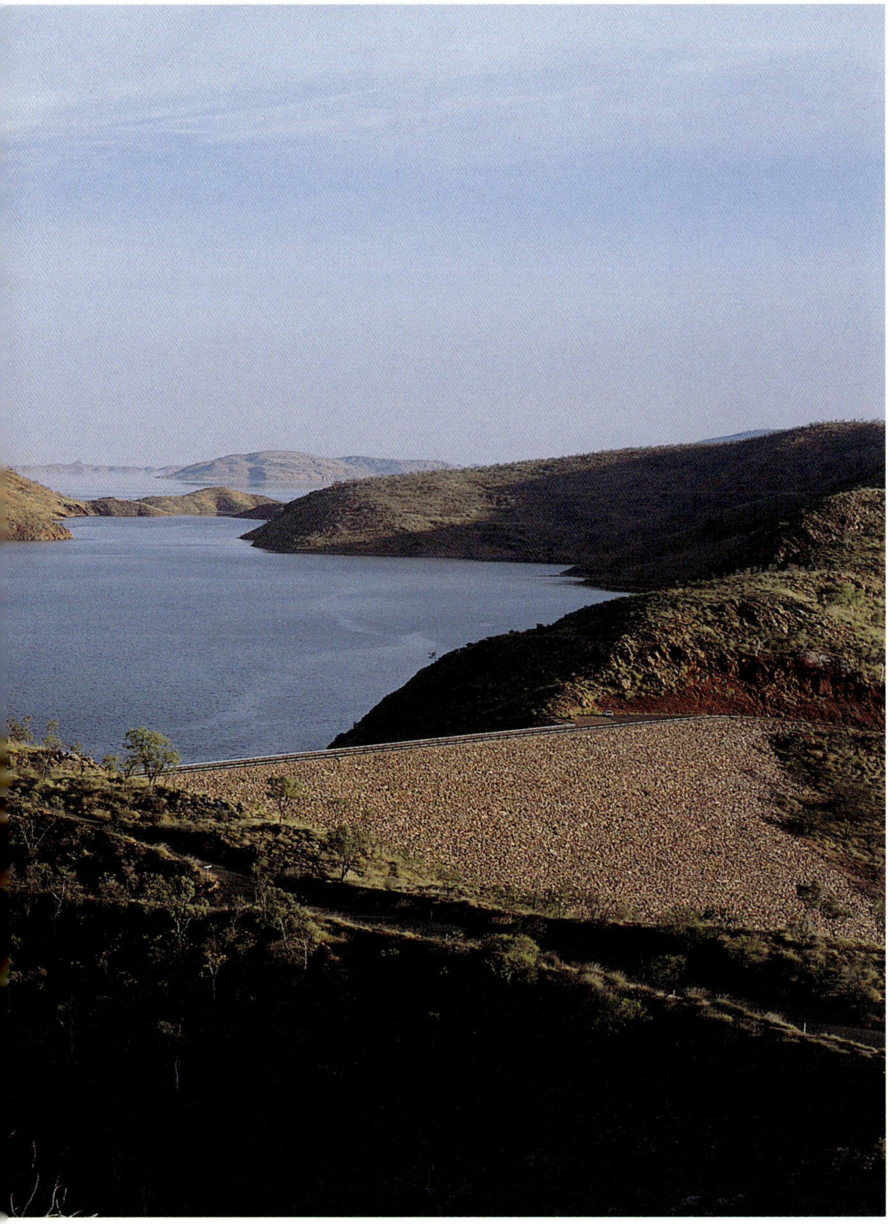

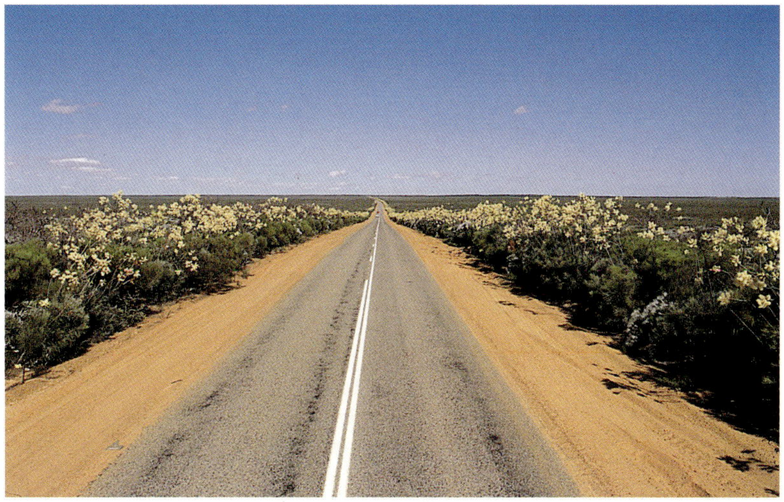

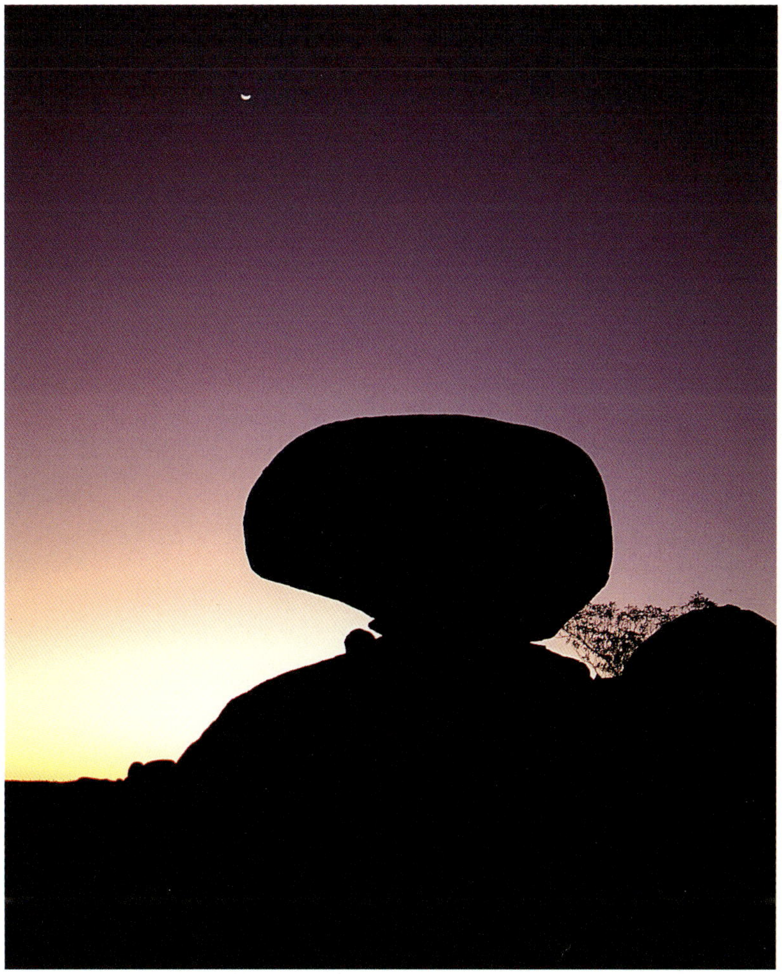

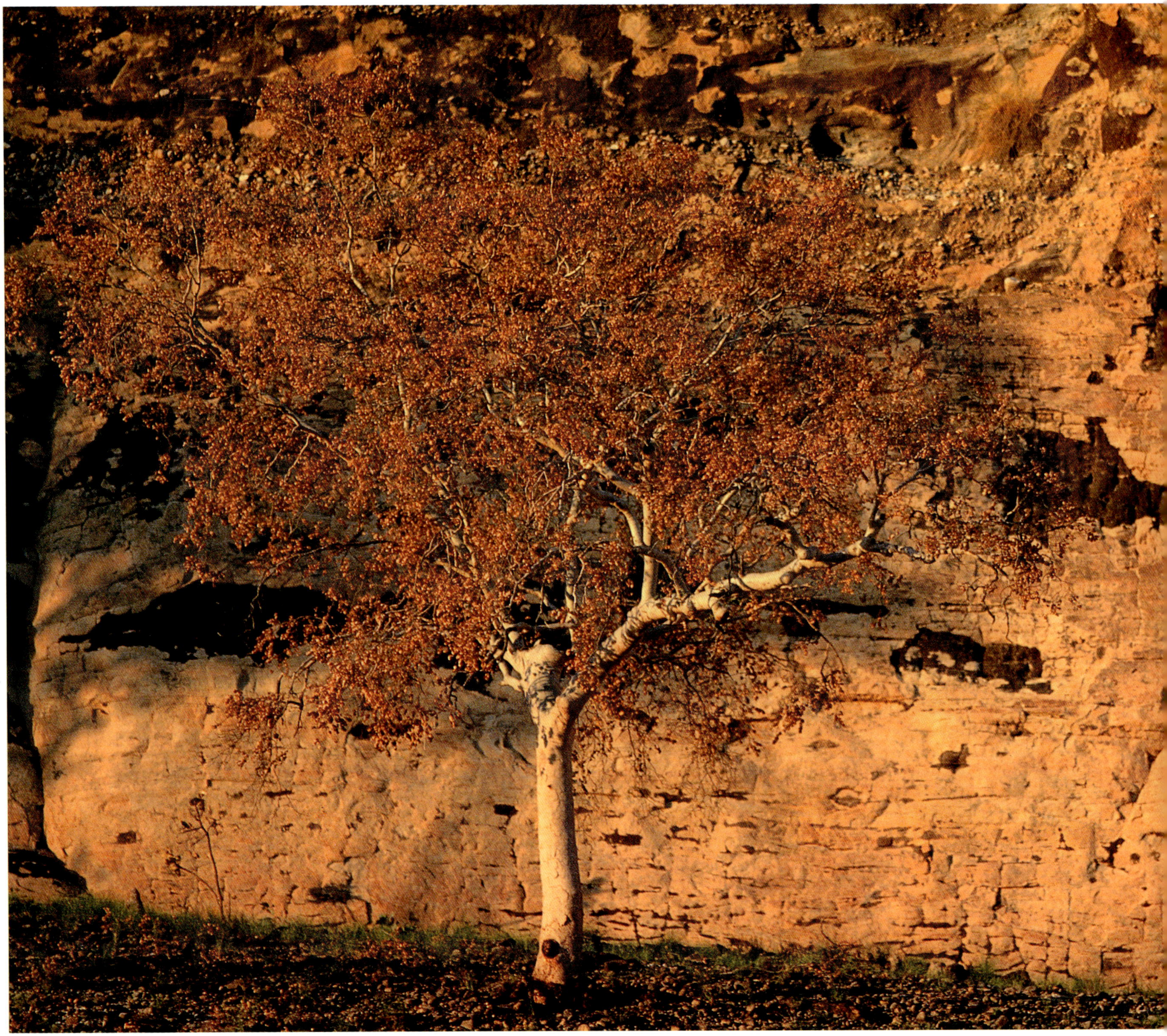

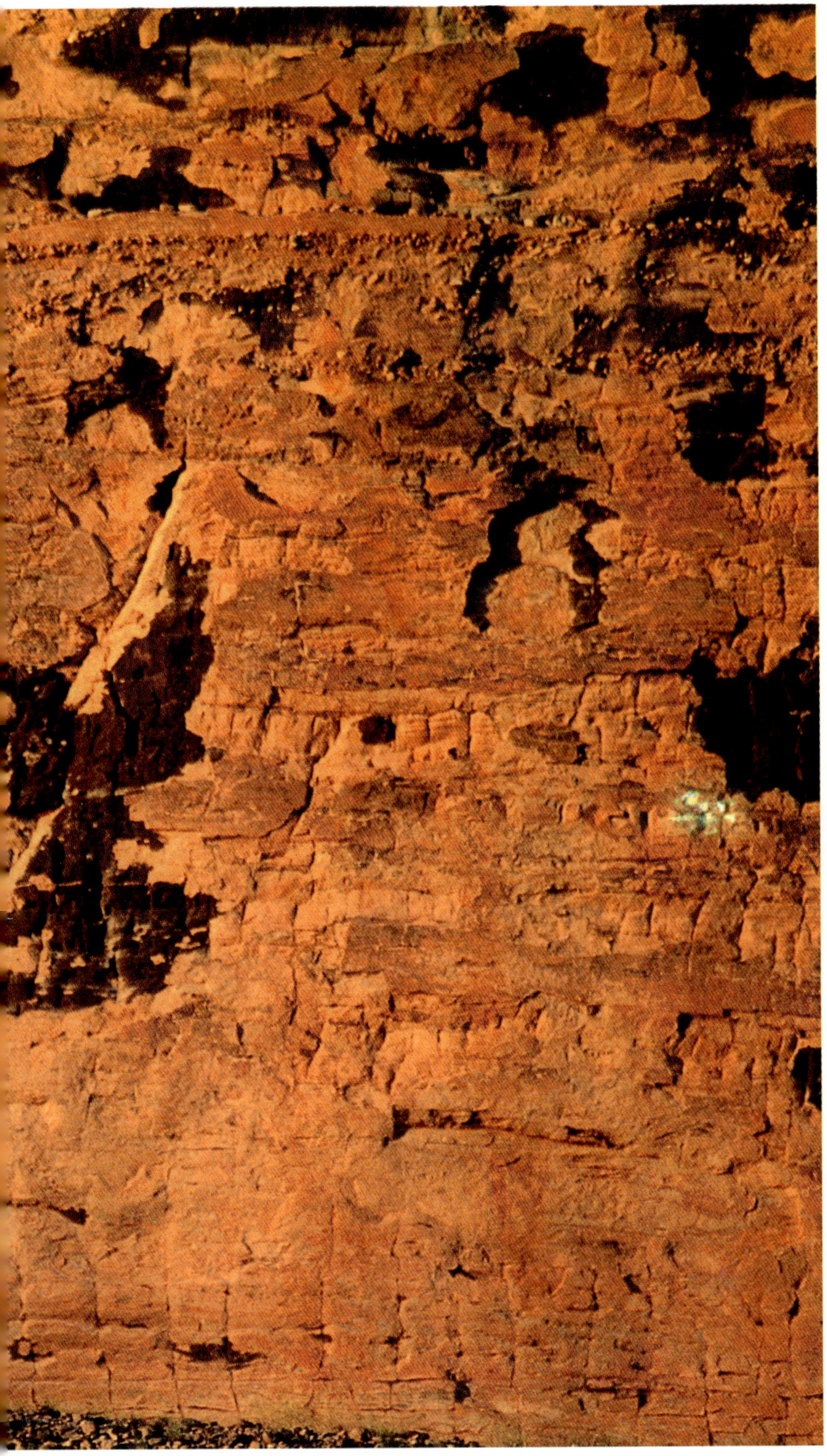

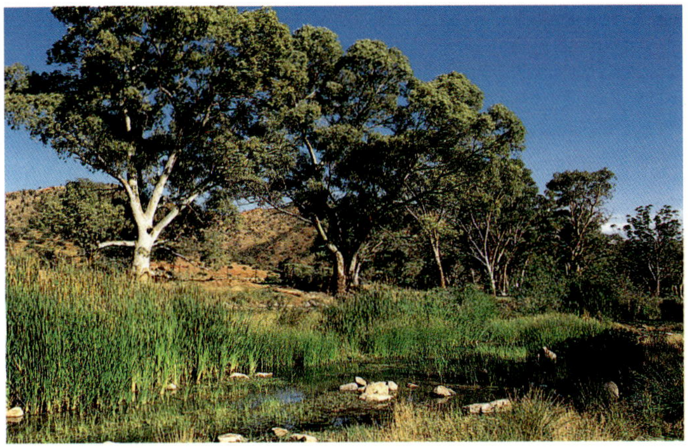

Left: The intense light makes the cragged, ancient sandstone wall at Gurrandaling in the Keep River National Park look ablaze. Even the lone tree seems to have succumbed to an auburn coating, but the strips of grass allow a cool respite in this fiery show.

Above: A little bit of water creates a welcome splash of green in this semi-lush oasis within a barren and tawny Territory landscape.

Below: A bright sky raining through the fronds of tall-growing palms creates the cool, tropical feel that is found at Rockhampton's Botanic Gardens.

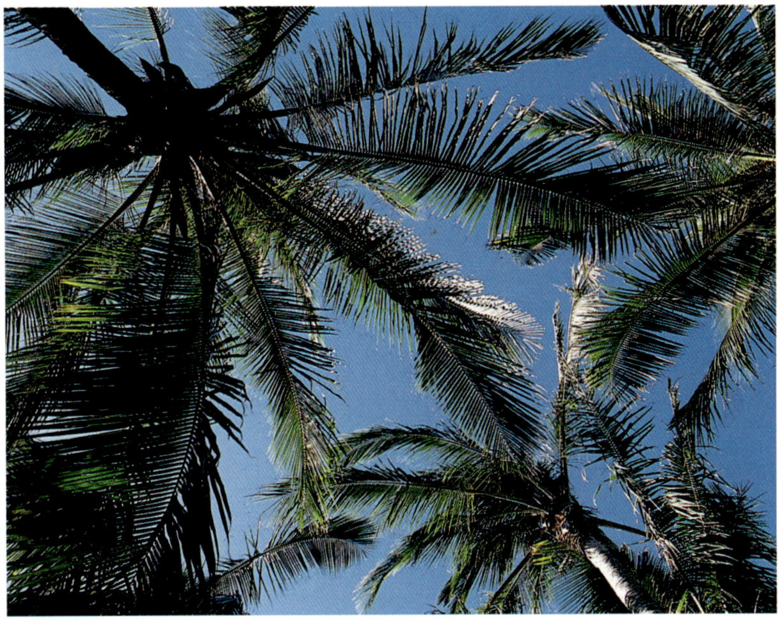

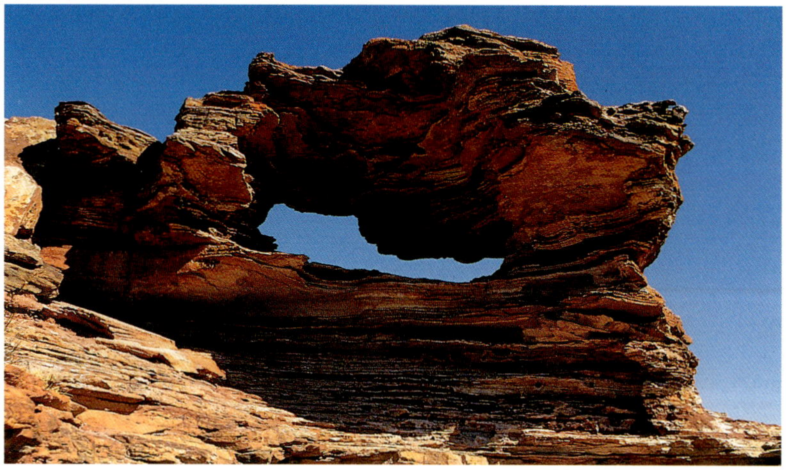

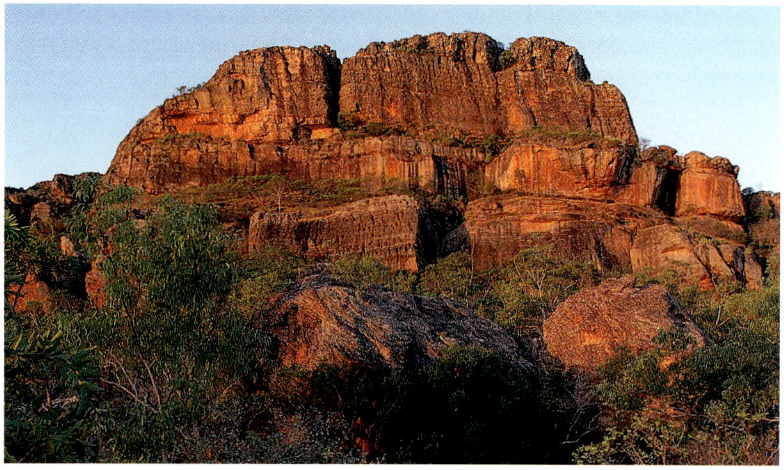

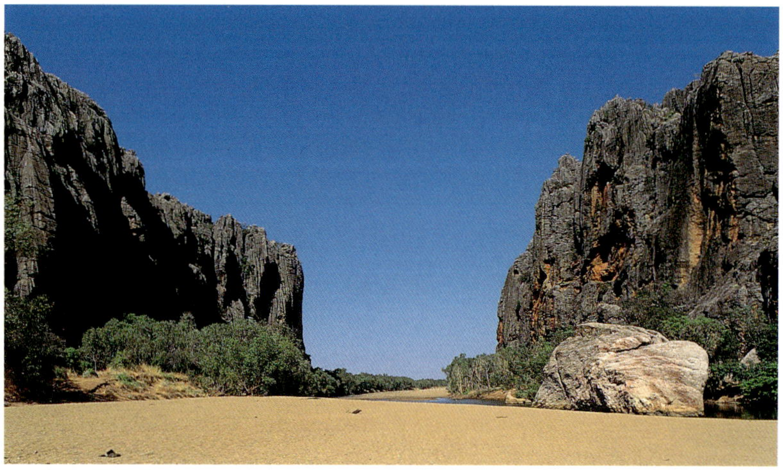

Left: The red and cream strata in the rock that forms Nature's Window in Western Australia's Kalbarri National Park illustrates how fragile sandstone can be moulded by the weather into fantastically jagged shapes.

Left centre: The ancient, dark, brownish-red Nourlangie, a majestic sandstone outcrop in the Northern Territory, still stands tall, despite the elements, above the tree lined ground.

Left bottom: The dark-grey limestone walls of Windjana Gorge in Western Australia were eroded by water to form this sand-lined ravine. Most of the outback rivers flow sporadically, and at Windjana the water height is subject to the season.

Right: In the cooler seasons, the softening tones of vegetation can almost hide the ochre sandstone plateau that surrounds the Keep River, but the deep clefts are still visible by dark shadows cast from the sun.

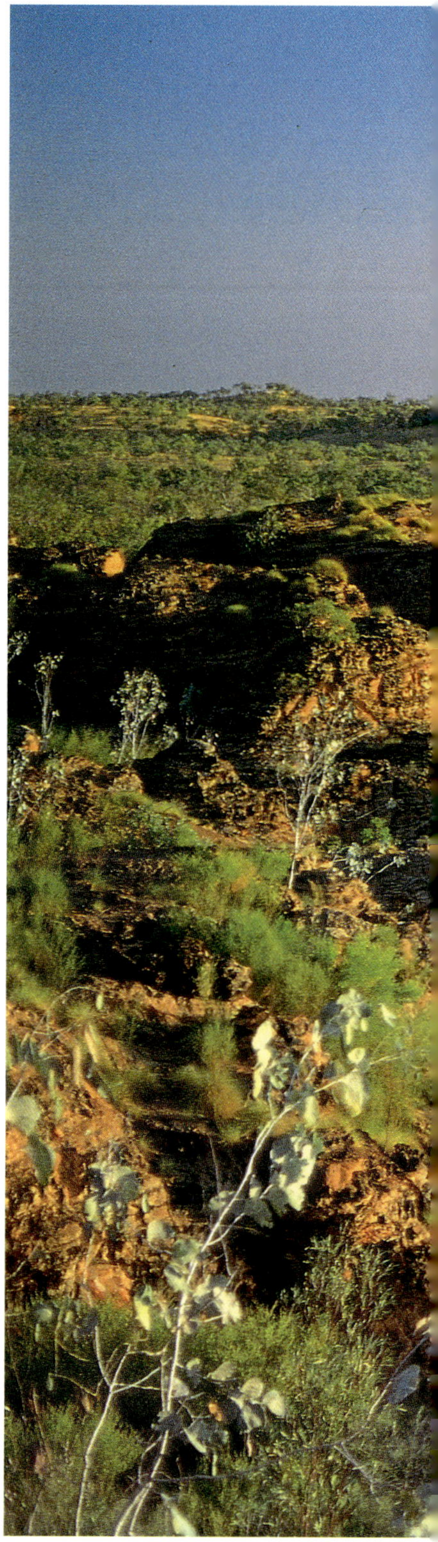

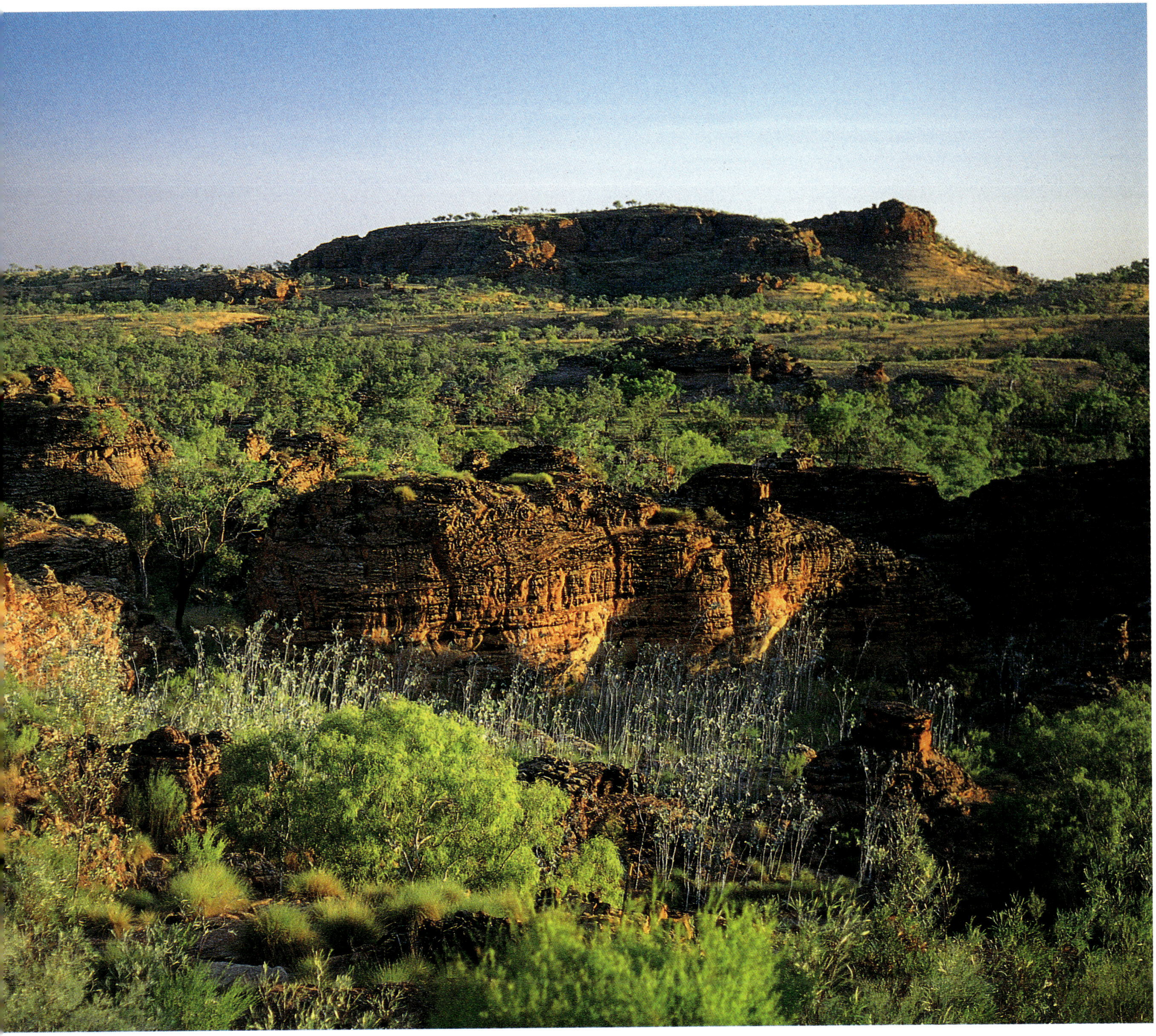

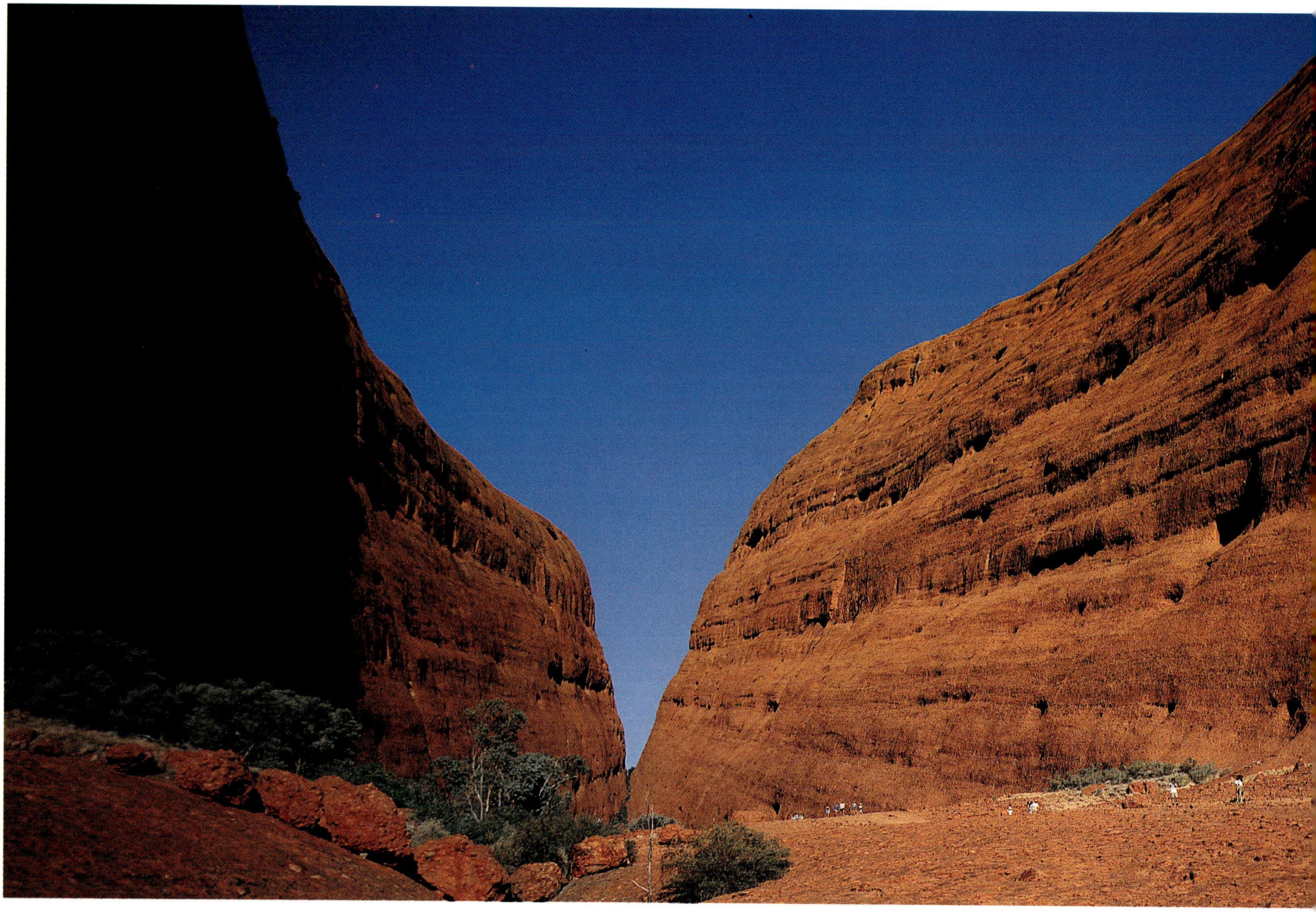

ABOVE: At Australia's heart monumental sandstone outcrops like Katatjuta (once known as the Olgas) leave little doubt as to why this region is called the red centre.

OPPOSITE TOP: The colour surrounding the bridge over the Burdekin River explains why early settlers were awe-struck by the intense blue of the mysterious southern land. The sky and water nearly appear as one, separated only by the lush green of the land.

OPPOSITE BOTTOM: The rock art of Aboriginal artists has always embodied earthy pigments, particularly the brick-red of the outback.

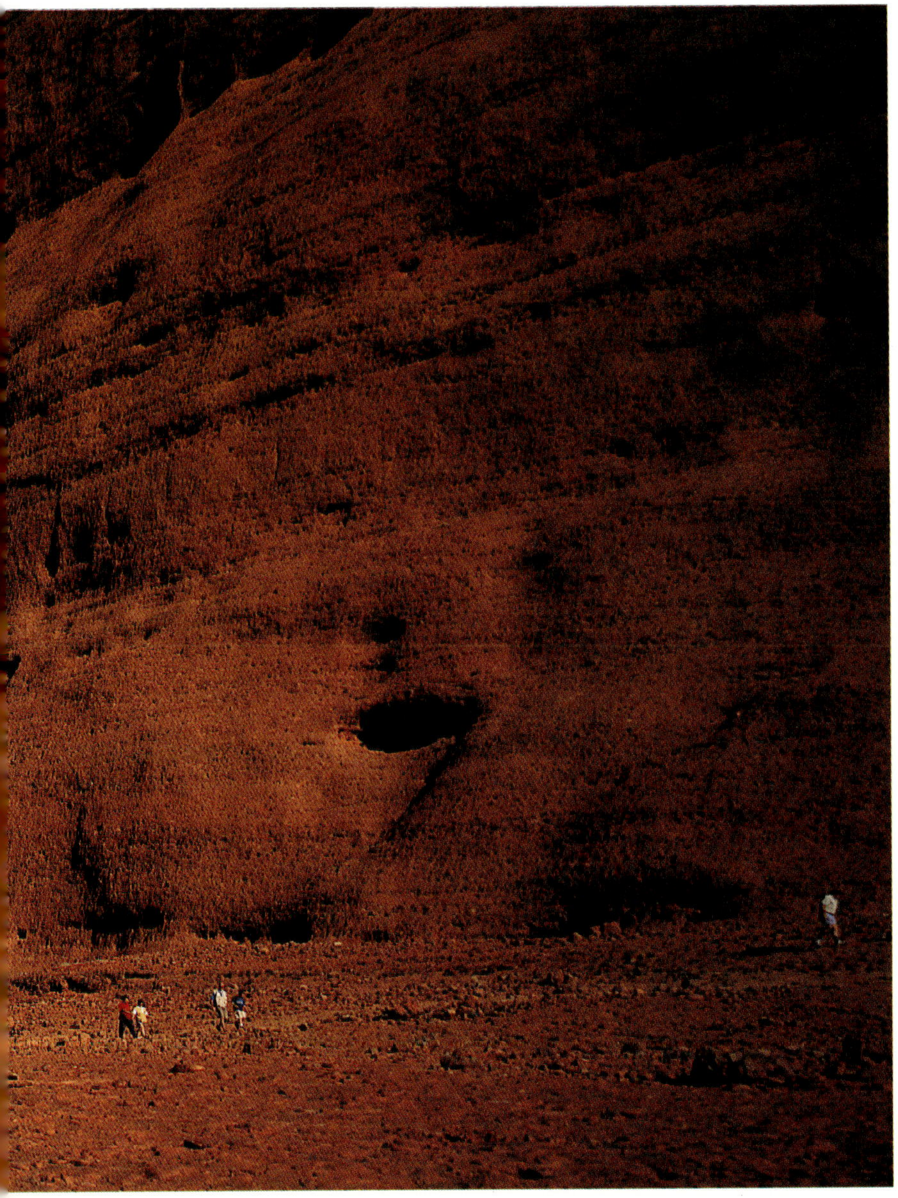

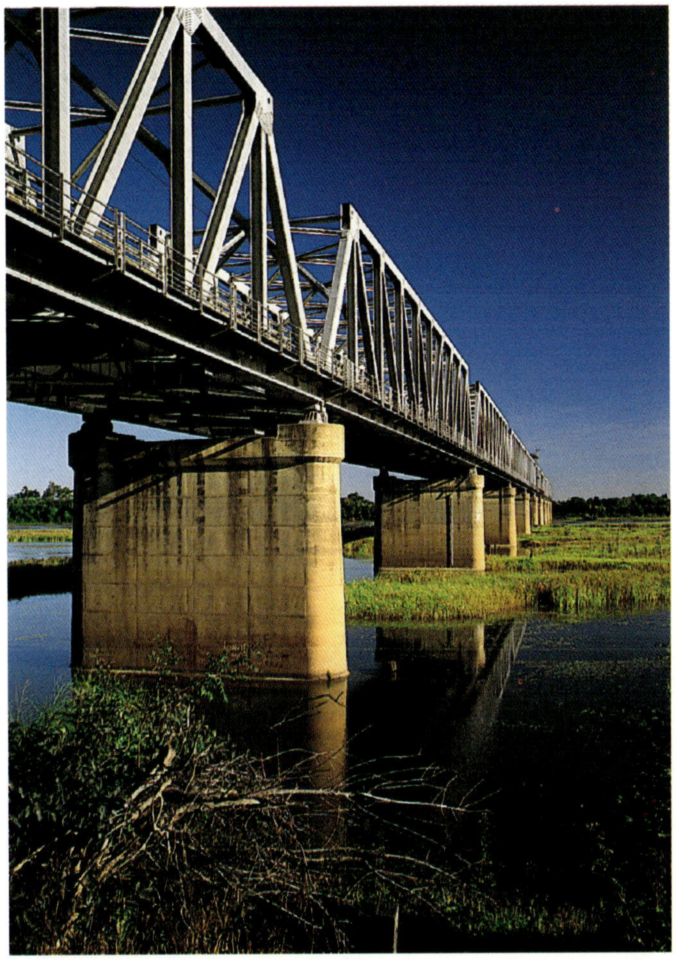

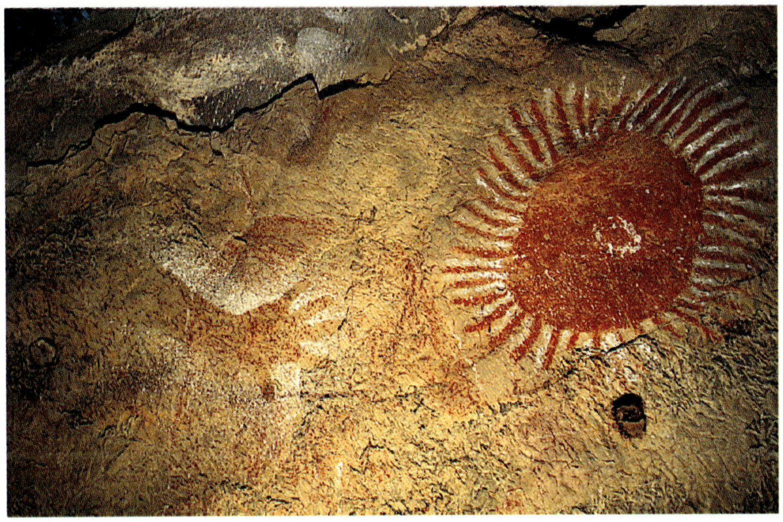

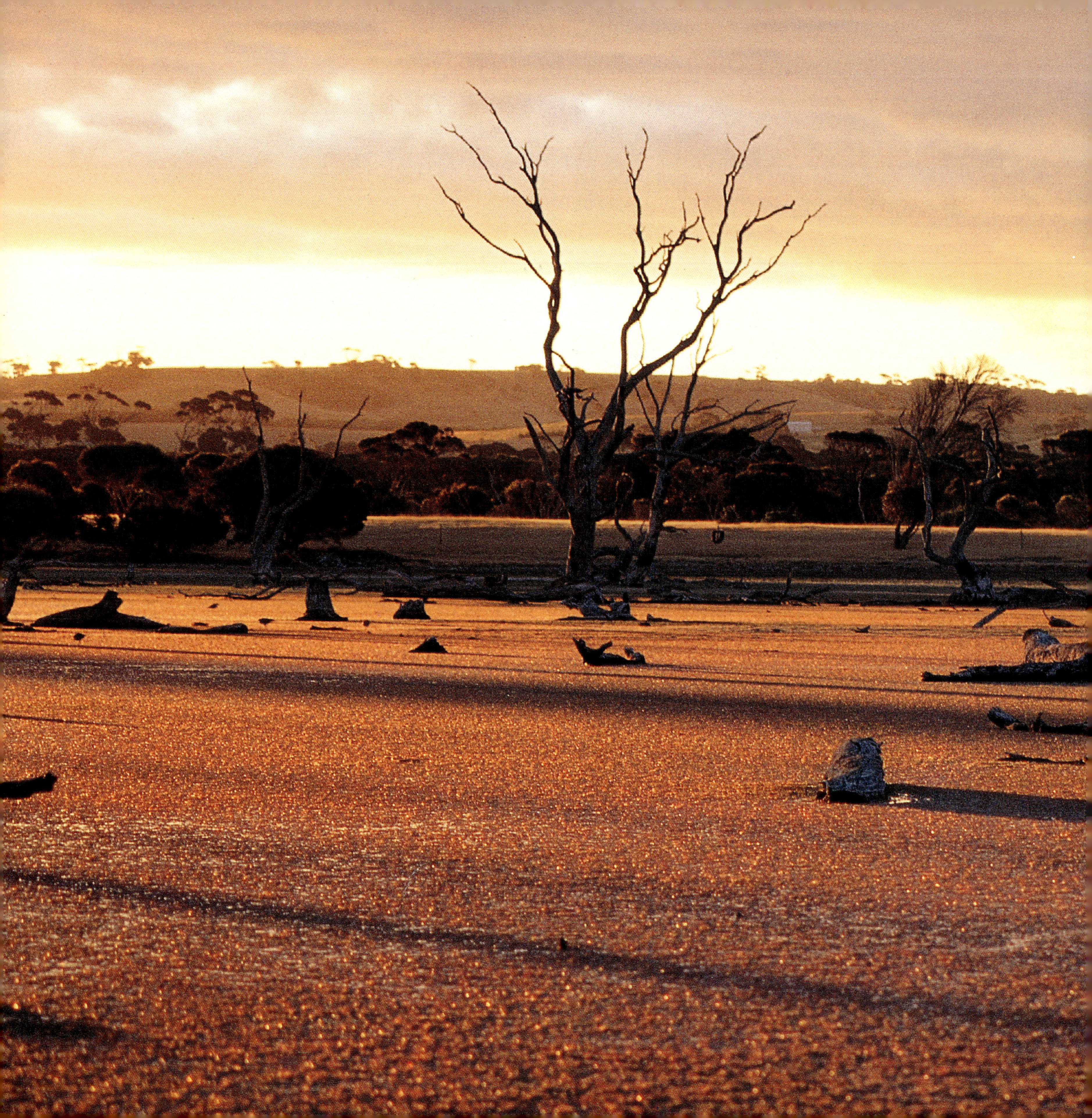

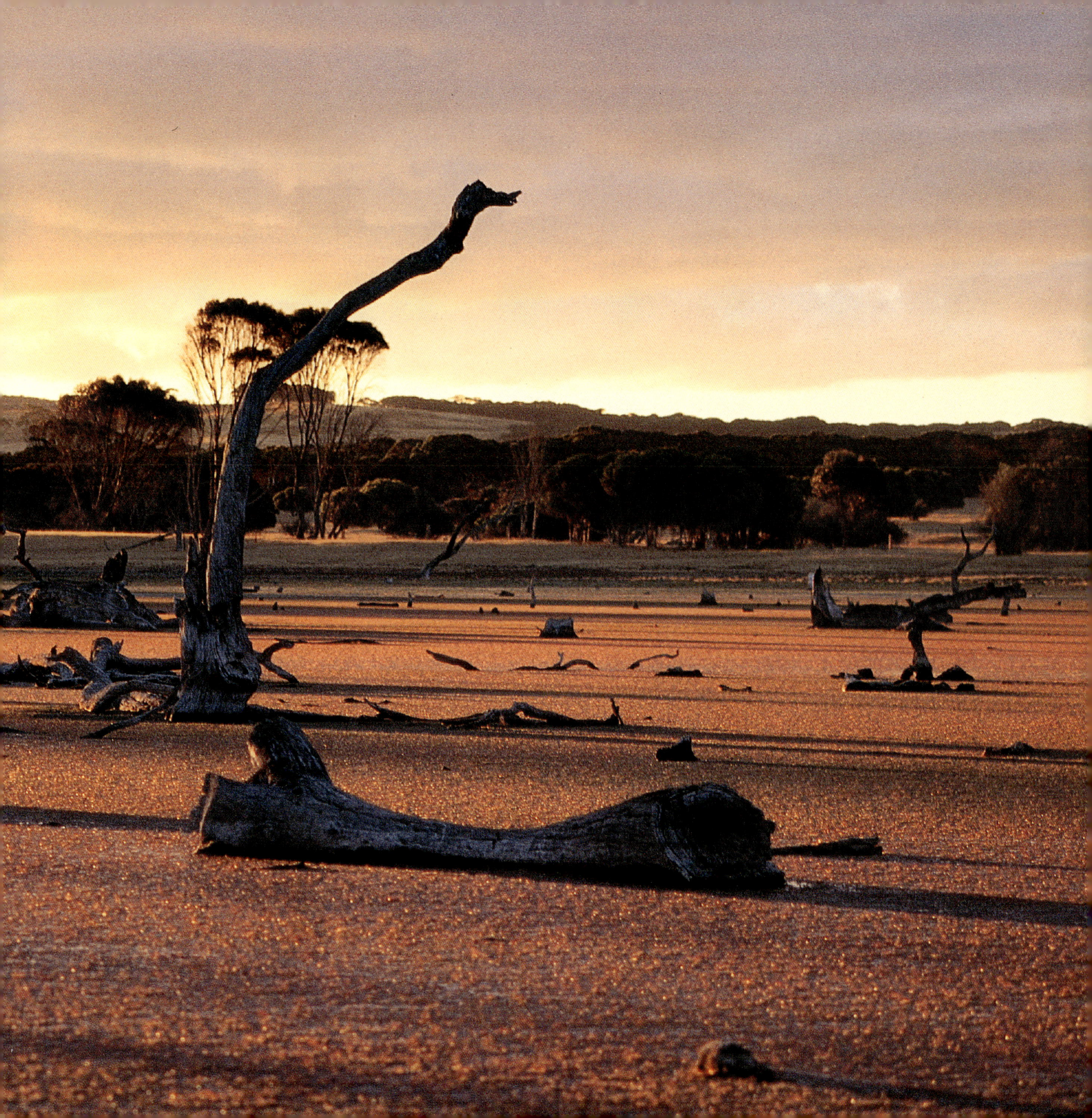

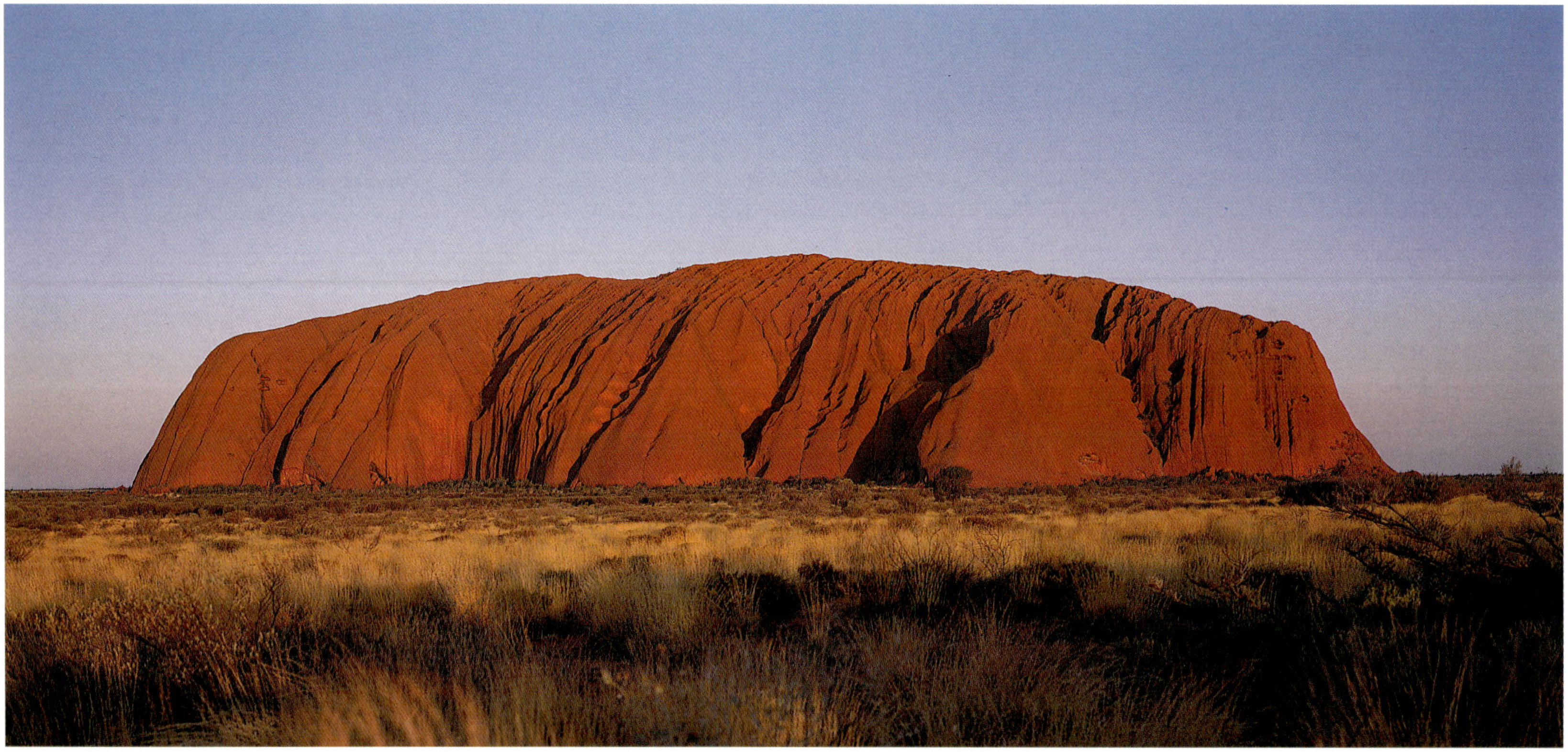

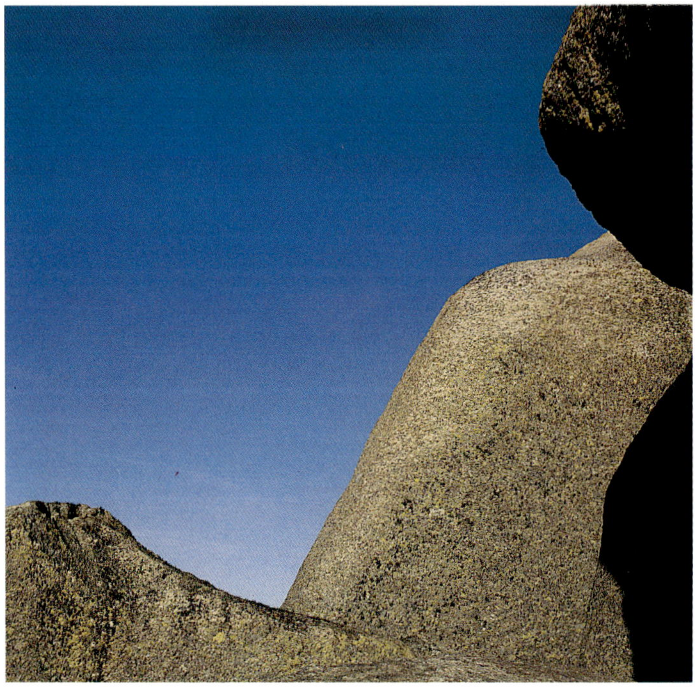

PREVIOUS PAGES: A warm evening light transforms the gentle greys and greens of a marsh at Emu Bay into a panorama of rust and brown.

ABOVE: Many moods and characteristics of the giant monolith Uluru are unveiled at different times of the day. The rock's colour shifts from pale mauves, pinks and even blues, but is best recognised in this exquisite rust colour backed by the pale evening sky.

LEFT: Solid beds of granite create distinctive forms and texture on the landscape. These tors at Mount Buffalo National Park in Victoria typify the smooth, rounded surface that can change from this warm golden-brown to a pinkish-grey in different light.

OPPOSITE TOP: A spectacular outcrop at Rainbow Valley in the Northern Territory reveals the almost unlimited variations of red dirt and the wild blue yonders. While the rock and sky dominate the scene, it is muted greens, greys and purples that enhance the glow.

OPPOSITE BOTTOM: The Breakaways are so-called because the sweep of the terrain, enhanced by the dark reds, softer creams, ochre and brown tones, which gives the impression that they broke away from the Stuart Range.

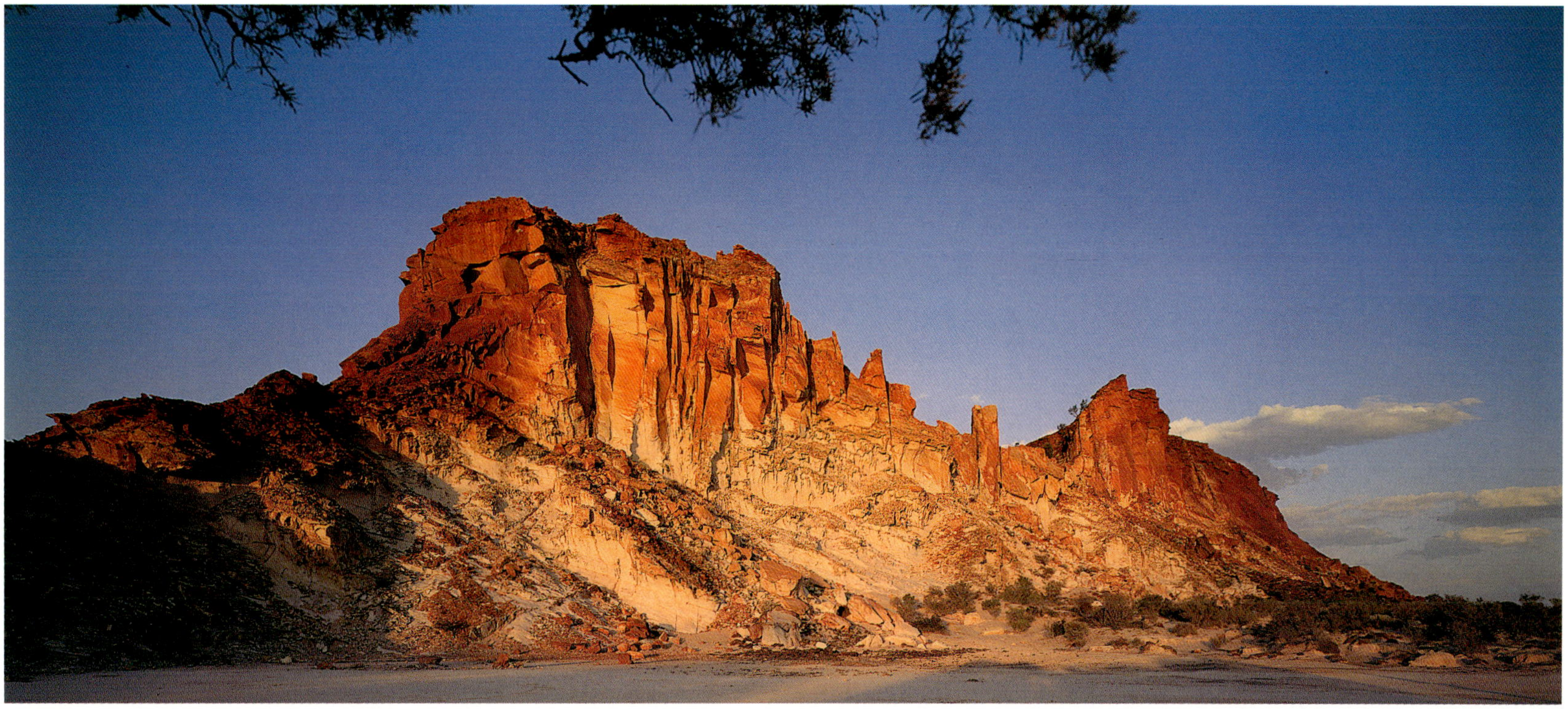

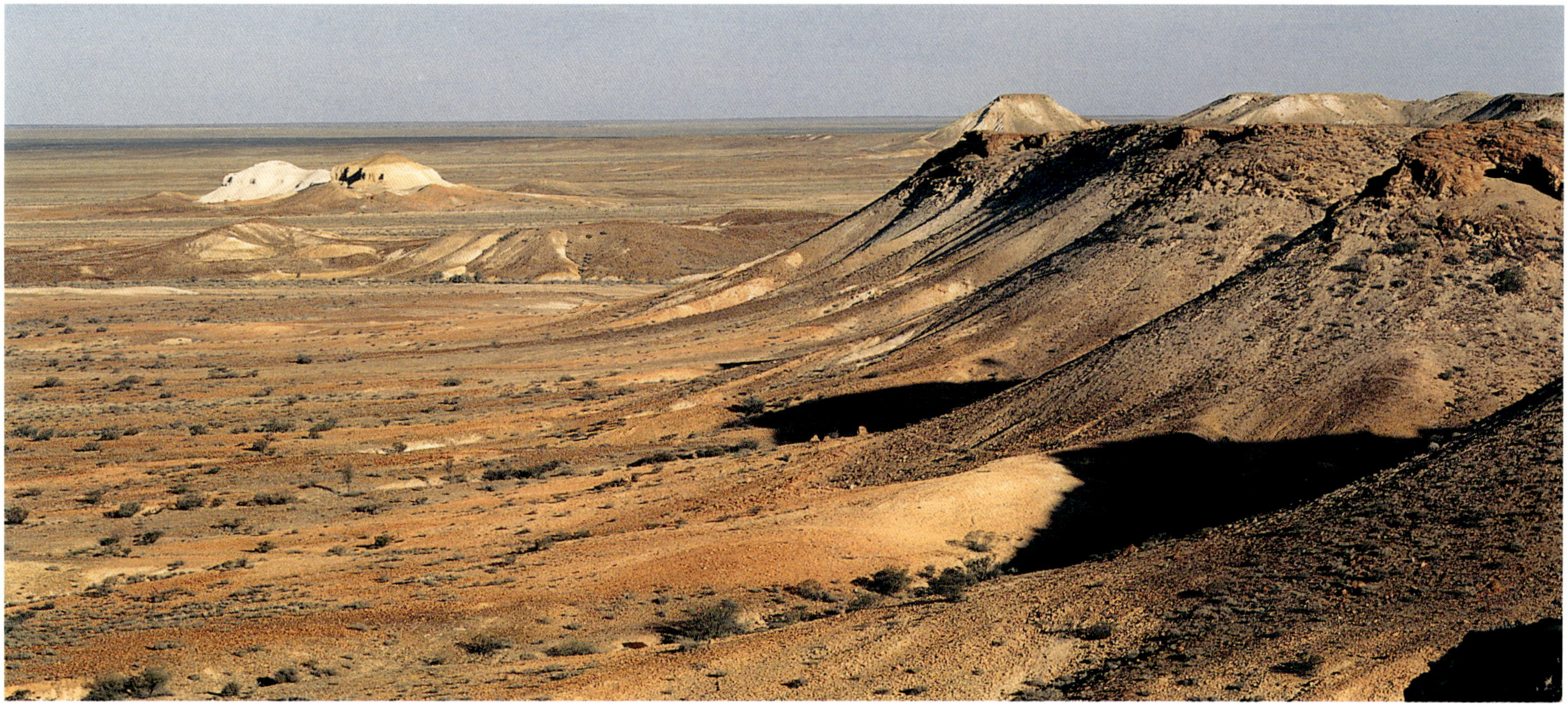

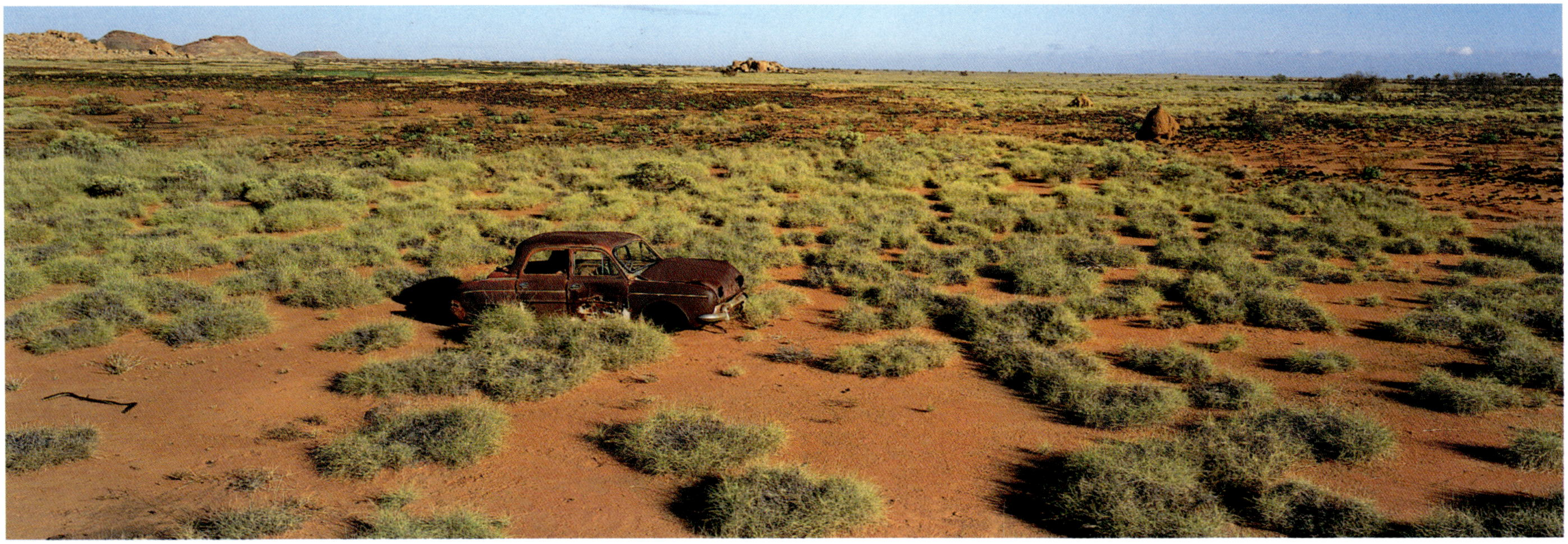

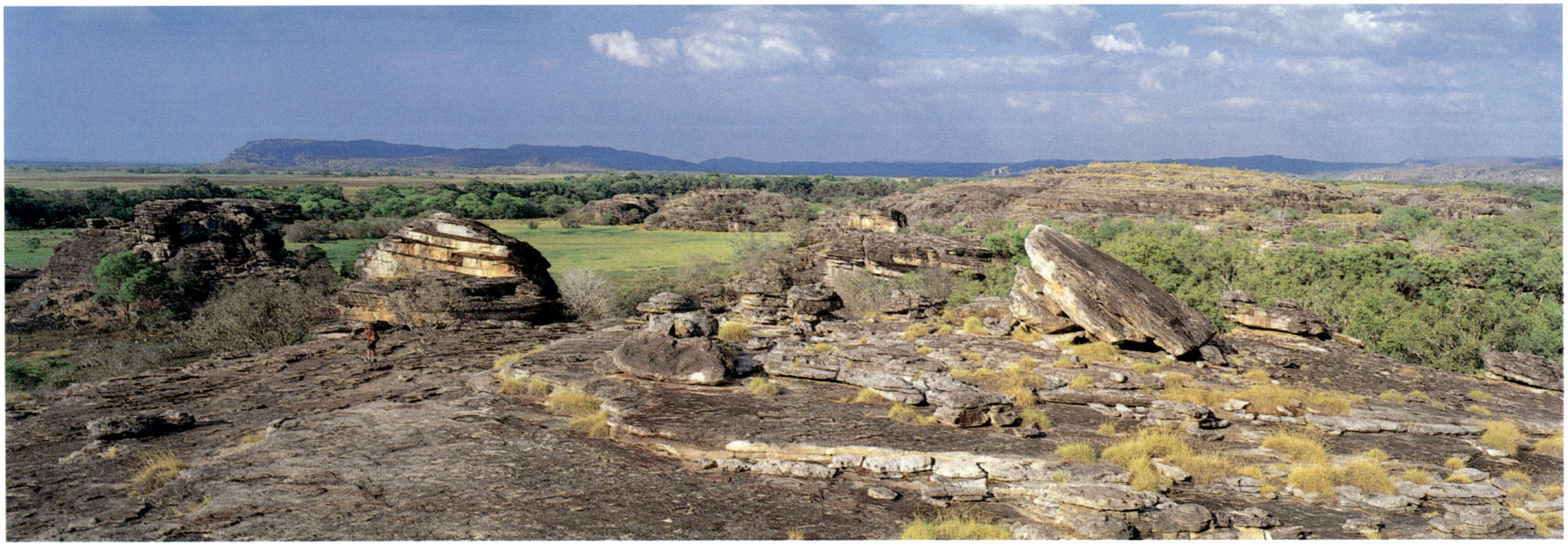

TOP: The Great Sandy Desert near Broome, which features deep red ancient rocks, is far removed from the usual image of sand dune deserts.

ABOVE: In the Kakadu National Park the rugged Ubirr rocky outcrops are softened by a pastel sky and rich green flora, watered only by wet season rains.

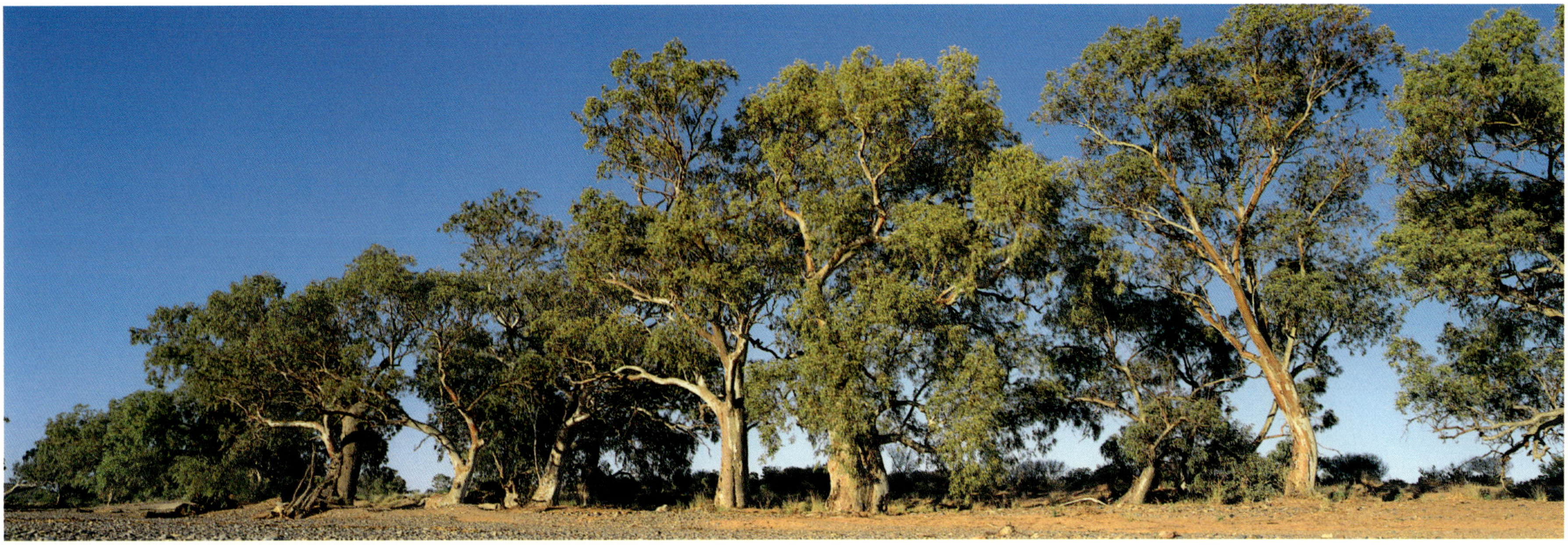

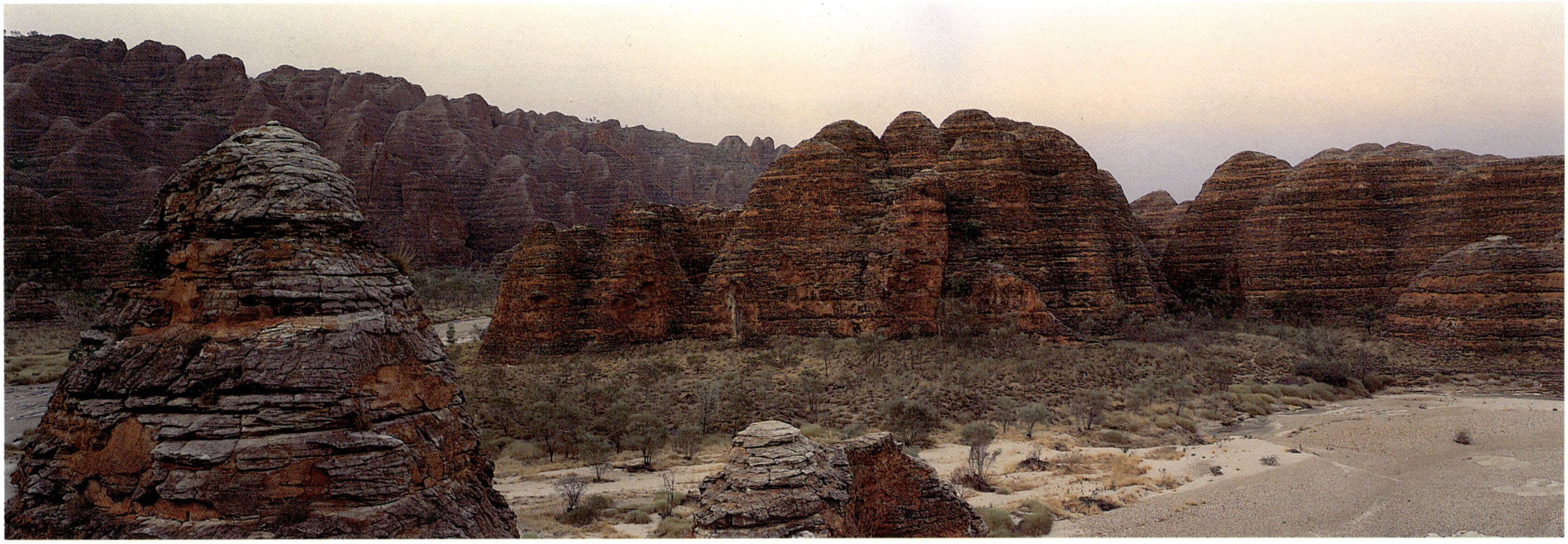

TOP: Hardy eucalypts at Tea Tree Creek near the Gammon Ranges add life to a dry scene. Despite the outback's aridity, the landscape is often softened by vegetation.

ABOVE: The Bungle Bungle Range at Purnululu National Park in Western Australia usually glows dark red, but on this cloudy day they adopt a much more cosy feel.

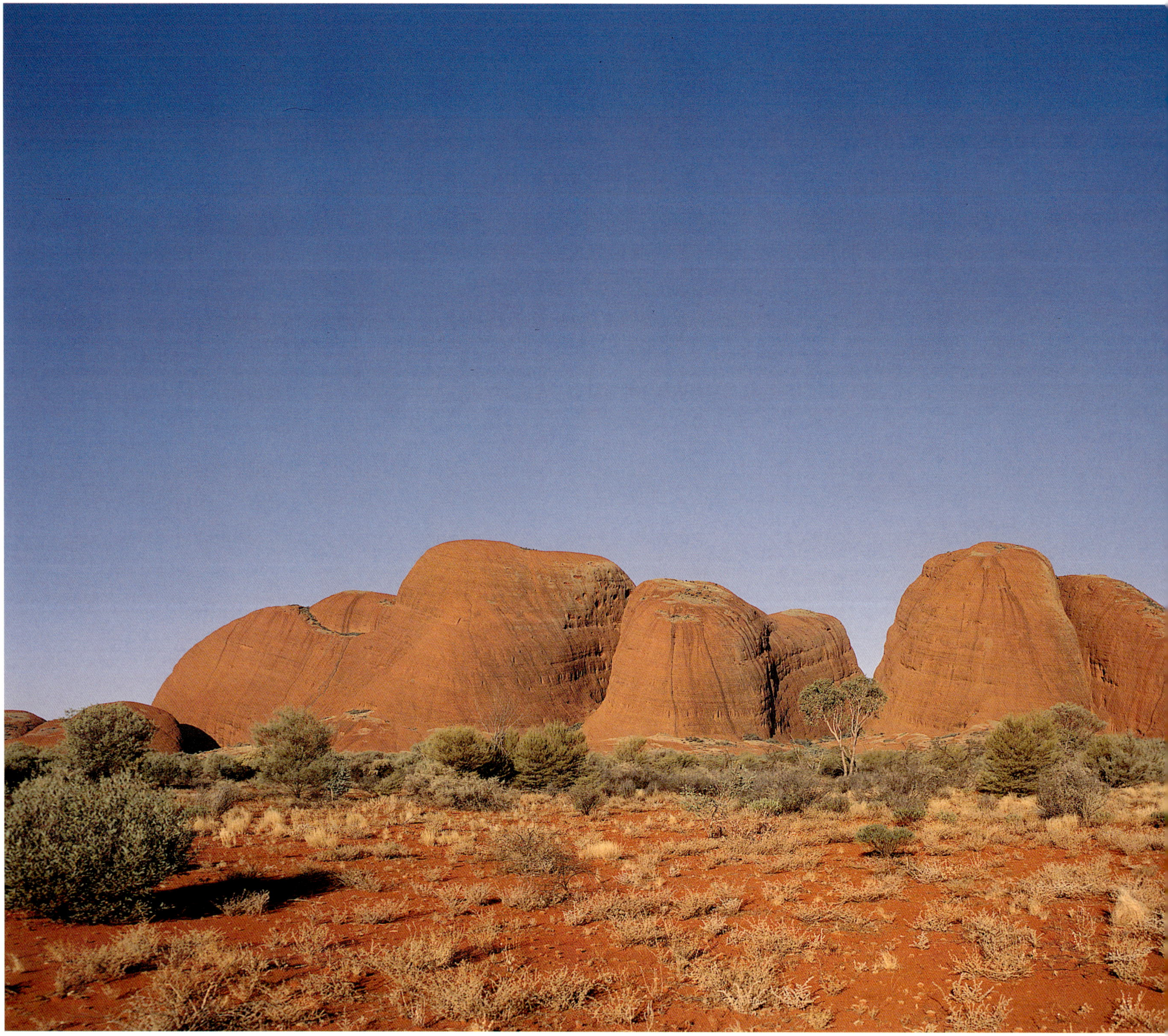

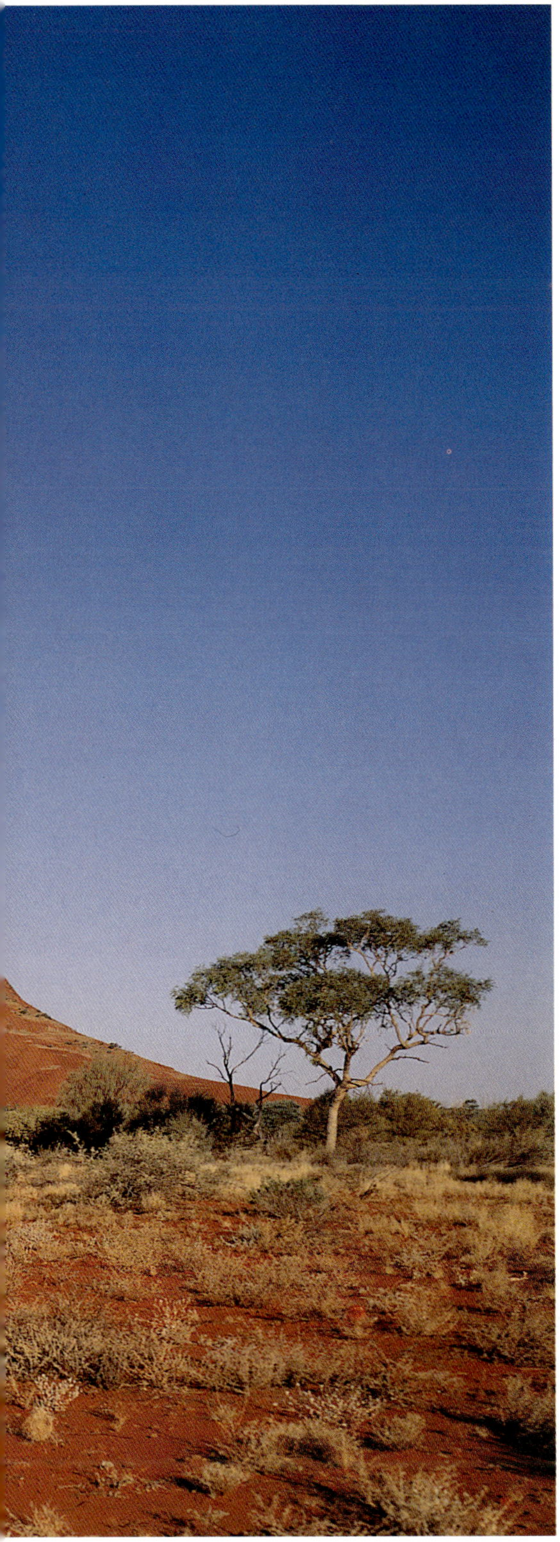

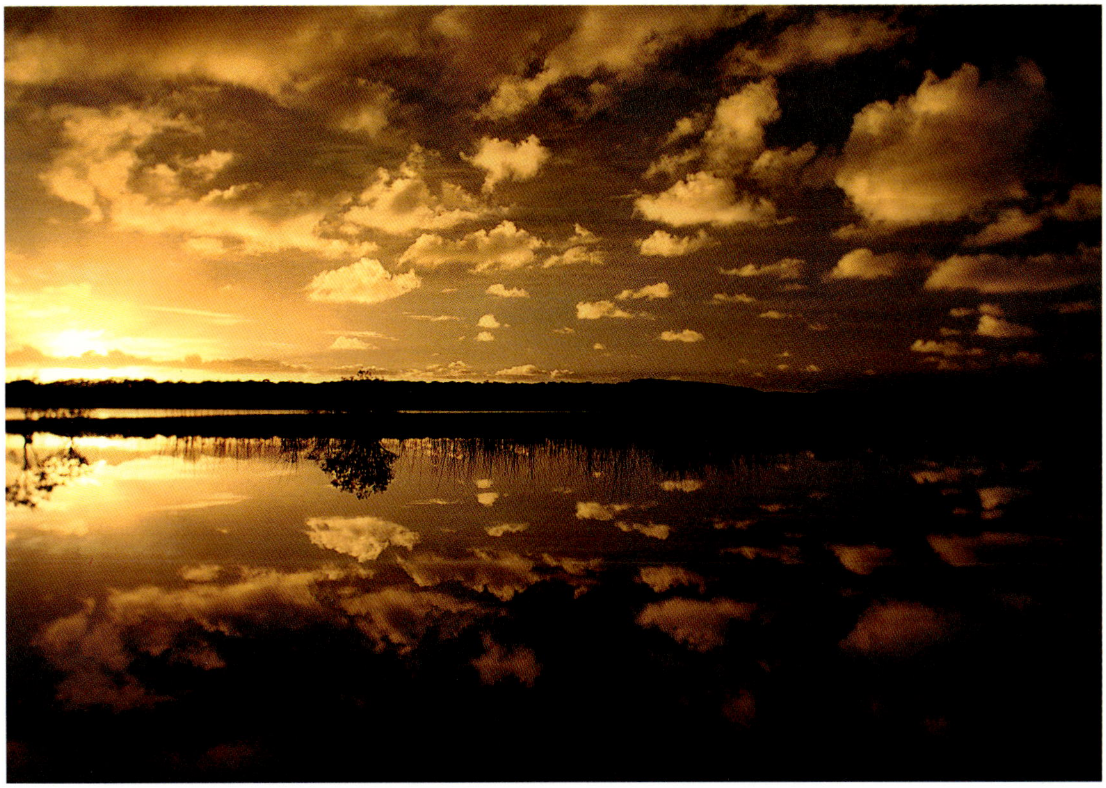

Left: The distinctive humps of Katatjuta—the name of which means 'many heads' in the local Aboriginal dialect—rise boldly from the nurturing earth towards an enfolding blue. These dramatically-coloured sandstone peaks represent the essence of the centre of the country, and even the landscape seems to be heading towards them.

Above: At day's end, a low evening light transforms the blue waters of Lake Boomanjin on Fraser Island, off the Queensland coast, reflecting the broad canopy of clouds, which are gold-flecked by a dying sun.

Following pages: Geikie Gorge in northern Western Australia displays a refined colour in its banded rock. The 14-kilometre-long gorge was forged by the Fitzroy River over many millions of years.

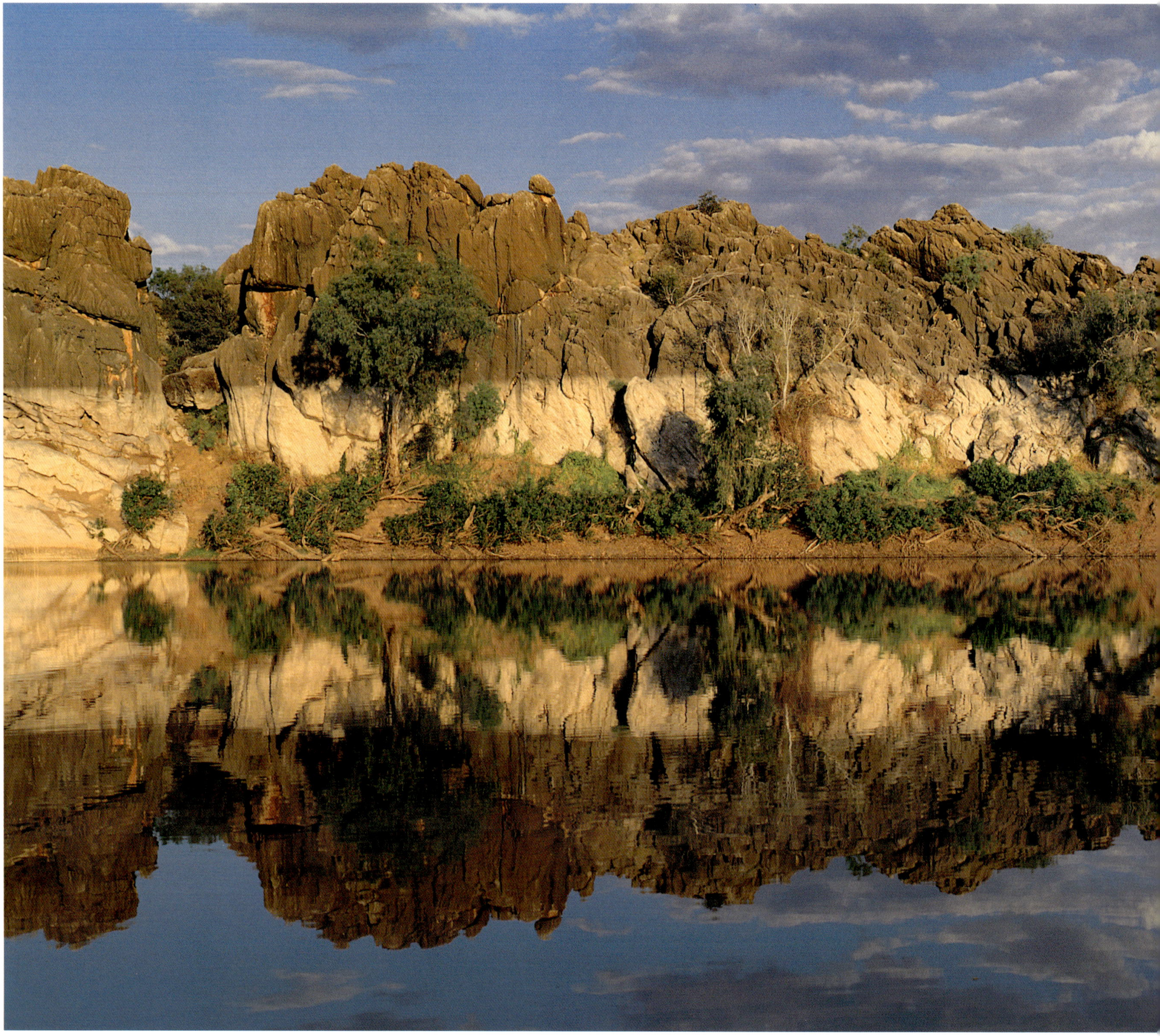

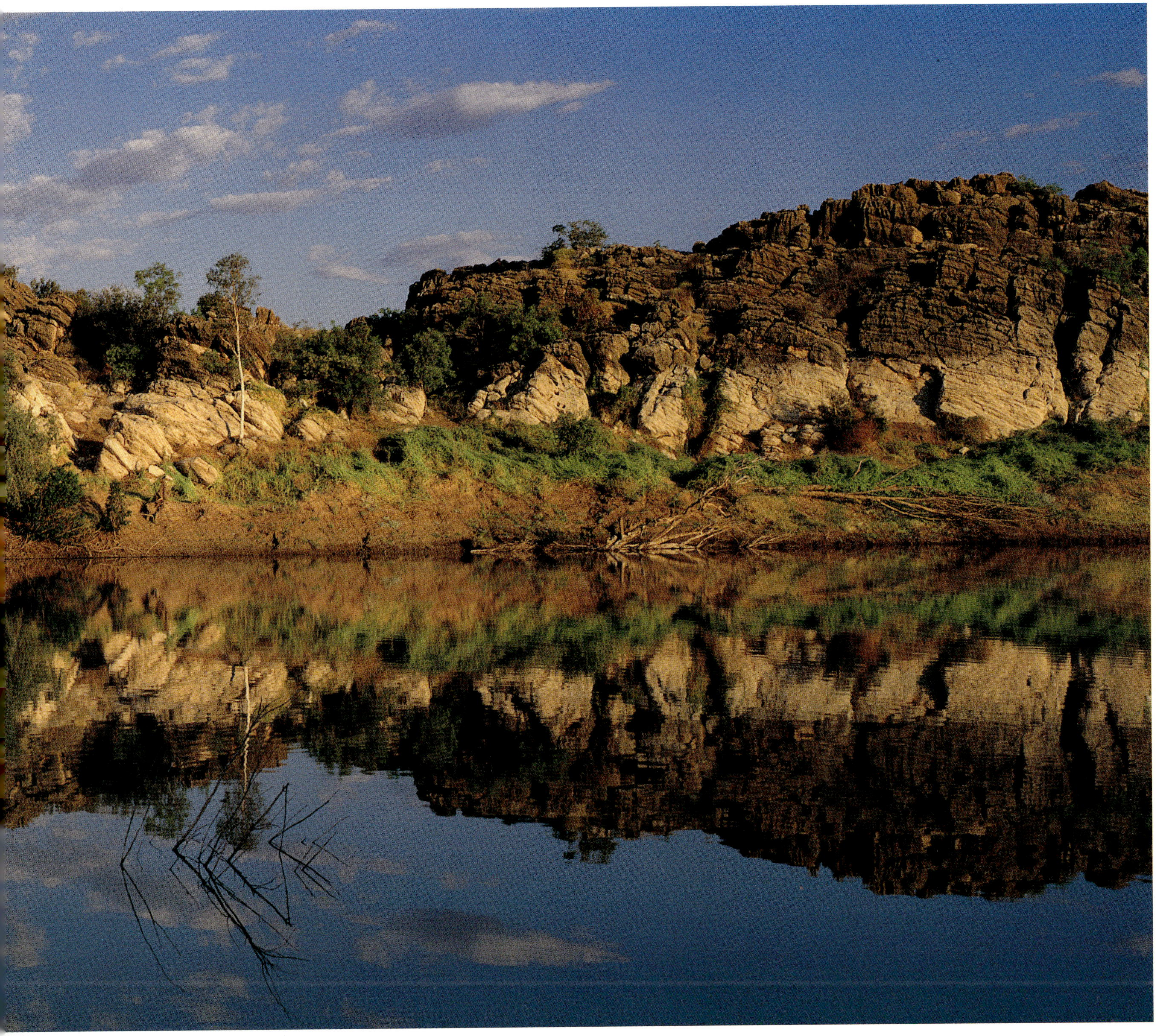

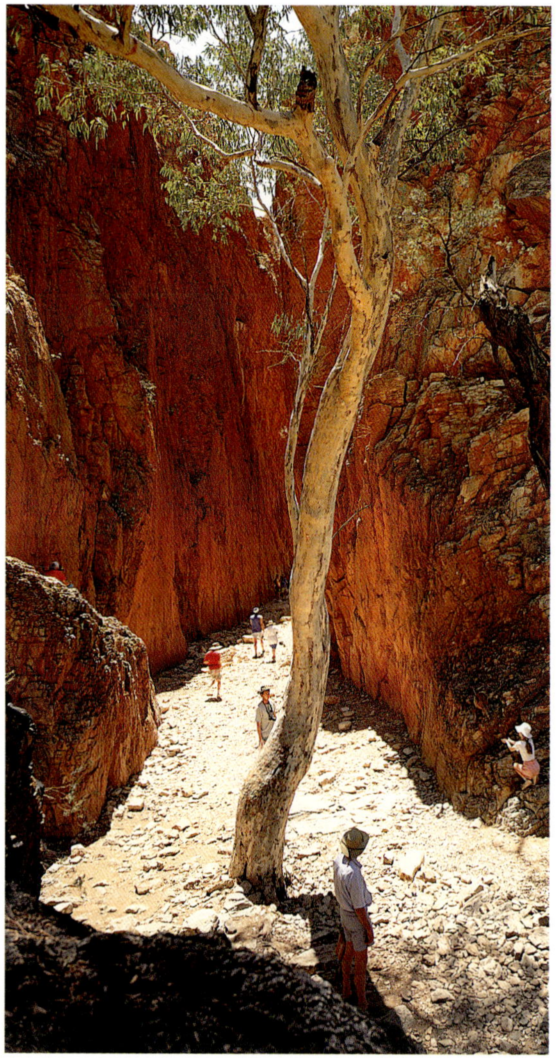

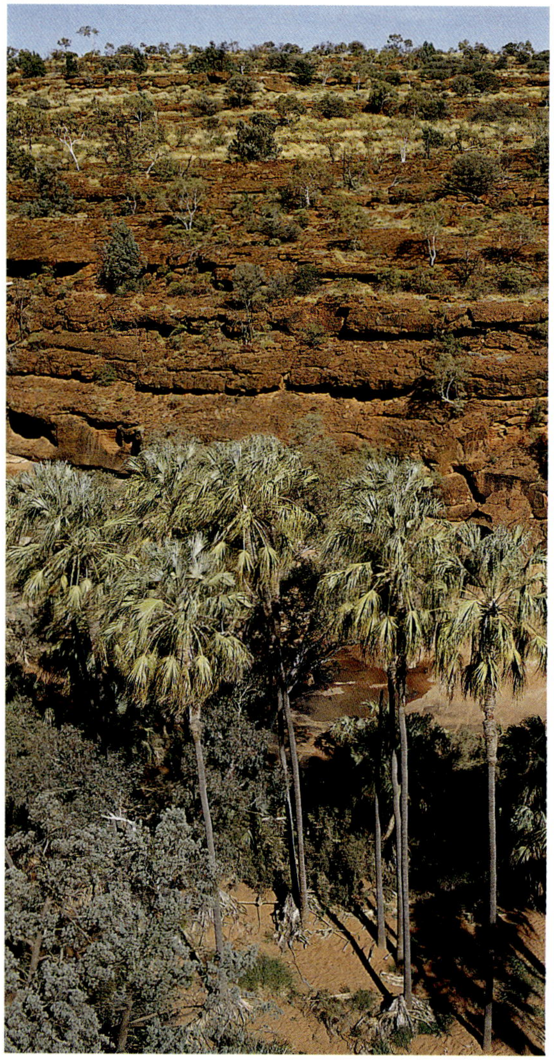

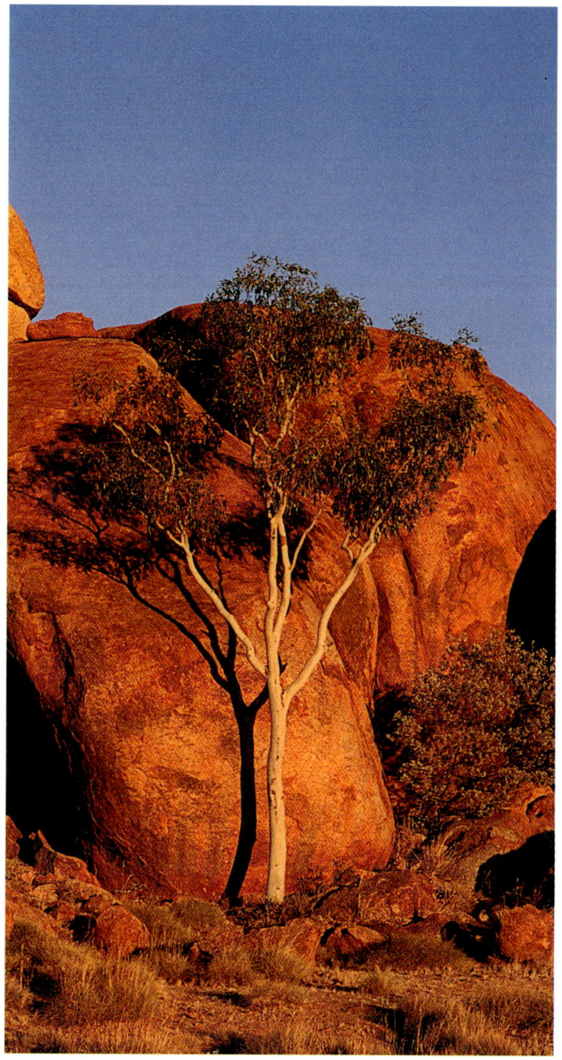

ABOVE LEFT: Nothing should grow out of the rocky floor of the narrow Standley Chasm in the Northern Territory, but a sturdy eucalypt finds a site to thrust its way up between the 100-metre high russet walls.

ABOVE CENTRE: In nearby Finke Gorge the khaki of the cabbage palms provides a striking contrast against dark-brown cliffs. These slow-growing trees defied all odds, notably the continent's vast climate changes over hundreds of year, to survive.

ABOVE RIGHT: A lone pale spindly gum tree has found a dramatic backdrop in the Devils Marbles' hot coal-colour. Despite its barren appearance, Australia's red heart supports a lot of vegetation which has adapted well to the harsh conditions and stretch high to take sustenance from both the sky and the earth.

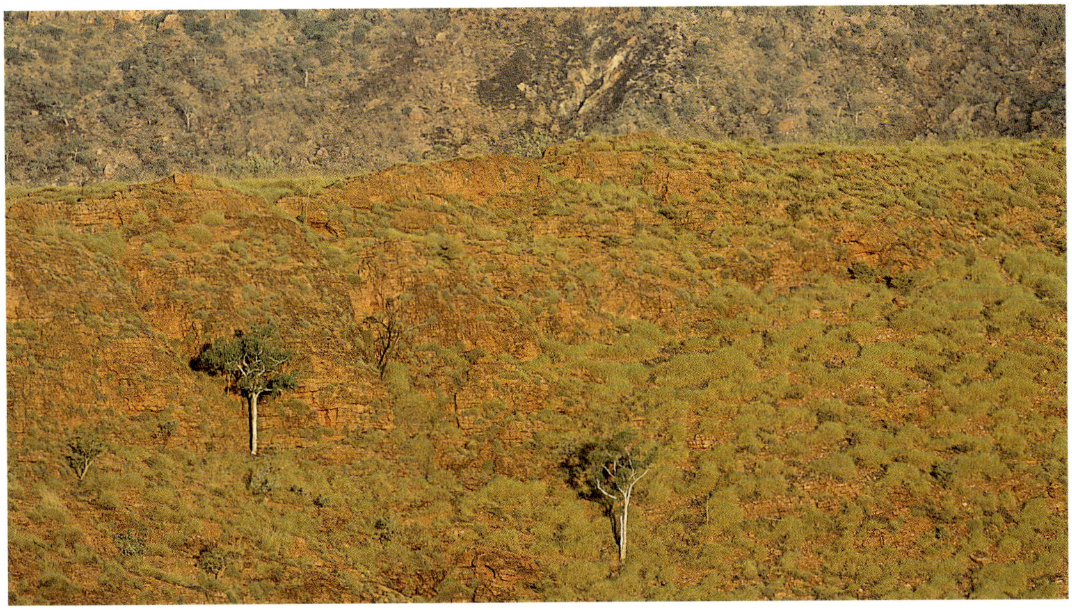

Above: The red and green combination creates a curious orange on the banks of Lake Argyle. The seasonal rains of the tropical north allow scrubs and isolated trees to grow.

Below: These appropriately-named ghost gums near Alice Springs seem to bow their almost white-barked trunks in reverence to the strength of the sky. These trees, like the grasses and scrub which surround them, seem to have been bleached by the fierce outback sun.

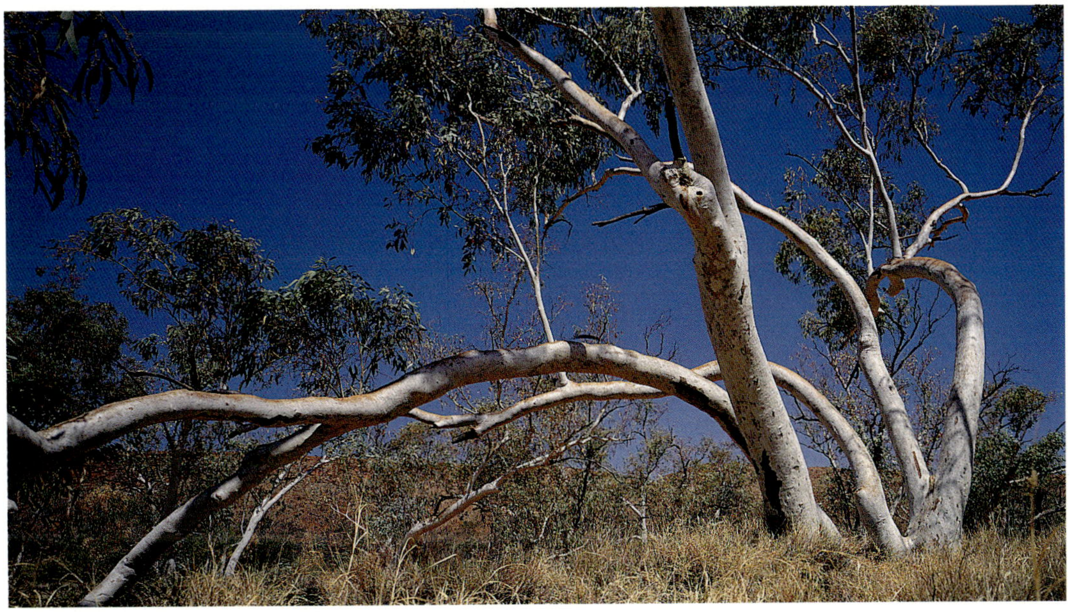

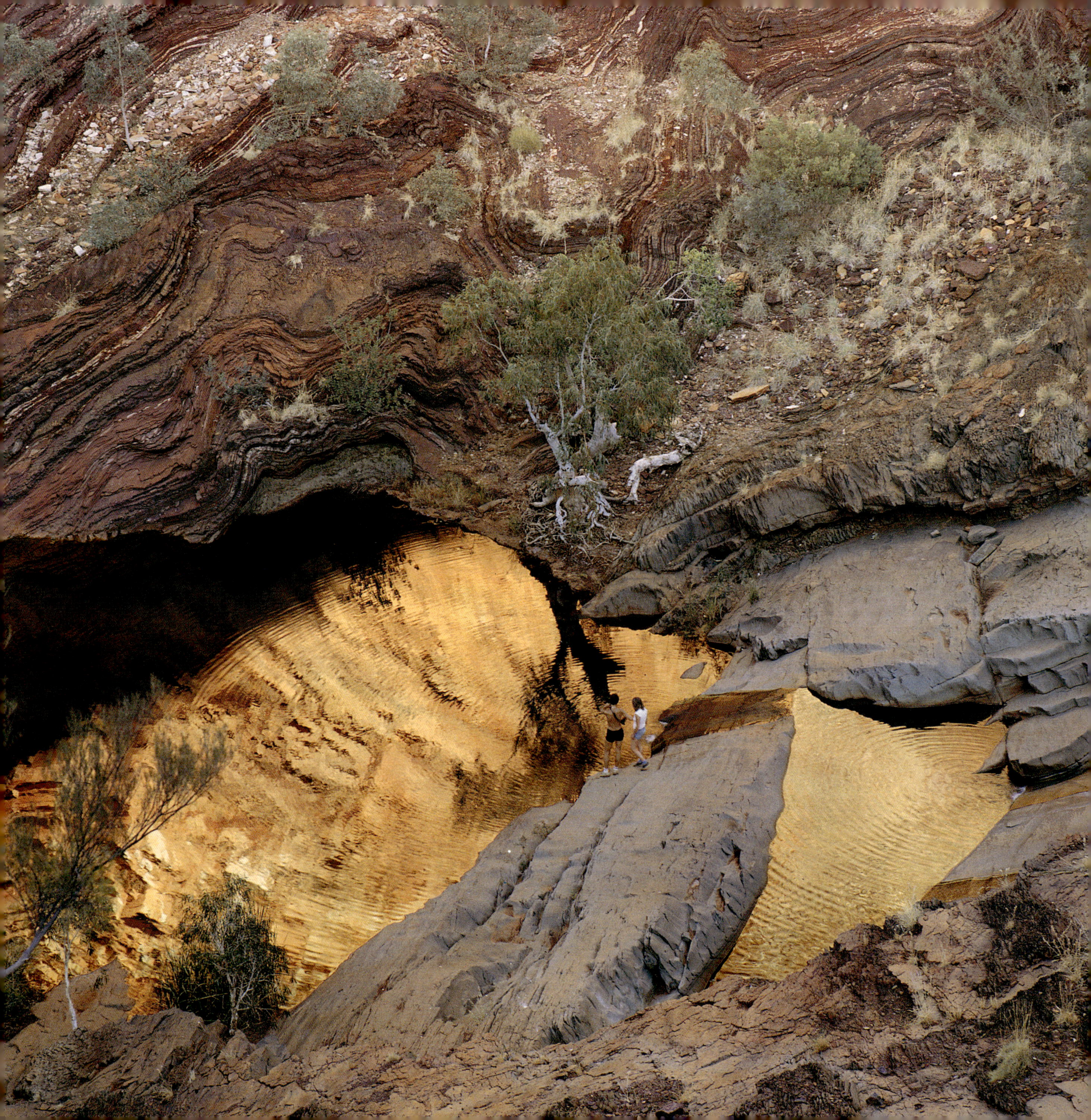

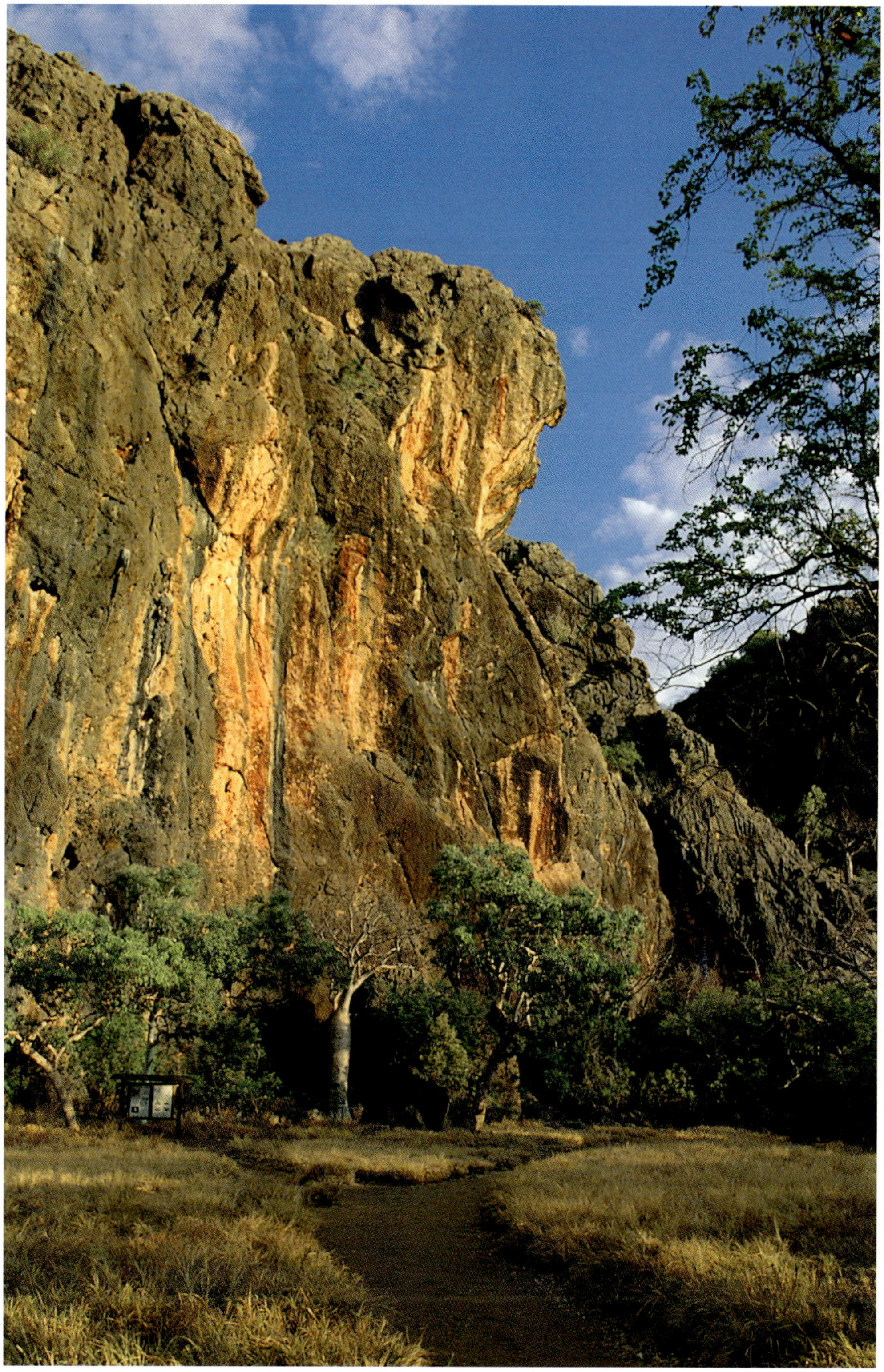

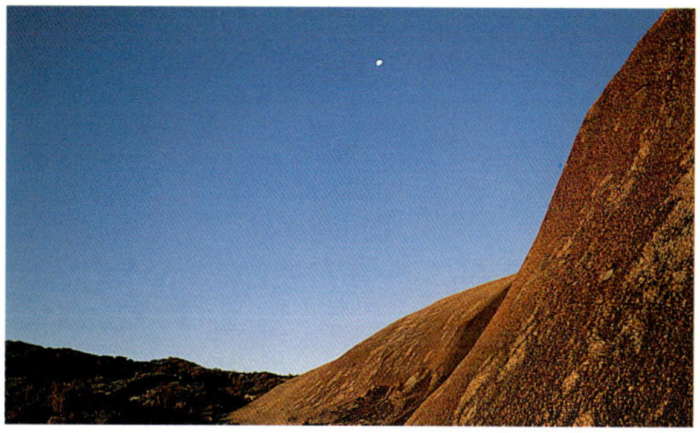

Opposite: The 3000-million-year-old rocks of the Pilbara are stunningly revealed at Hamersley Gorge. Swirls of reddish-brown display the incredible antique richness, but a younger glow is cast on the water below where the colours mix with the bright light.

Left: A prehistoric limestone reef was transformed into a 750-metre-long cavern at Tunnel Creek in the Kimberleys by the ravages of time. The emerald trees are dwarfed by the dramatic orange, red and brown precipice in a regal light.

Above: The Remarkable Rocks are fascinating boulders on Kangaroo Island, off South Australia's coast. Even the moon can't resist a peak at their imposing forms from behind its blue curtain.

Below: In this particular light the strange shapes and smooth surface of the Remarkable Rocks appear a deep terracotta colour against the soft sky, despite the fact that they are composed of warm-brown granite.

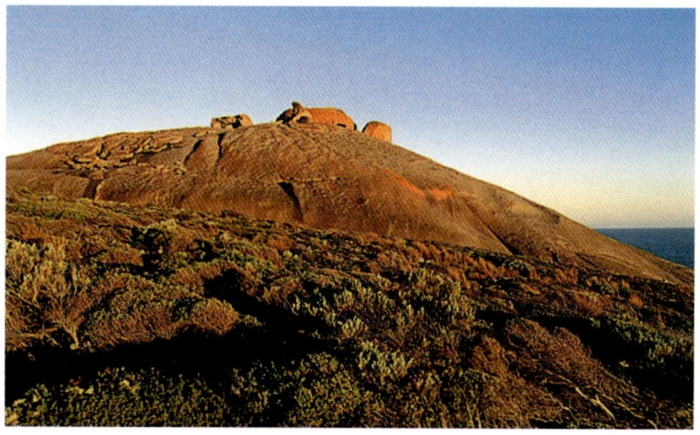

Right: Above this broad river near Hervey Bay in Queensland the airy pink clouds cast by the sunset head towards the night sky just beyond the horizon, while streaks of gold from the fading sun shower the water surface. The delicate light of evening and early morning lends a magical touch to many of Australia's wide open spaces.

Right bottom: At Pine Creek in the Northern Territory, the pastel pinks, blues and lilacs of the evening sky softens a stark and dry scene. This light also adds an ethereal touch to the spindly marsh trees that await a drink from the seasonal rains.

Far right: The fresh morning light of a new day covers the terrain surrounding the town of Tennant Creek. The ubiquitous red dirt, dotted scrubs and trees and clear sky seem to have been just brushed by clean new paints, giving the typical wide open spaces of the outback a new life.

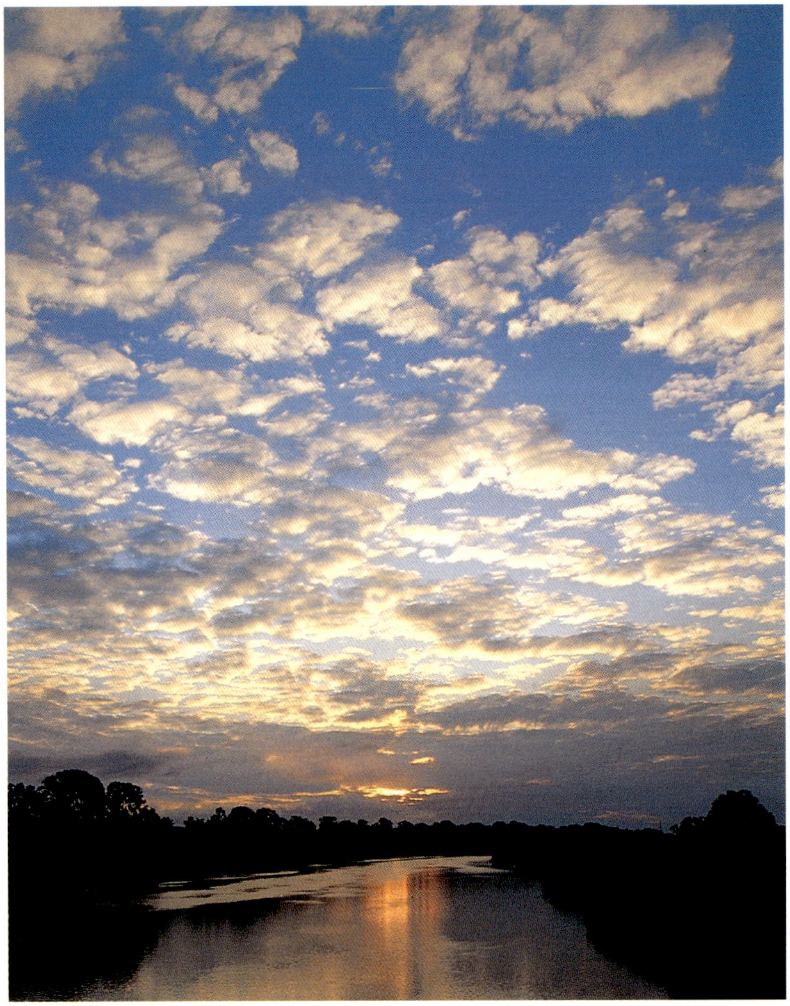

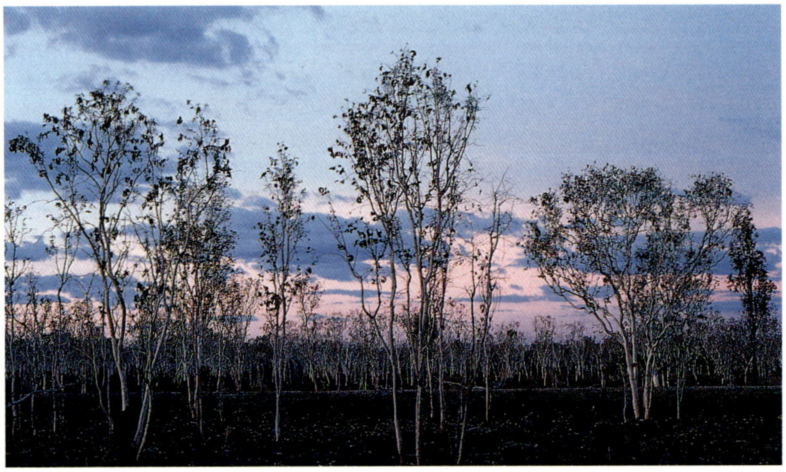

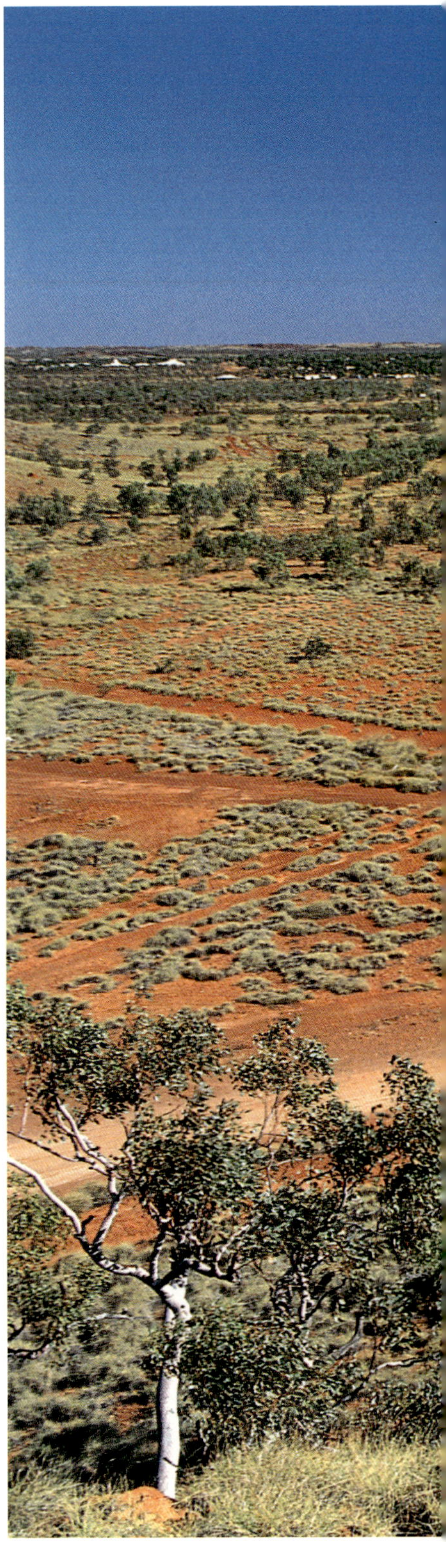

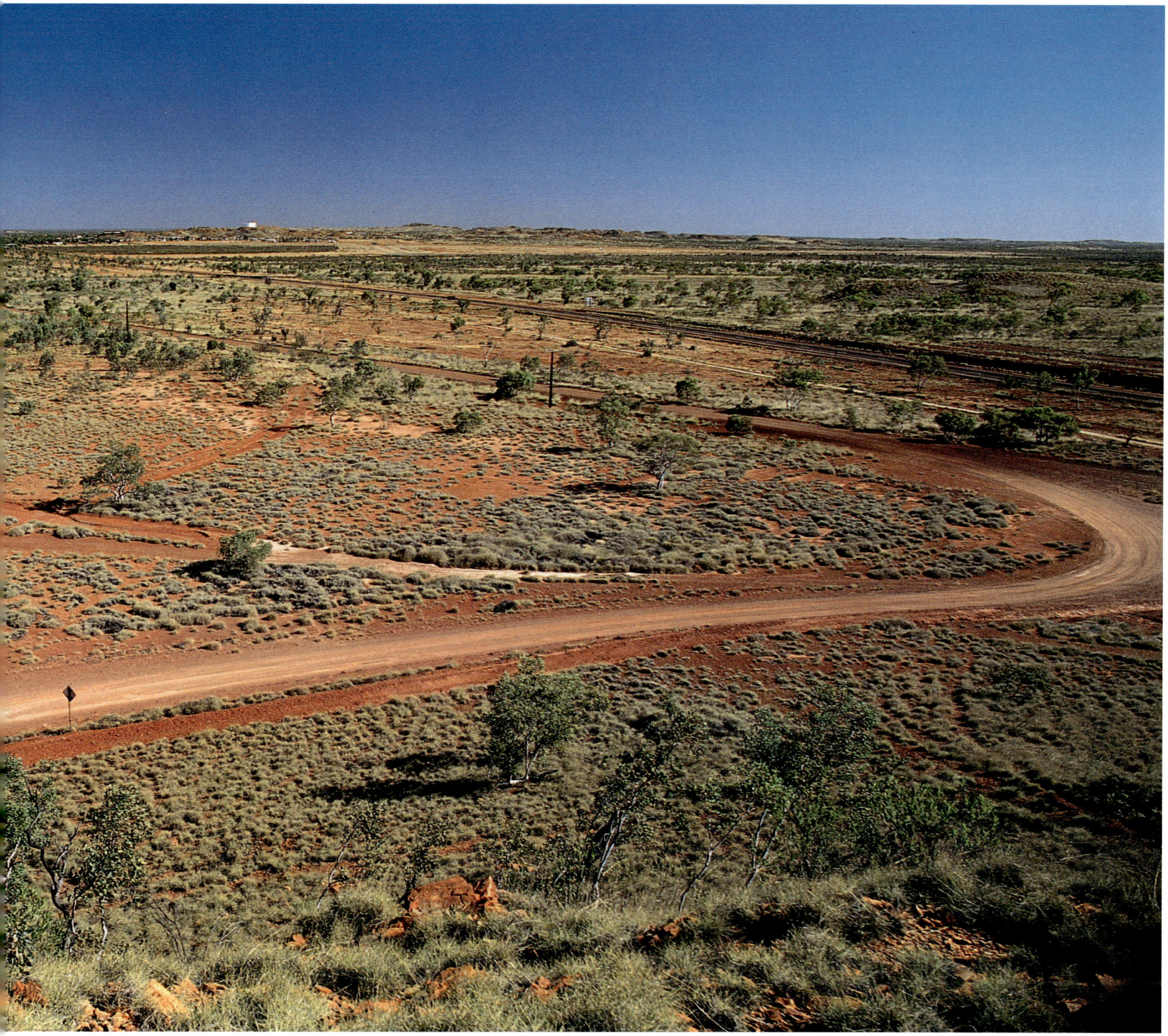

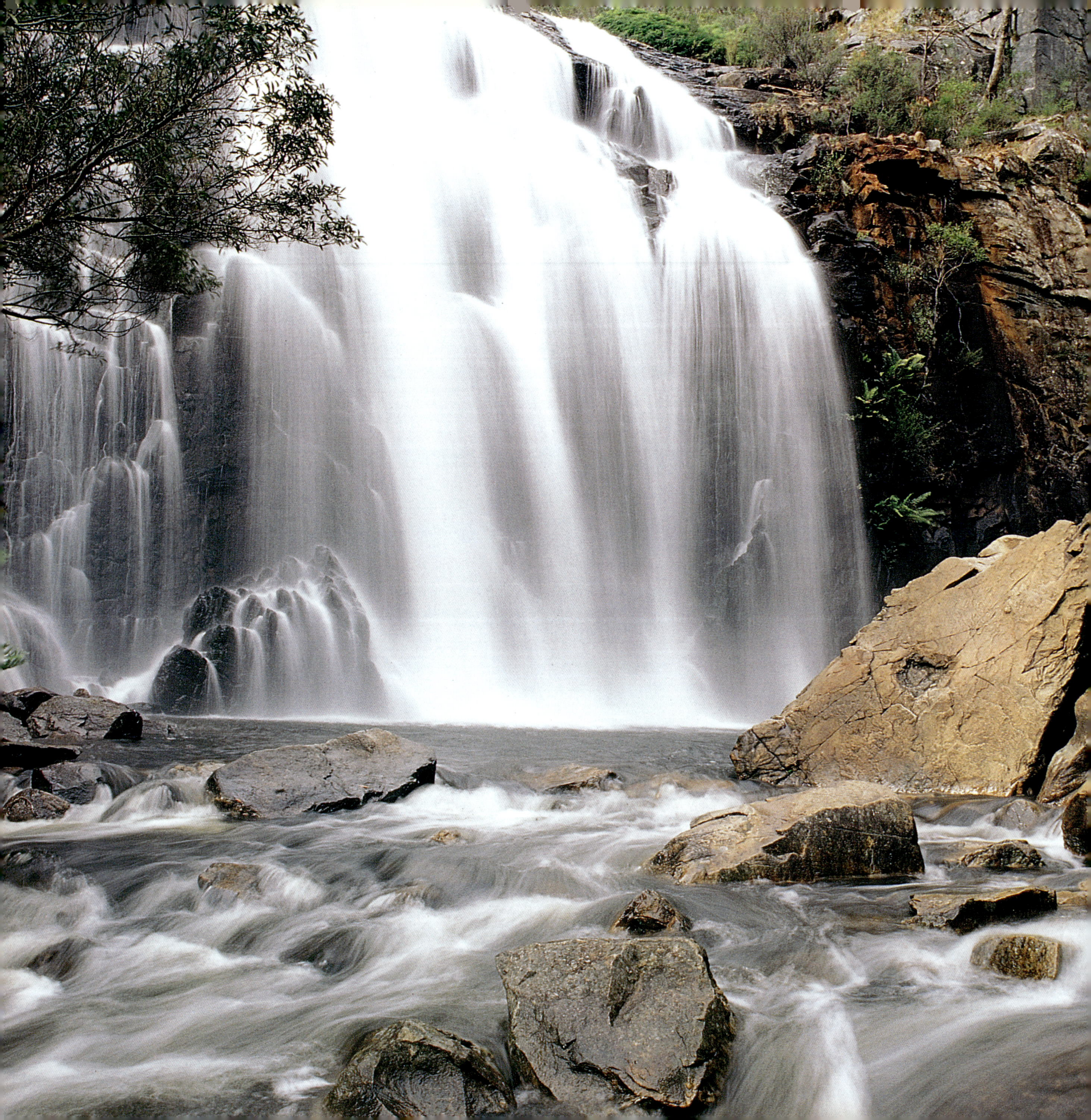

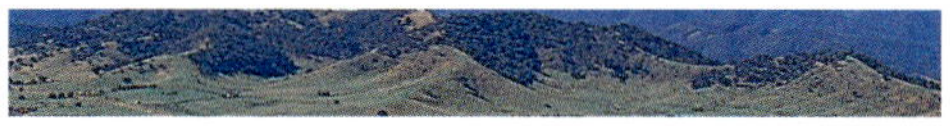

BLUE MOUNTAINS AND WHITE WATER

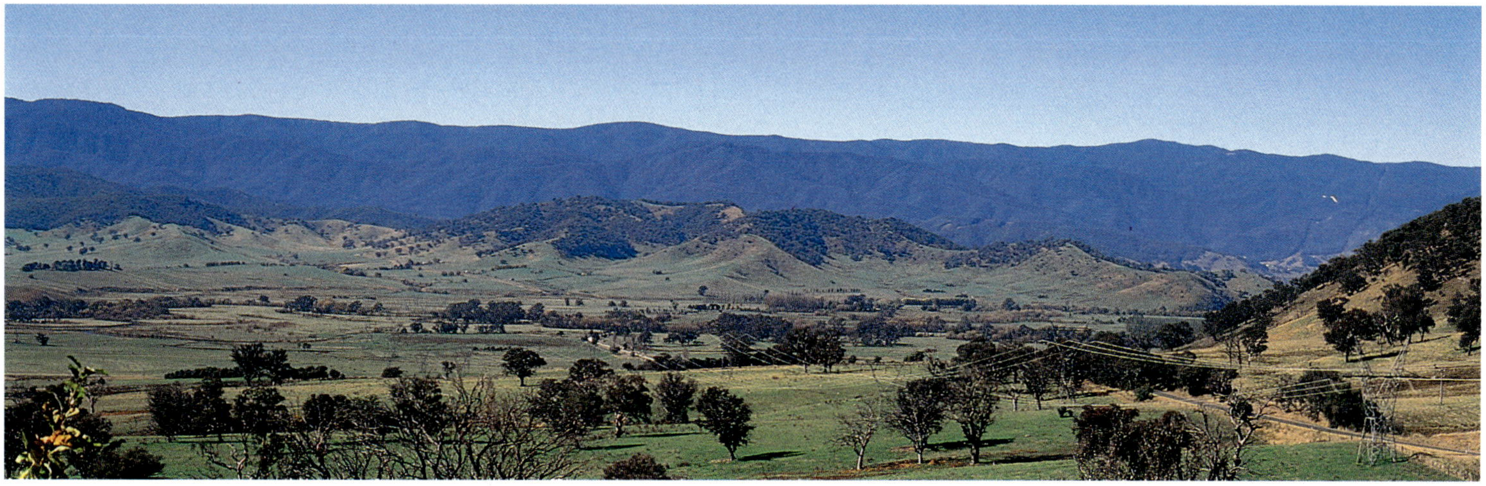

OPPOSITE: The opaque curtain created by the Mackenzie Falls at the Grampian (Gariwerd) National Park tumbles to the creek bed and turns the rocks it covers into a cool slate waterway.
ABOVE: Farmlands sweep the lowland beneath the blue peaks of New South Wales' Kosciusko National Park.

Australia's landscapes hold many topographical surprises. The continent is often described as the world's flattest, and the driest after Antarctica, in terms of annual rainfall. Yet around its well-watered fringes, particularly in the east and south, bluffs, mountain ranges, streams, rivers and lakes abound, giving much of the coastline cool hinterland retreats.

From the far north of Queensland to western Victoria the Great Dividing Range stretches its mighty arms. The 'Great Divide' is actually a series of hills, peaks and high plateaux that run along the east coast for almost 2000 kilometres. Tasmania, long separated from the mainland, also features windswept highlands—the origins of which were once the Great Divide and which are still connected, technically, by a bridge of hills lying beneath the strait between Victoria and the island state.

But many thousands of years of erosion have weathered Australia's mountains down in size dramatically. The continent's highest peak is in southern New South Wales and reaches a mere 2228 metres. Other worn upland areas are scattered throughout the continent, such as South Australia's Flinders and Gammon ranges and the Hamersley and Stirling ranges in Western Australia, and they each can hide and reveal surprises of bubbling cascades amidst the ancient rock.

Narrow creeks and streams, broad rivers, lakes, volcanic tarns and tumbling waterfalls provide splashes of white, grey and blue throughout the land, giving life to the barren regions. Interspersed are the subtle greyish-browns of hardy granite, the reddish-gold tones of easily eroded sandstones and the mountain flora of olive, bottle green, greys and browns. Emeralds brightens the tropical rainforests and in winter snow and ice envelope the alps, transforming the blue mountains into scenes reminiscent of Europe rather than the widely held images of a sunbaked Australia.

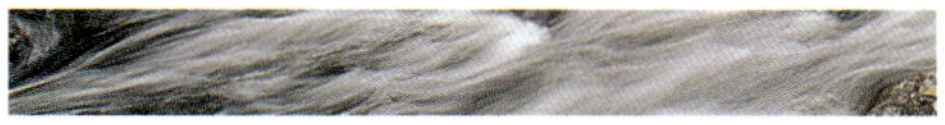

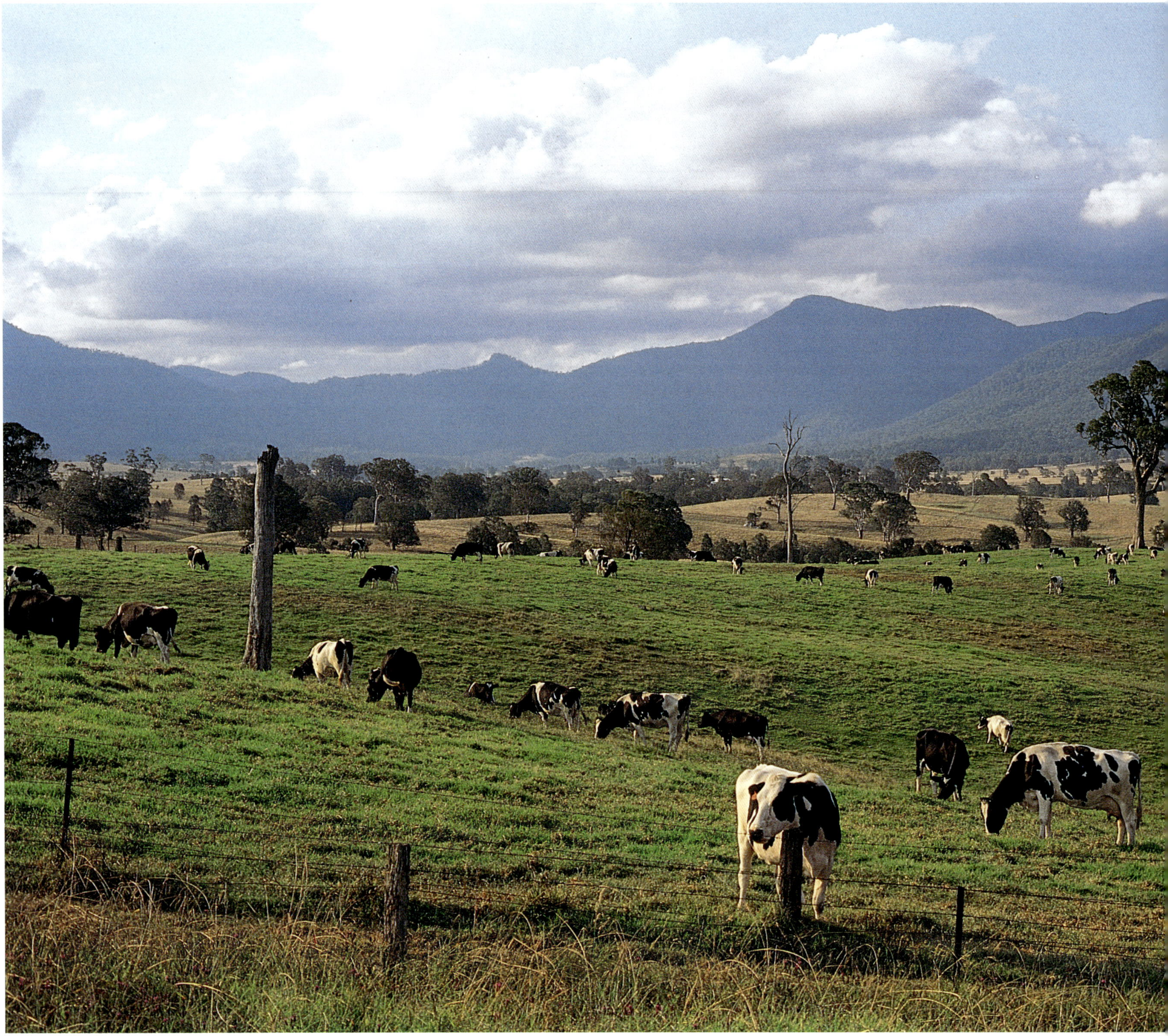

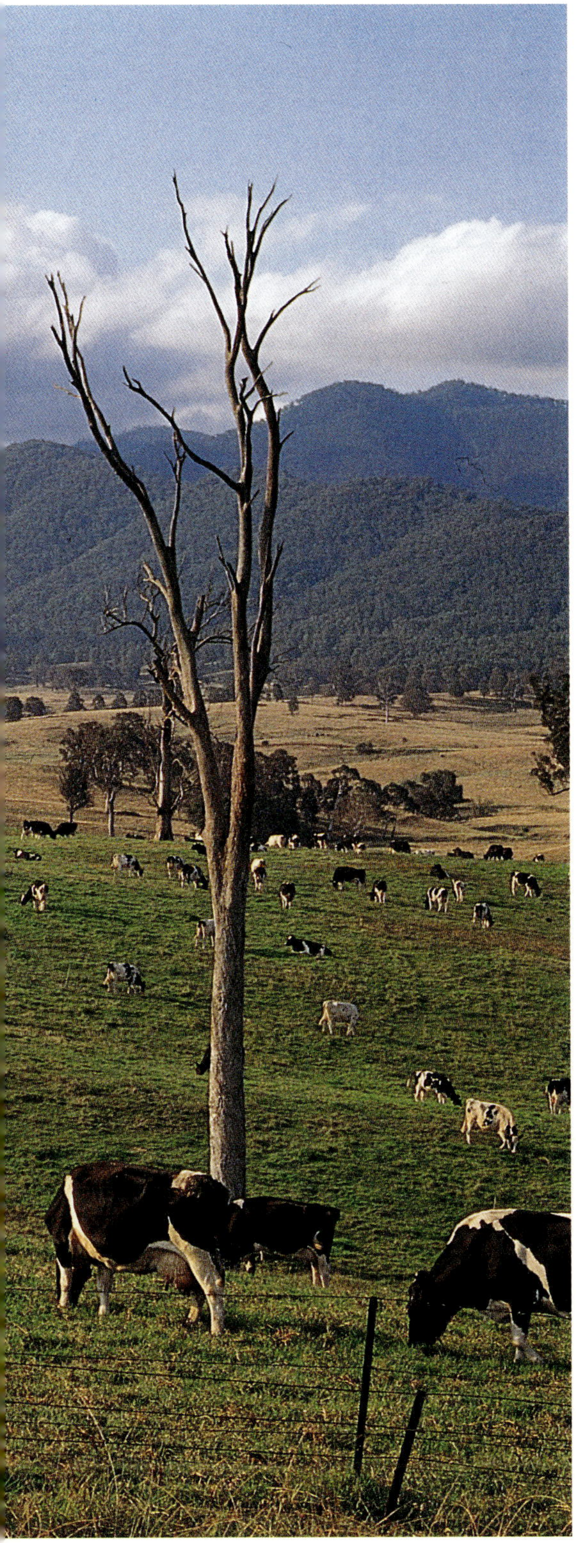

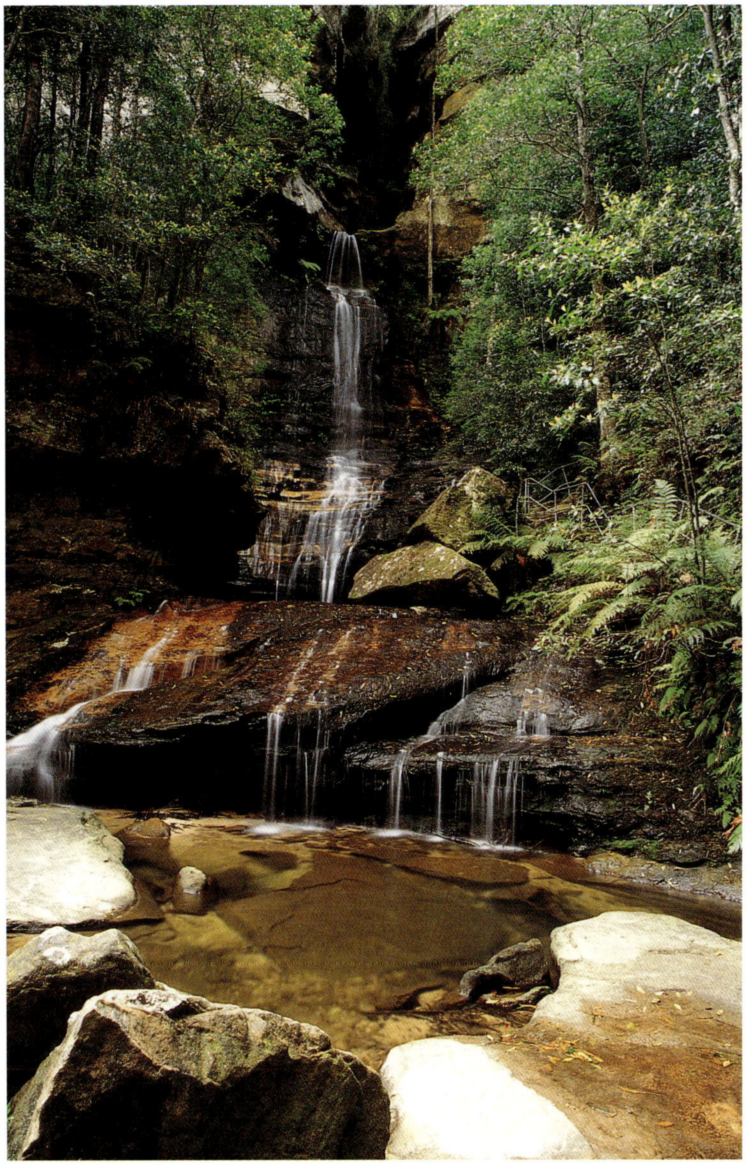

LEFT: The fertile land that runs along the narrow eastern coastal belt is used for intensive farming, such as dairying. Overlooking these tranquil scenes are the sturdy peaks of the Great Dividing Range.

ABOVE: Rivulets of white cascade down the Valley of the Waters in the New South Wales' Blue Mountains. The water, trees, ferns and mosses create a delightfully cool and verdant environment.

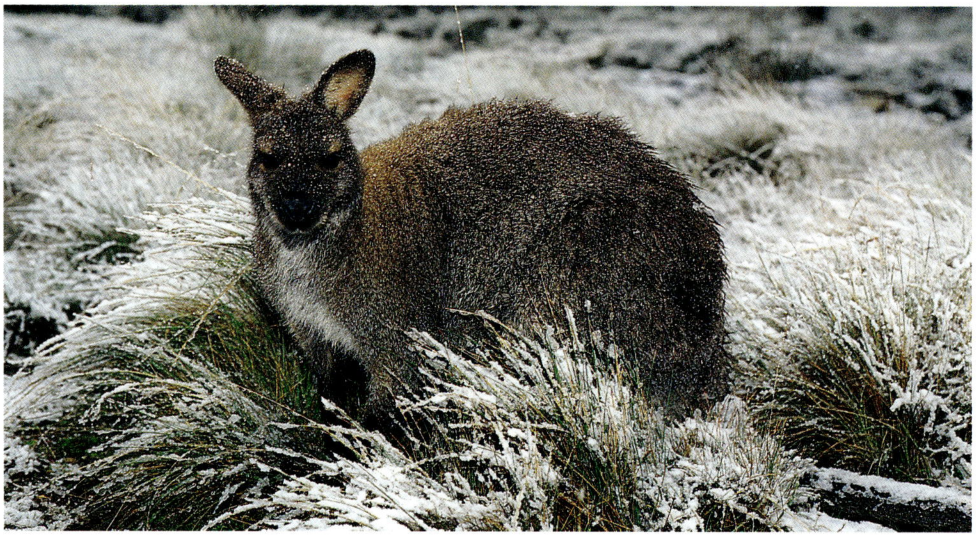

ABOVE: Tasmania's Cradle Mountains contains some of continent's most rugged environments, but is often cushioned with snow during winter. This wallaby has adapted well to the frosty conditions.

BELOW: Beerwah, the largest of the Glasshouse Mountains in Queensland, is composed of solidified lava as it was once part of a vast volcano. It seems to grow out from the lush green fields to touch the sapphire sky.

OPPOSITE: Russell Falls bubbles through the dense forests of Mount Field National Park in Tasmania.

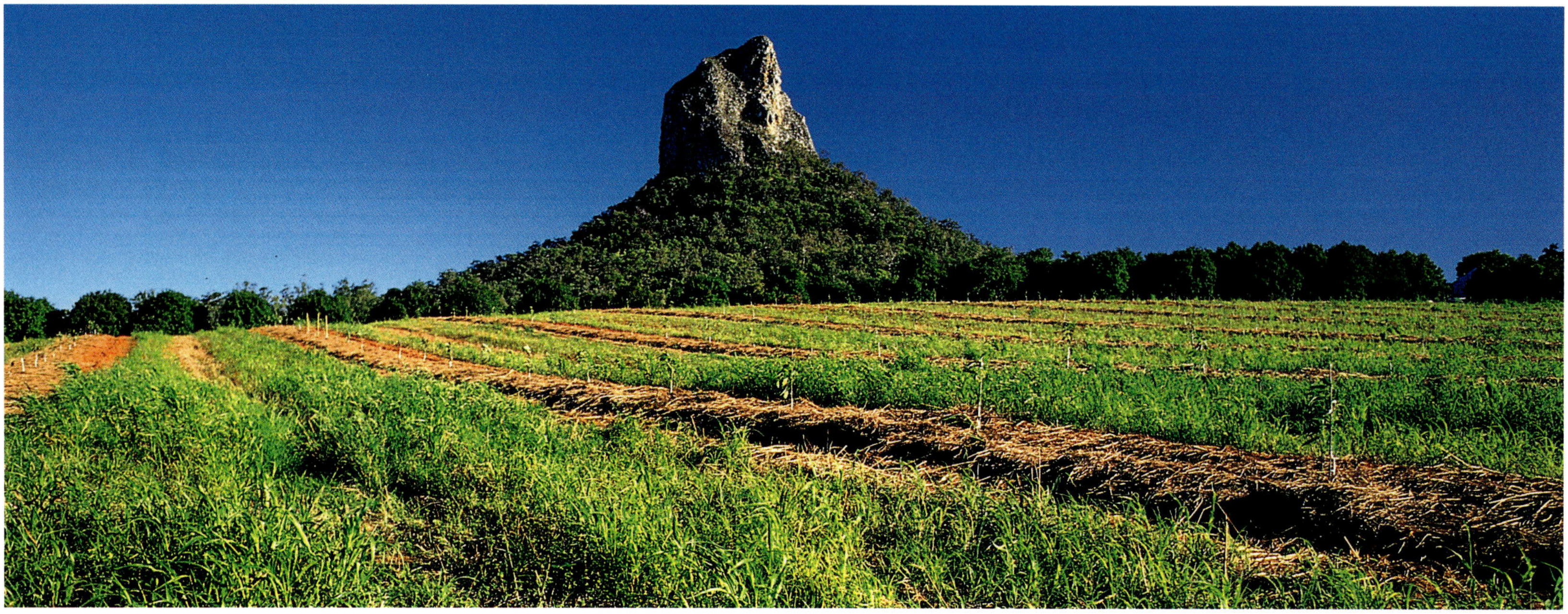

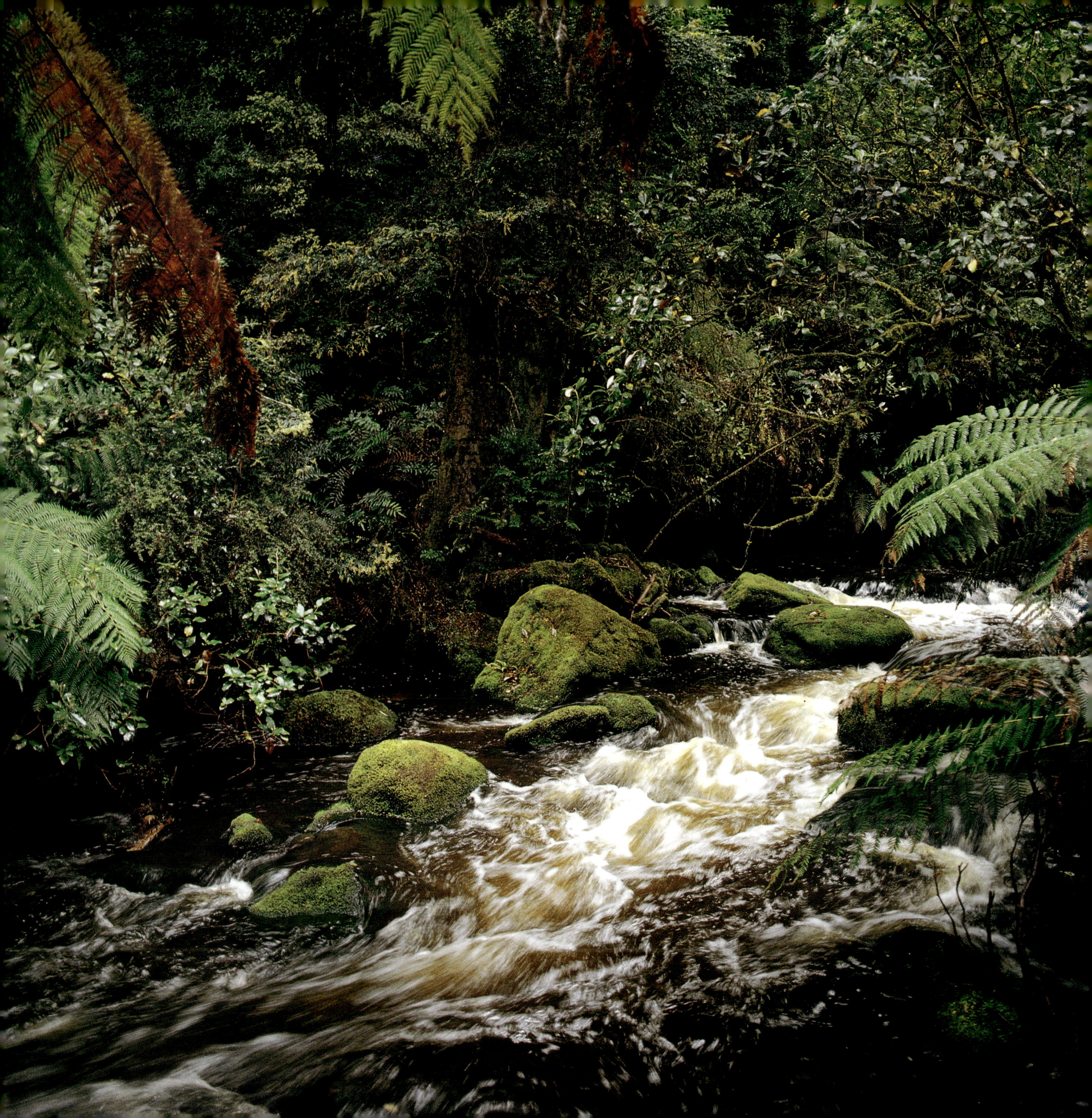

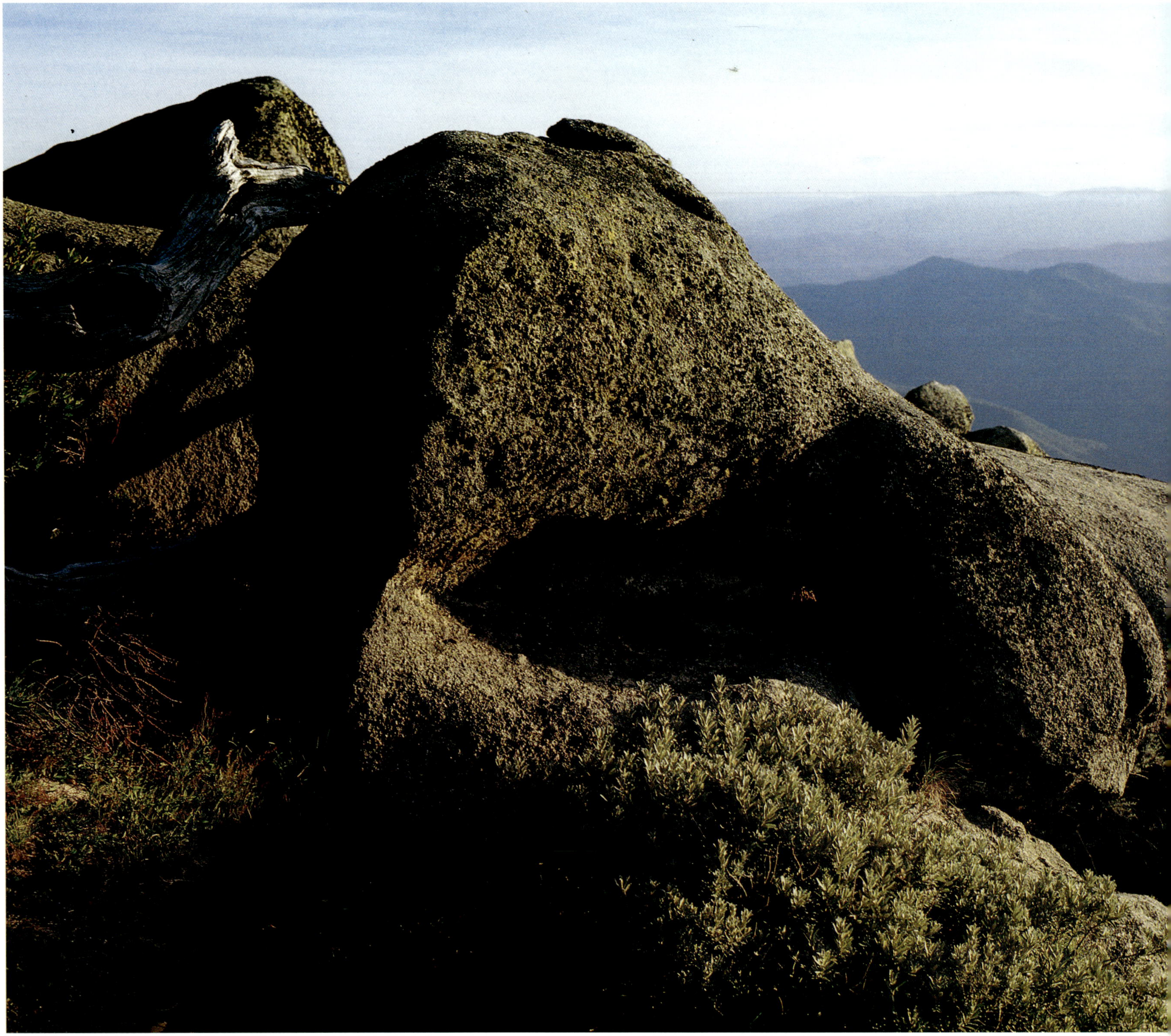

LEFT: Mount Buffalo National Park in Victoria reveals just one of the many striking variations of Australia's highland regions. The 1723-metre Mount Buffalo has monumental granite outcrops that present a solid front to the misty peaks in the distance.

RIGHT: Tamborine Mountain in the south-east of Queensland displays the verdant remnants of the area's original rainforests and eucalypt woodlands. The cool sky of billowing clouds hangs like a blanket above the lush green carpet of vines and trees.

BELOW: The Fortescue Falls in the wild and rugged Hamersley Range in Western Australia splashes its colour over the rocks it has been moulding into rounded shapes for centuries, before joining the deep still water in the gully below.

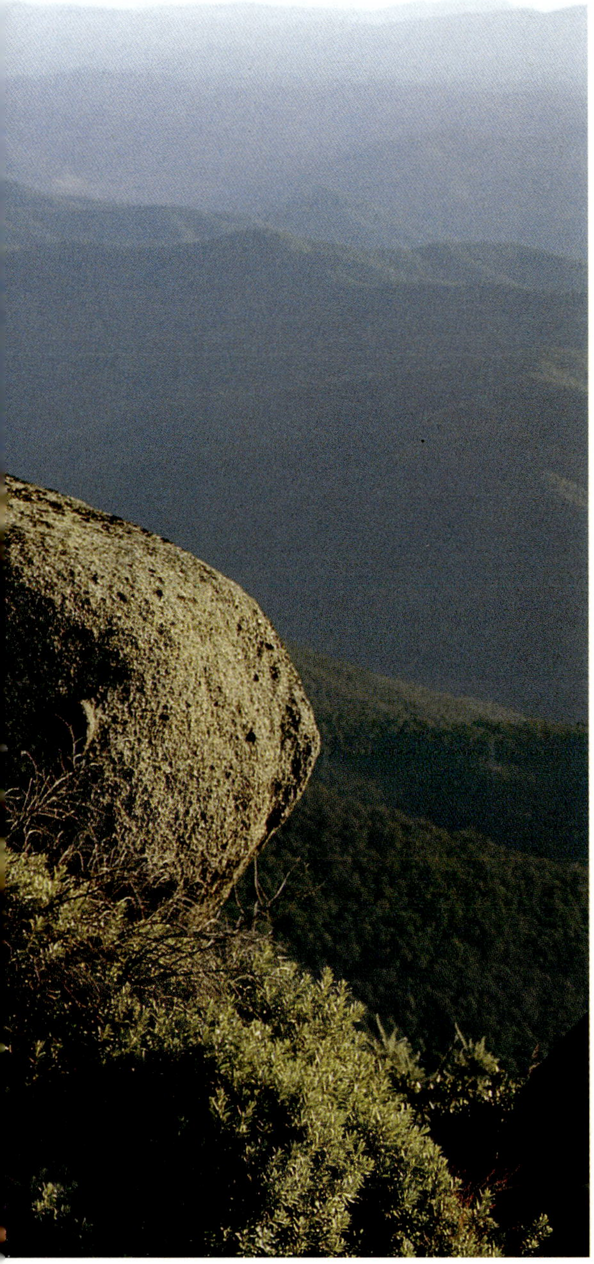

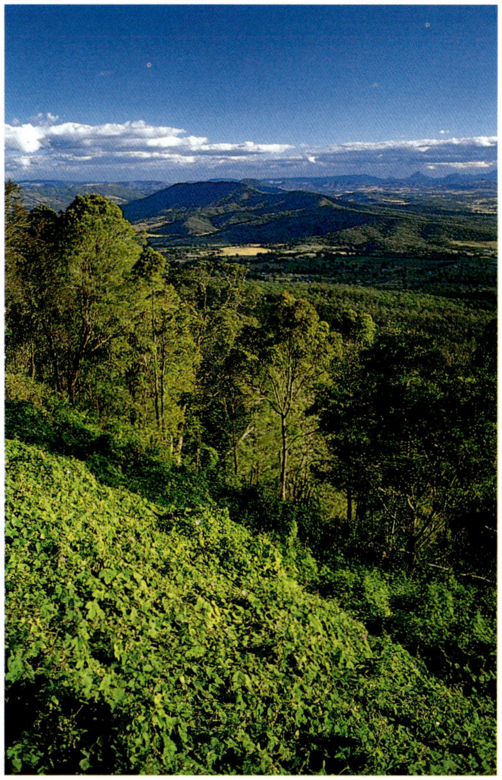

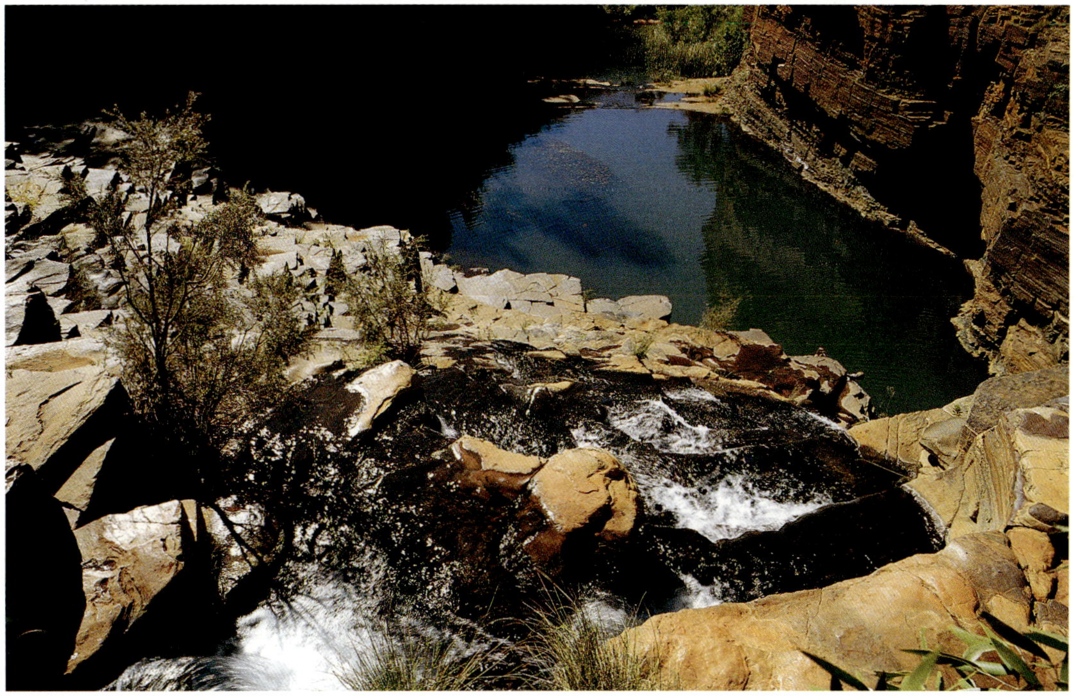

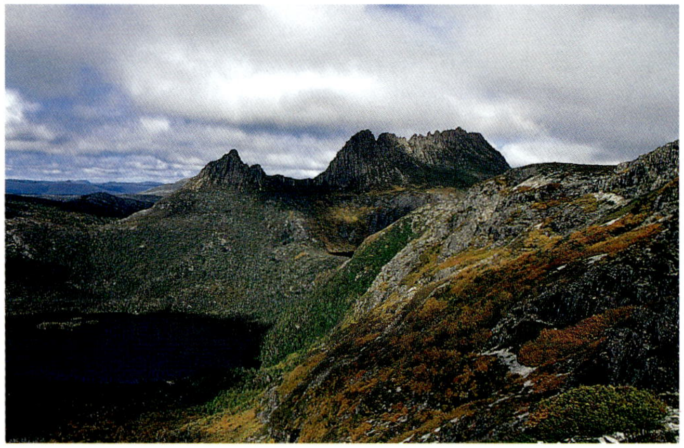

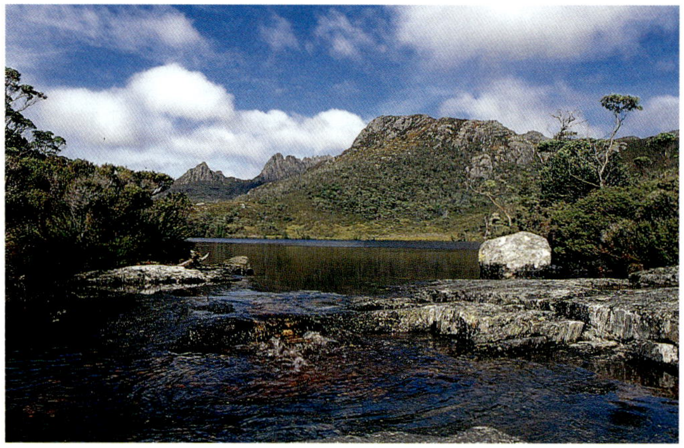

Above left: Dove Lake is a tarn of glacial water that nestle alongside Cradle Mountain within Tasmania's Cradle Mountain–Lake St. Clair National Park, one of the country's most spectacular regions.

Above right: The national park's stark, jagged peaks are clothed in hardy mountain heath and alpine grasses that touch the edges of the sparkling bubbling waterways. The whole area was World Heritage listed in 1982.

Below left: During winter the fall in temperature turns the 1545-metre Cradle Mountain's brown, green and gold tinges into icicles of snow, making the trees appear frosty blue.

Below right: With an elevation over 1600 metres, the dolerite peaks of Cradle Mountain turns the area into a stark and chilling landscape—a far cry from the country's arid climes.

Opposite: The serene Dove Lake belies the ferocious glaciation that swept through the craggy uplands to create the high rocky outcrops, deep valleys and lakes of the Cradle Mountain–Lake St Clair National Park.

Following pages: Tasmania's capital, Hobart, has its own high peak, the 1270-metre-high Mount Wellington.

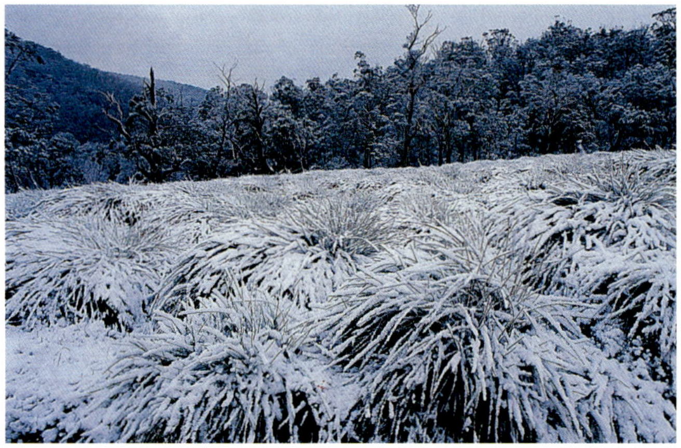

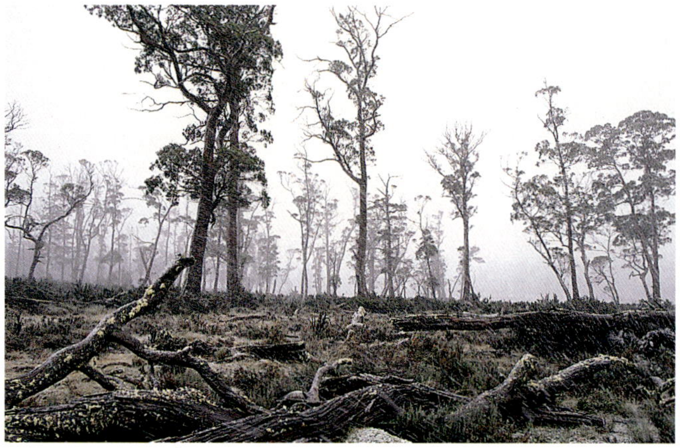

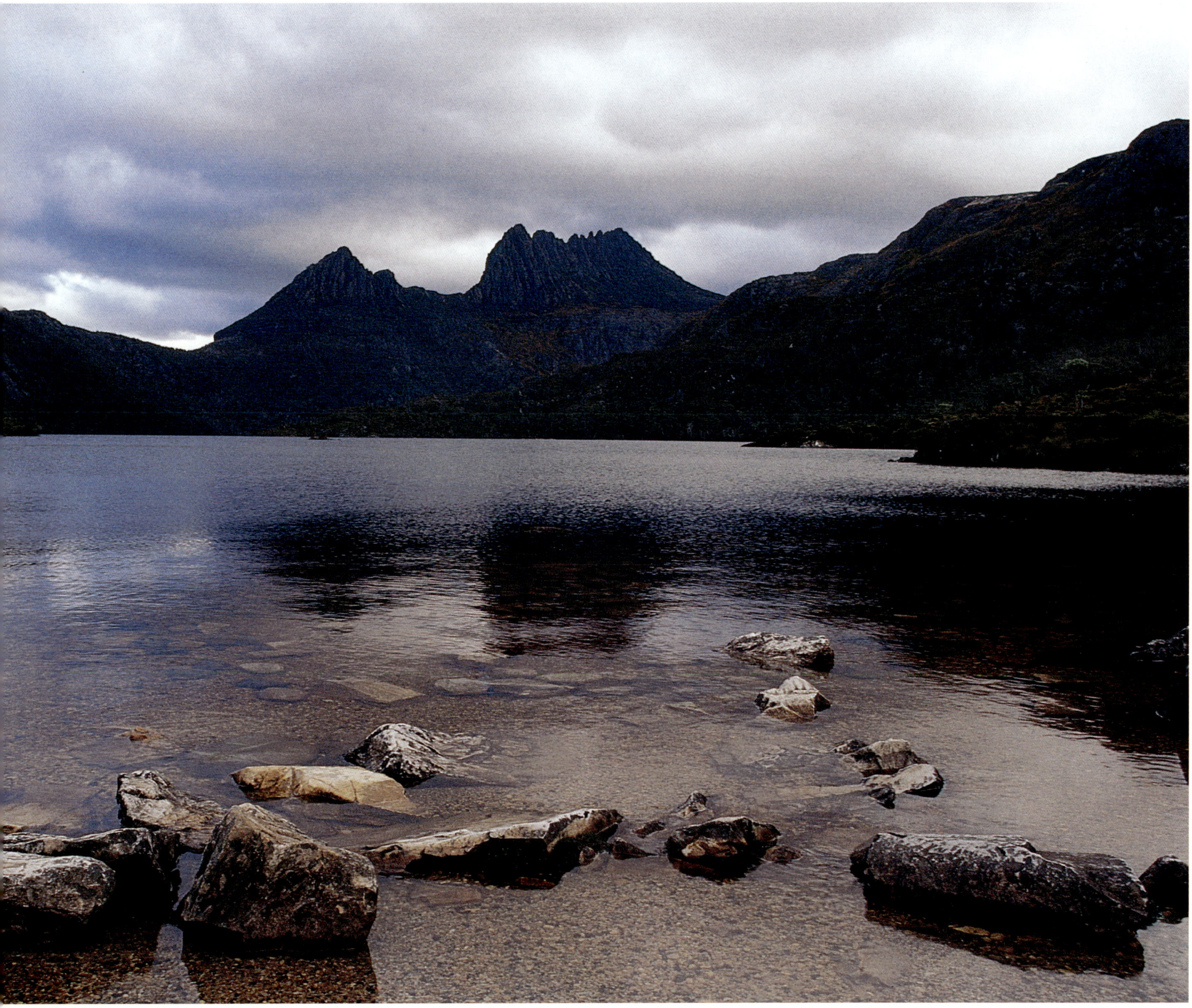

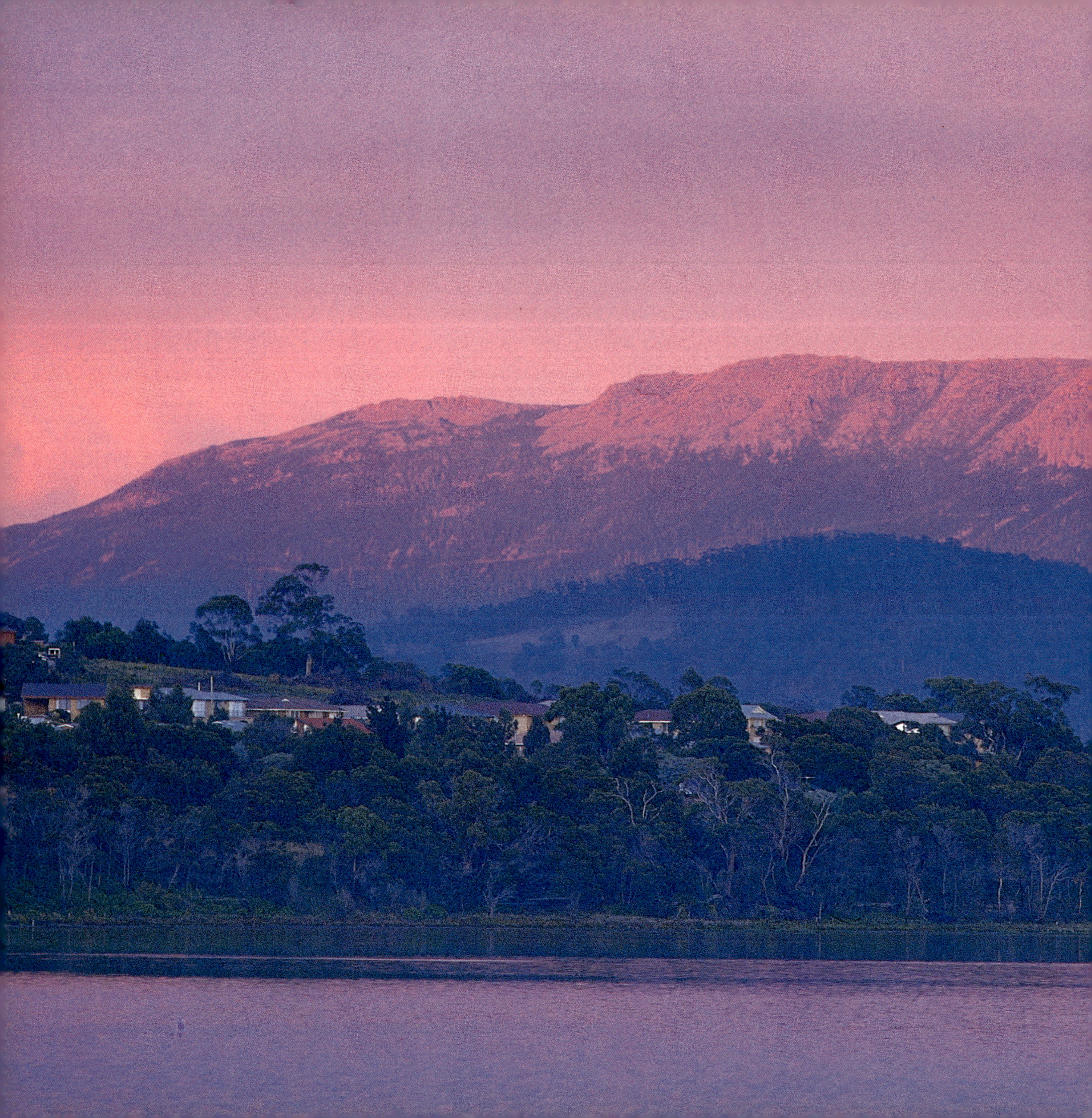

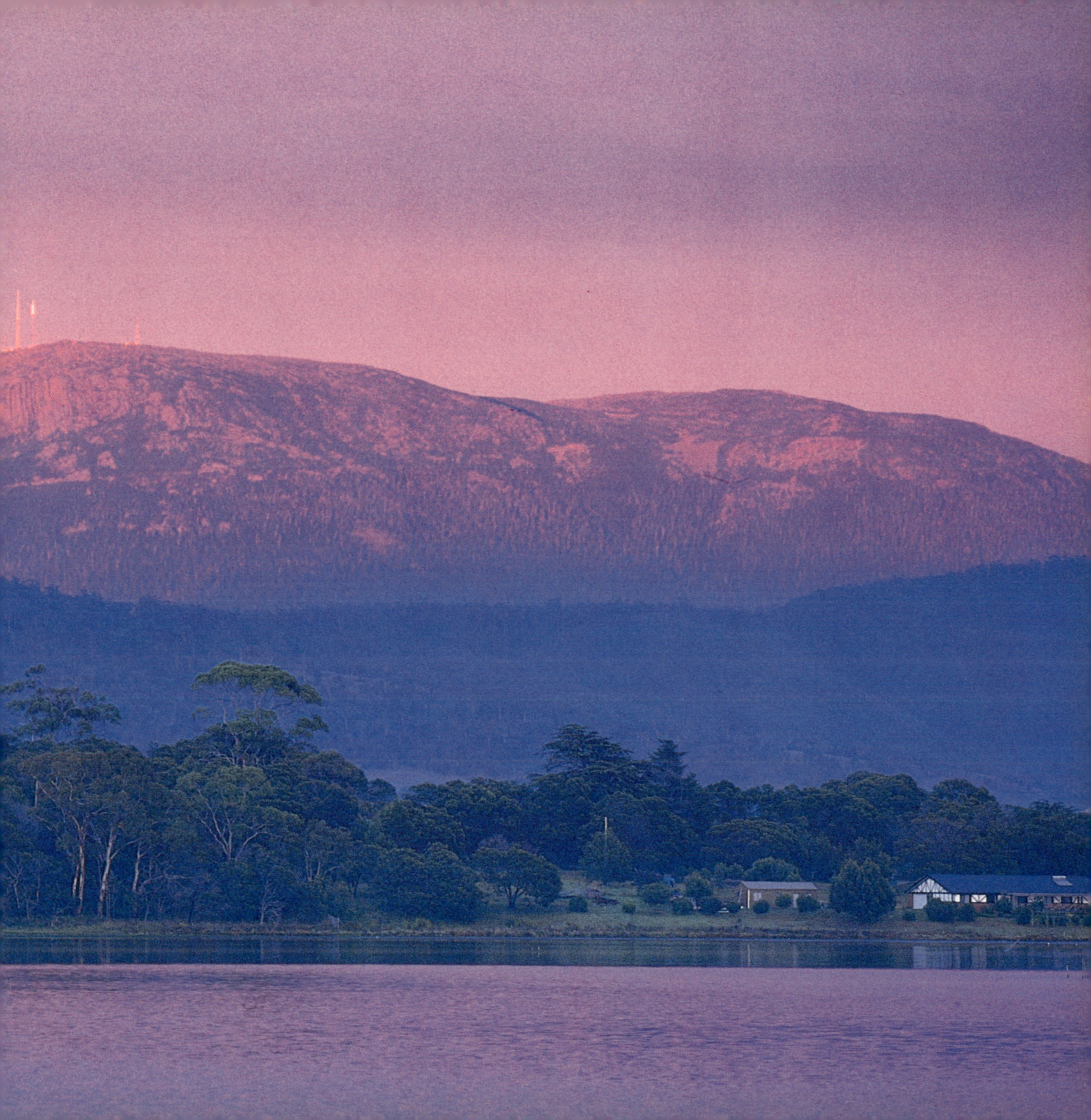

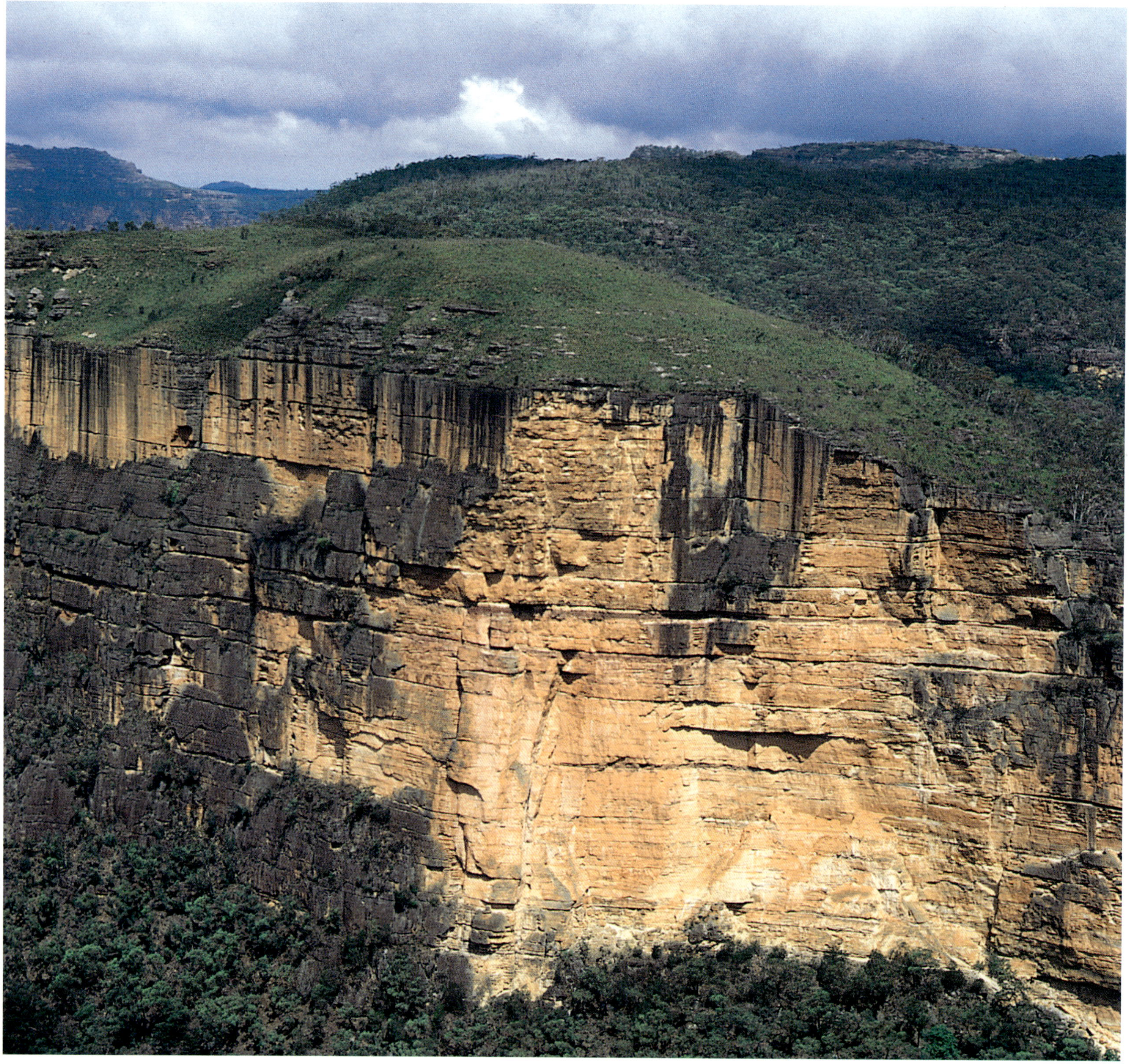

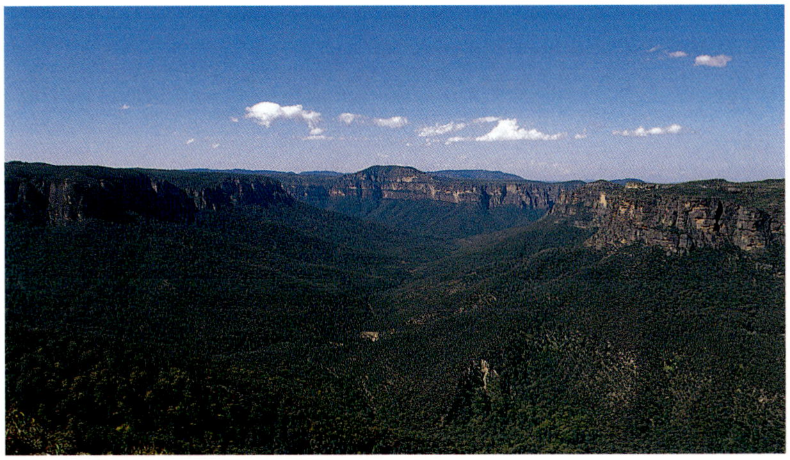

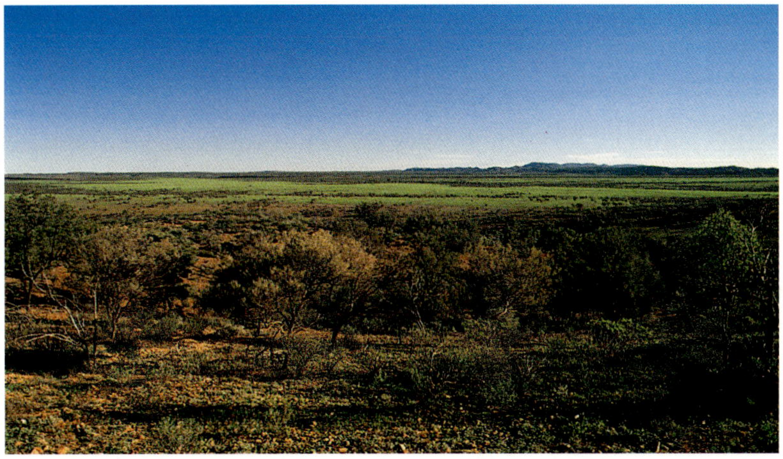

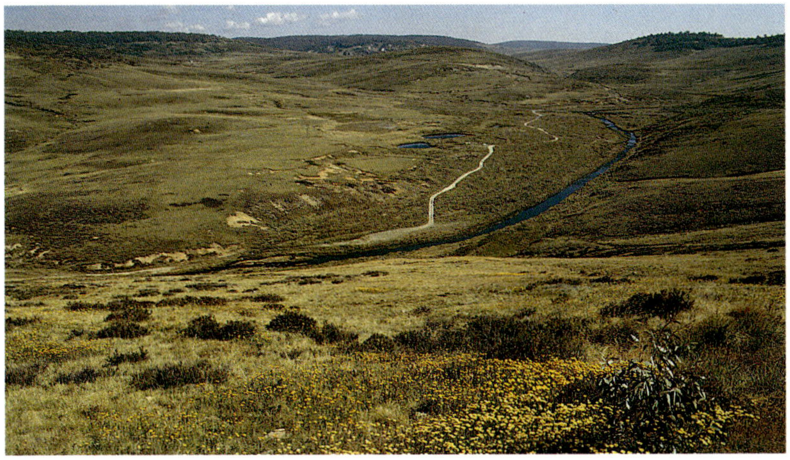

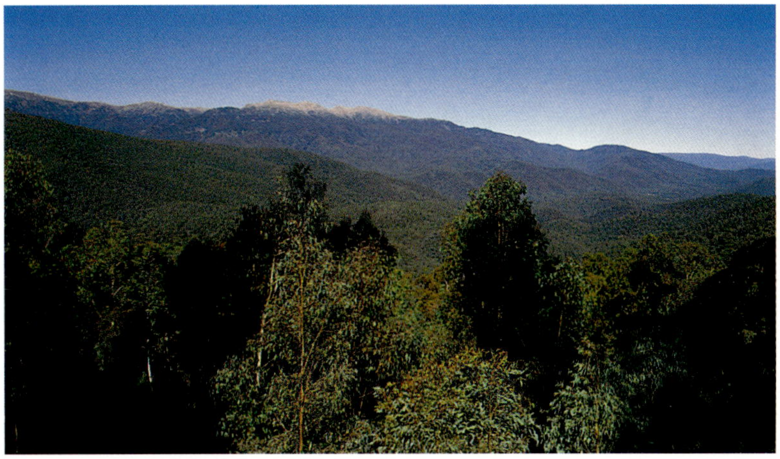

OPPOSITE: The Blue Mountains, west of Sydney, is so named because of the haze created from the distillation of the oil from the innumerable eucalyptus trees that lie within this wilderness region.

TOP LEFT: Nearby at Evans Lookout, the Grose Valley clearly displays the heavily-forested sandstone valleys, which fall from the deeply eroded and dissected plateaux to create the upland areas.

TOP RIGHT: The ancient mountains of the Gammon Ranges in South Australia display the same sheen as the Blue Mountains with a surprisingly vivid green flora amidst an otherwise arid red earth.

ABOVE LEFT: The rolling hills of the Kosciusko National Park behind fields near Kiandra support heathland vegetation that blazes with wildflowers like yellow paper daisies in spring and summer.

ABOVE RIGHT: Kosciusko National Park is where Australia's mountains reach their peak, and the view from Scammels Ridge Lookout on the Alpine Wall is a great vantage point to see the heights.

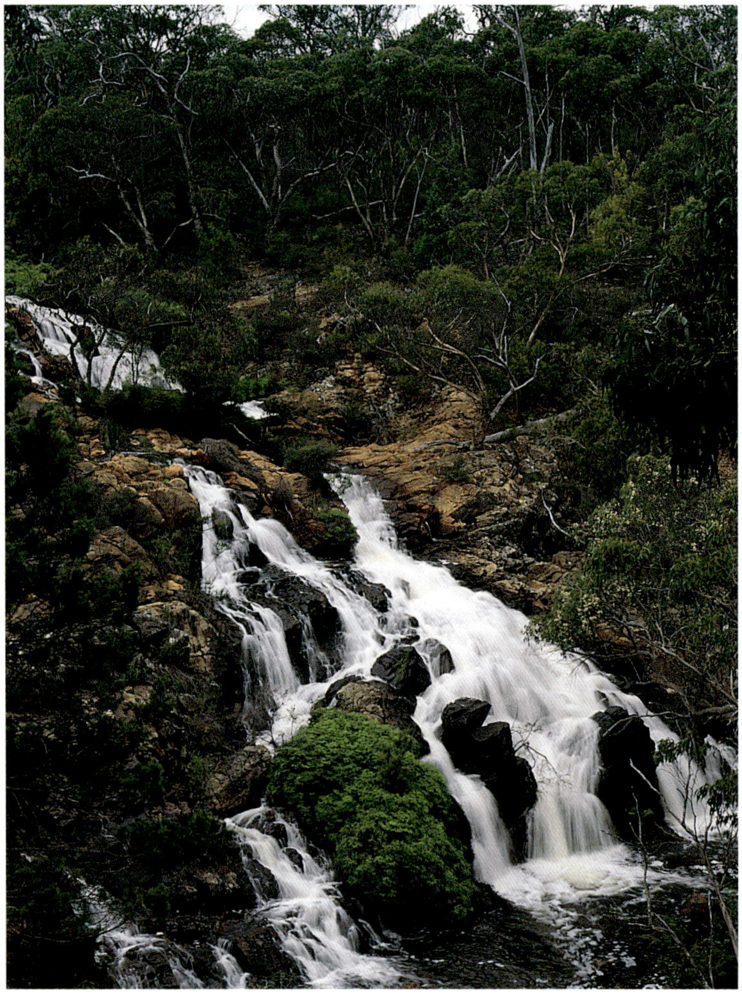

Left: The crystal-clear cascades that make up the Mackenzie Falls in the Grampians (Gariwerd) National Park create a very different image to Australia's reputation as a flat and dry continent. The water falls quickly over the park's red and brown sandstone rocks, swamping everything that lies in its path.

Left below: The Atherton Tablelands in Queensland hosts a veritable feast of cascades, like the Murray Falls between Cardwell and Tully.

Below: The highland area of Bright in the north east of Victoria lies between two of the state's major upland regions. An abundance of rain in the area means that its streams are rarely dry.

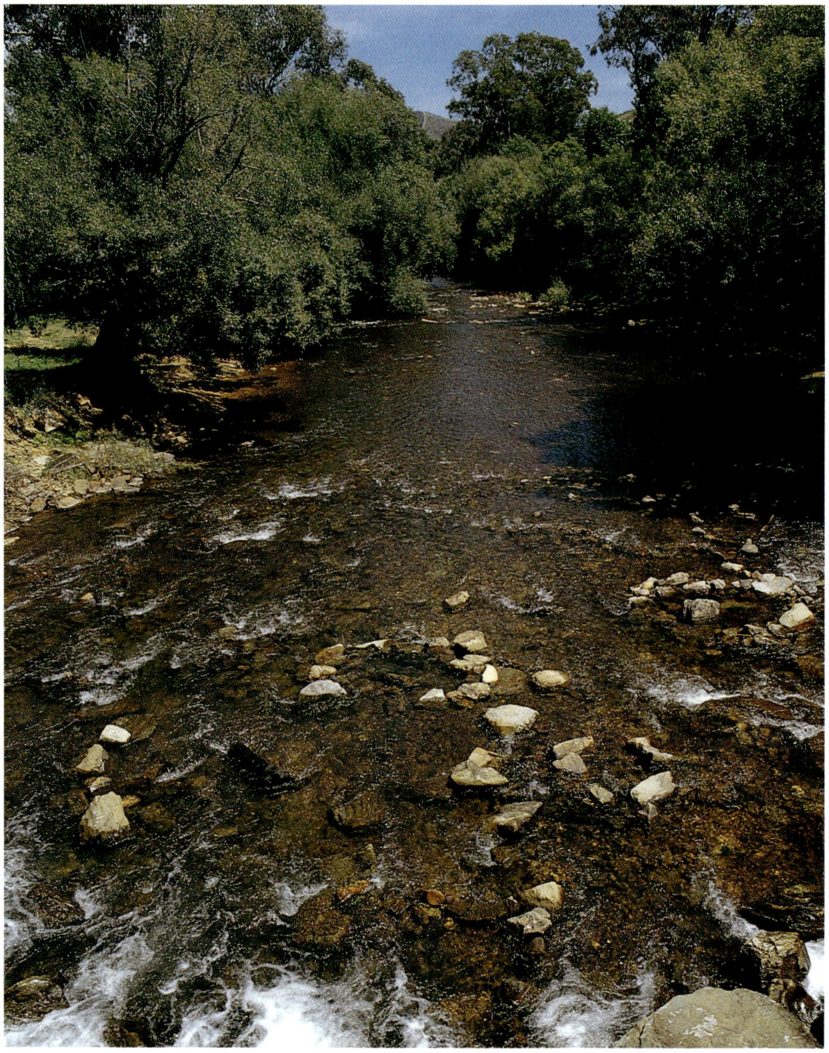

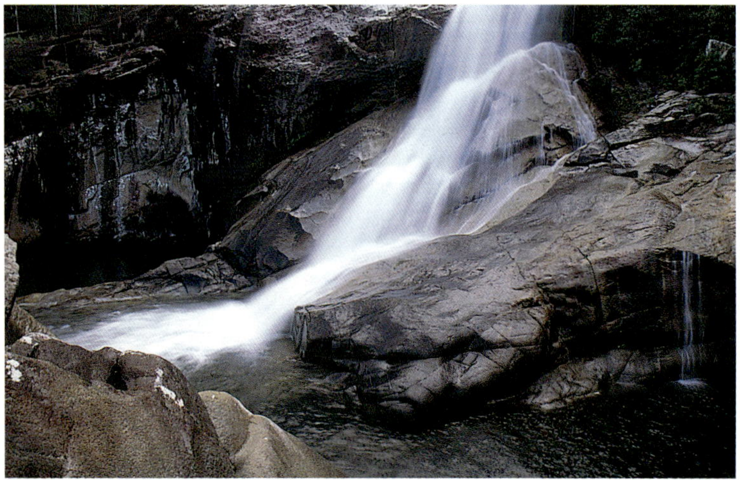

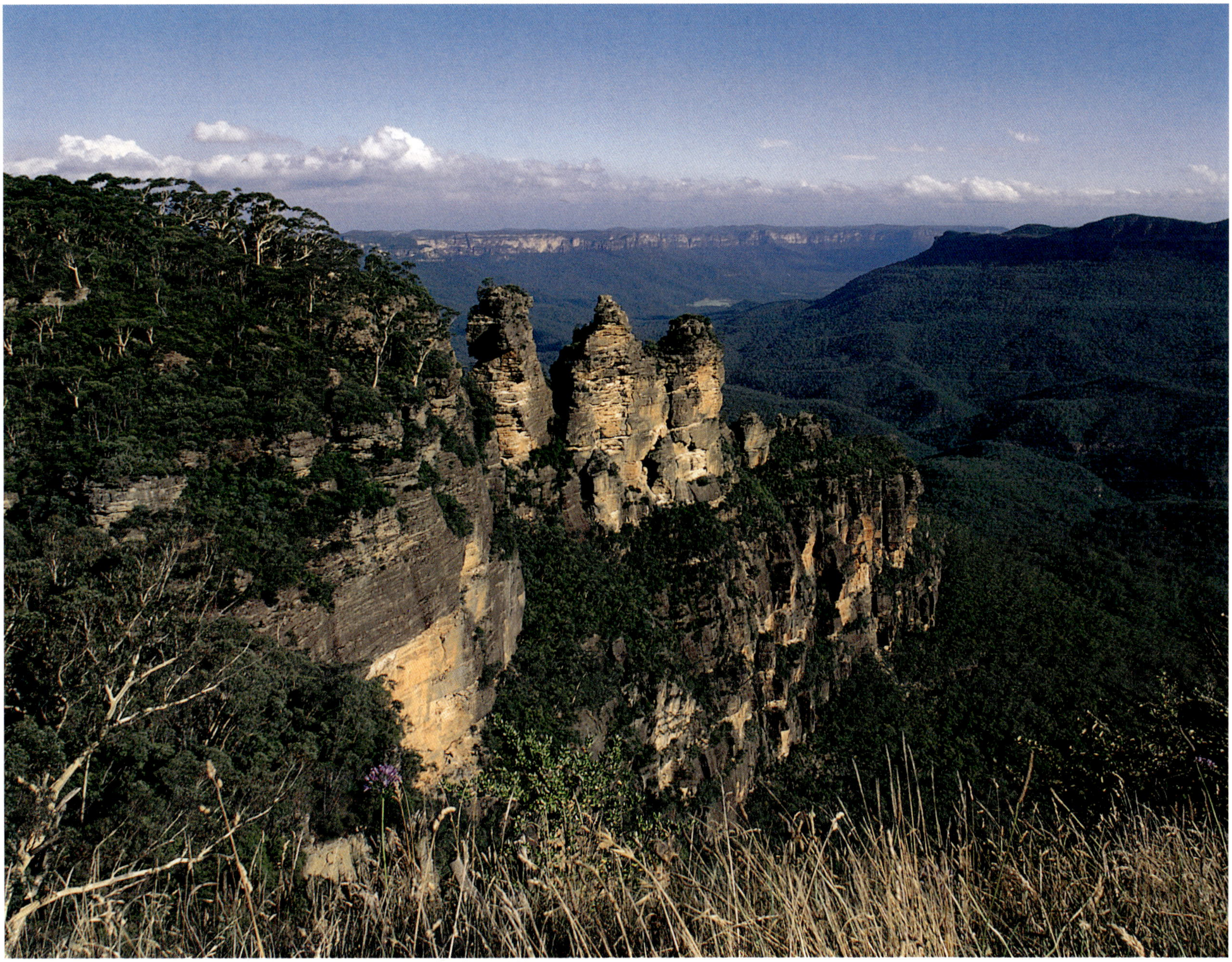

ABOVE: The famous Three Sisters, which overlook the dense, deep-green forests of eucalypts in the Jamison Valley, are rocky formations of golden-brown sandstone in the Blue Mountains. The name of the mountains is somewhat misleadingly until viewed from a distance.

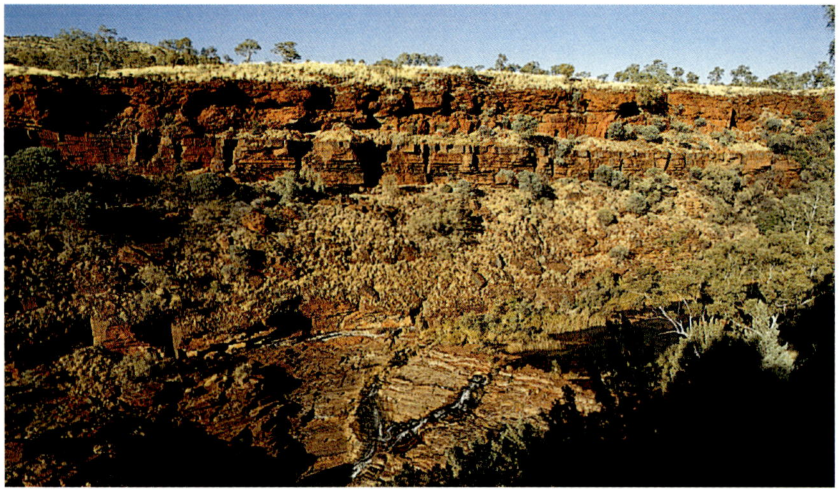

ABOVE: The arid landscape of Western Australia's Hamersley Range is tickled by streams and waterfalls that partly slide beneath the banded rocks of terracotta, grey and cream.

BELOW: A clear mountain stream playfully tumbles over dark granite boulders in Victoria's Mount Buffalo National Park.

RIGHT: In the south east of Queensland lies the scenic Lamington National Park, where green hills roll towards distant blue peaks.

FOLLOWING PAGES: The Millstream Falls of the Atherton Tableland is a screen of white pouring over a shelf of basalt surrounded by damp, lush fertile plants that resist the onslaught of the flow.

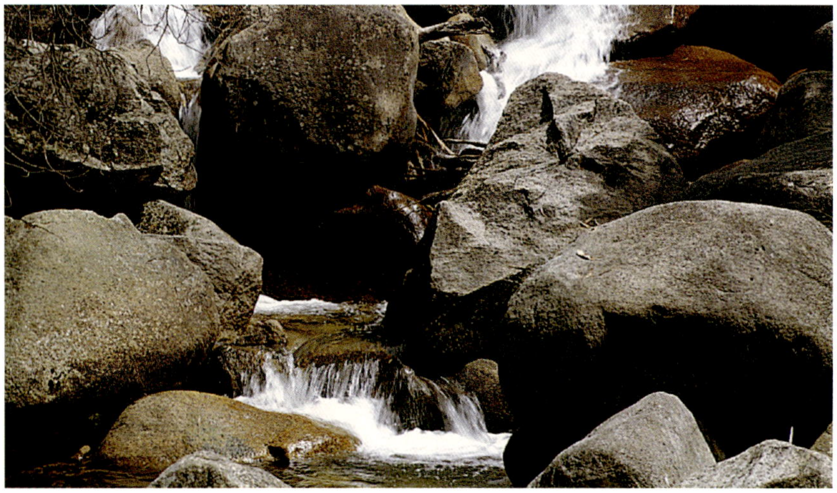

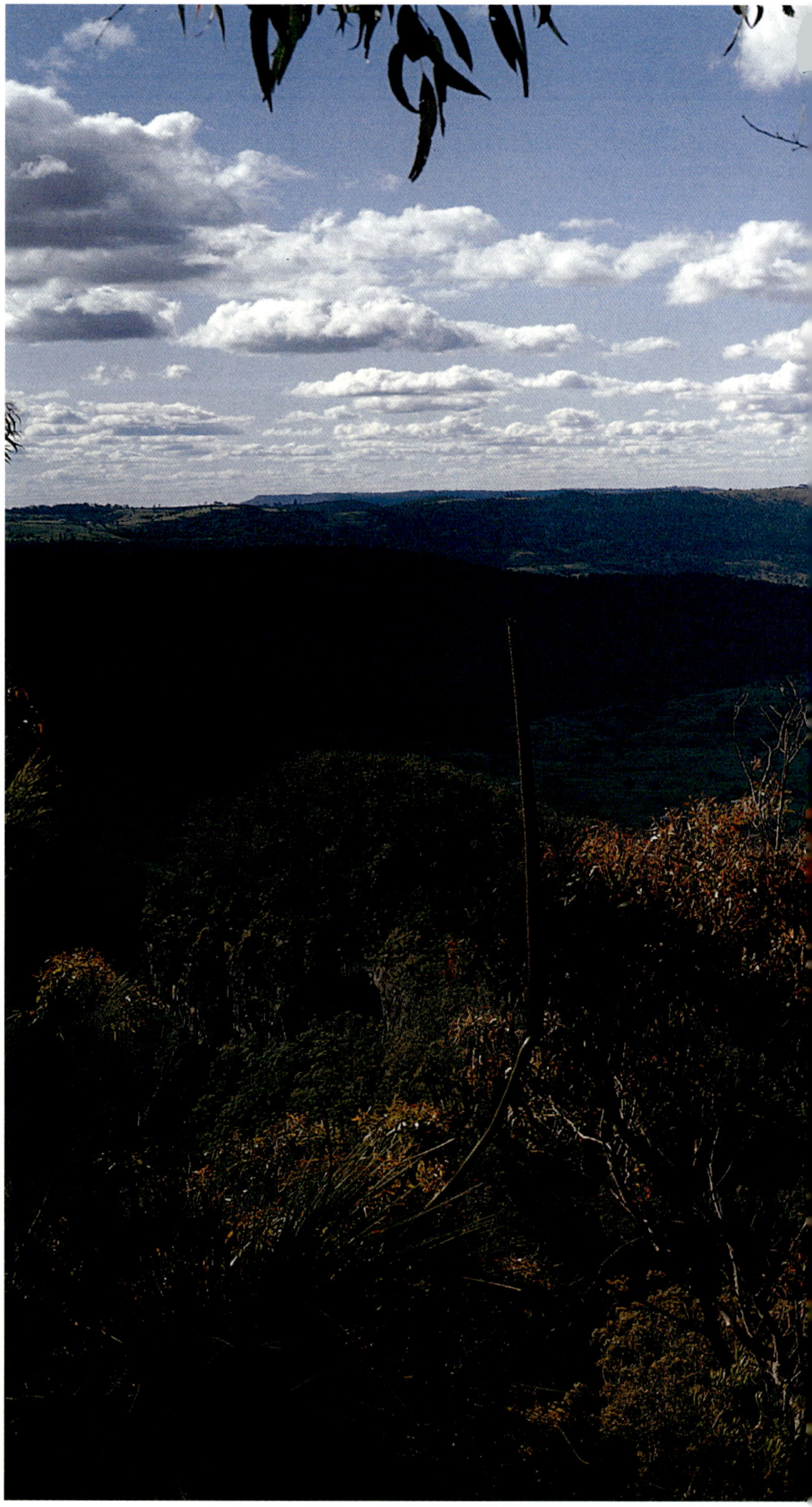

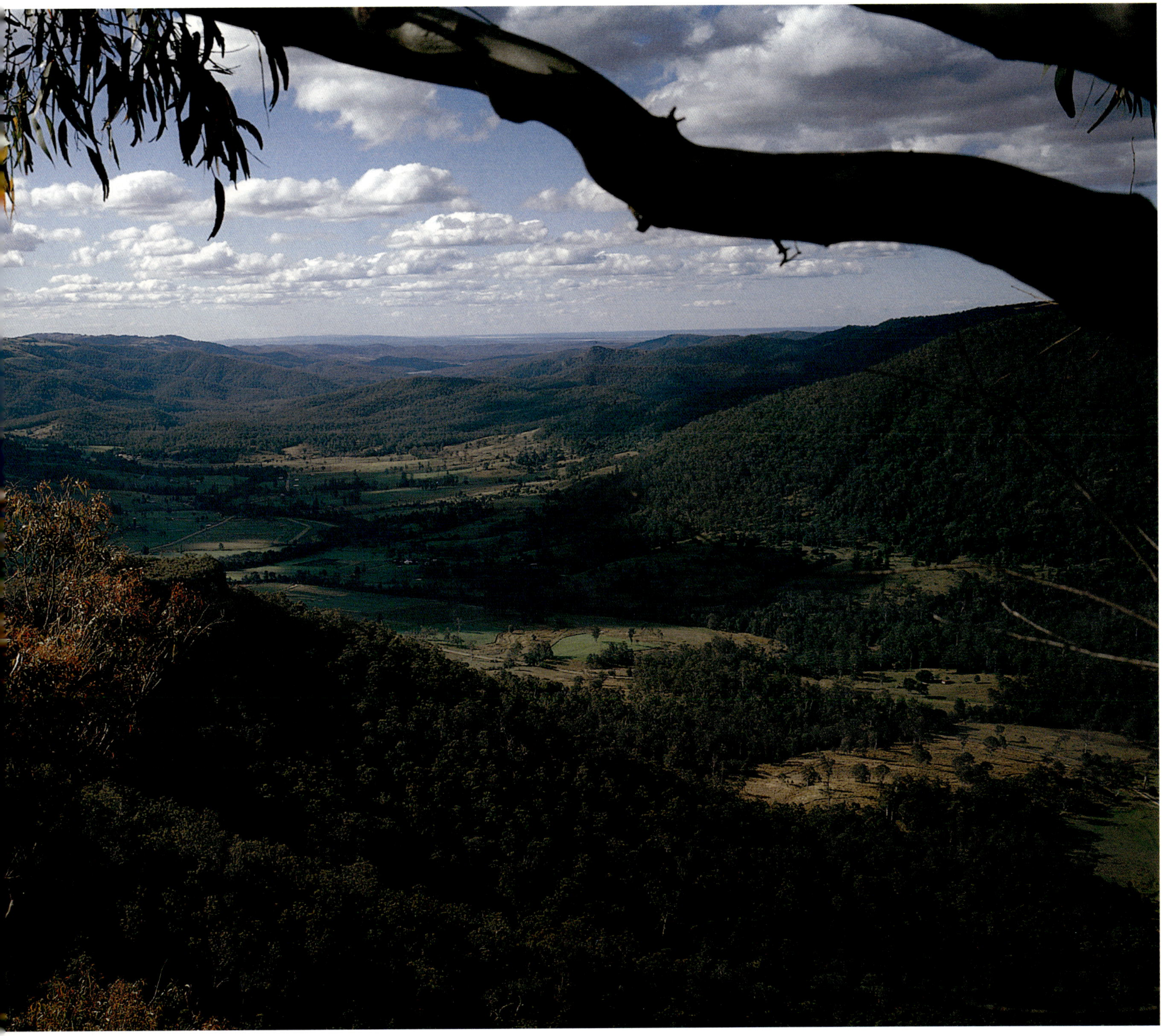

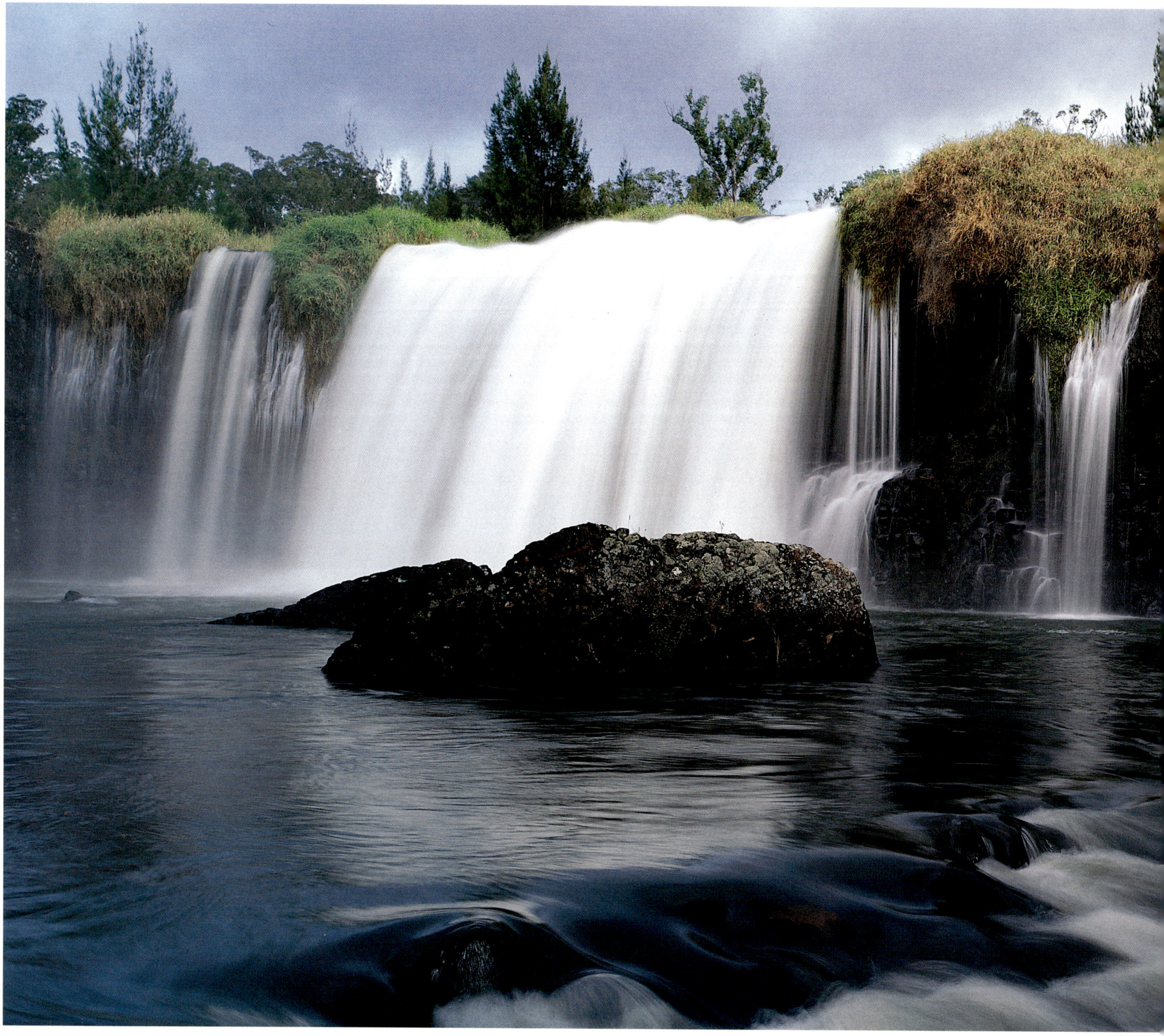

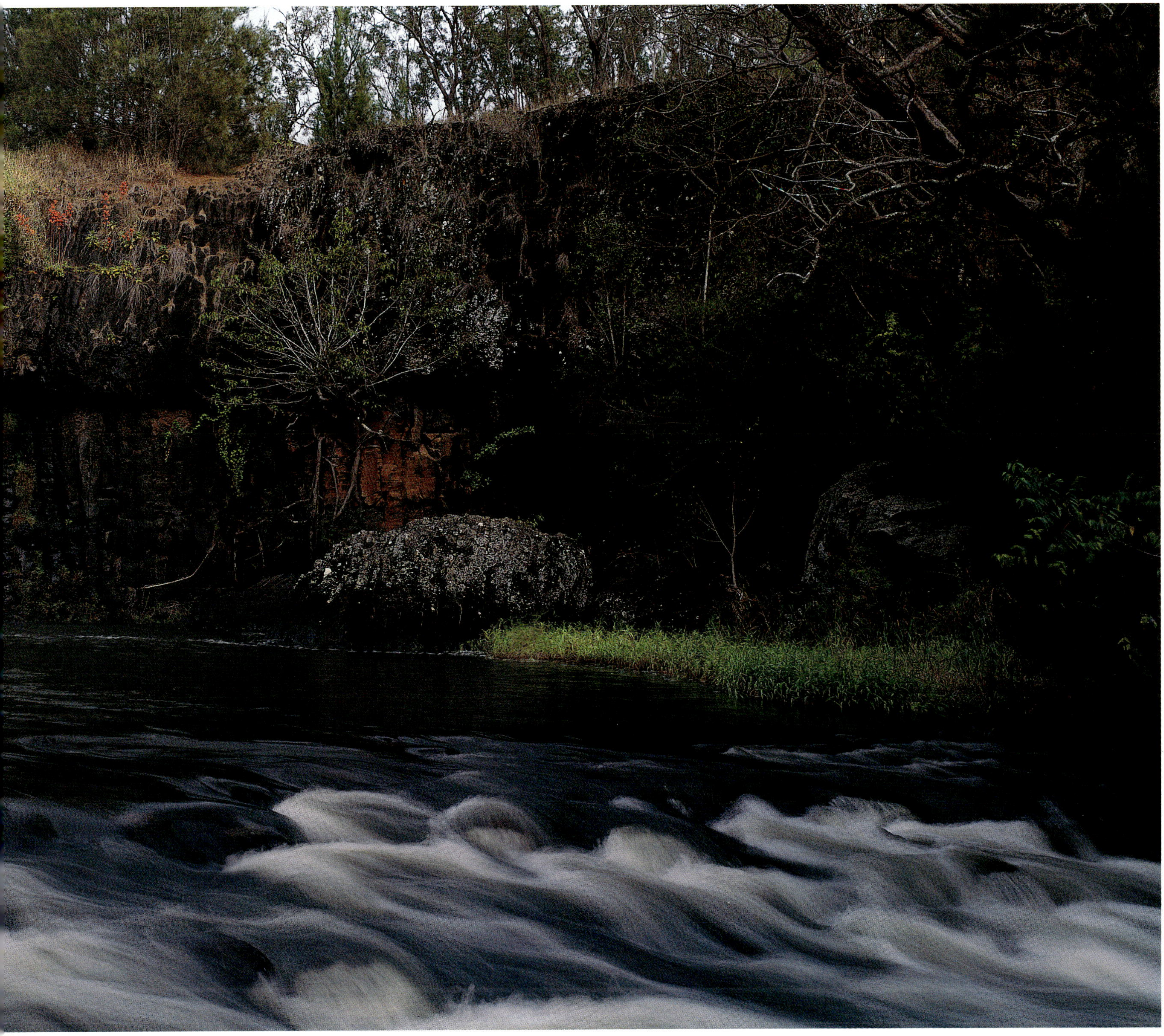

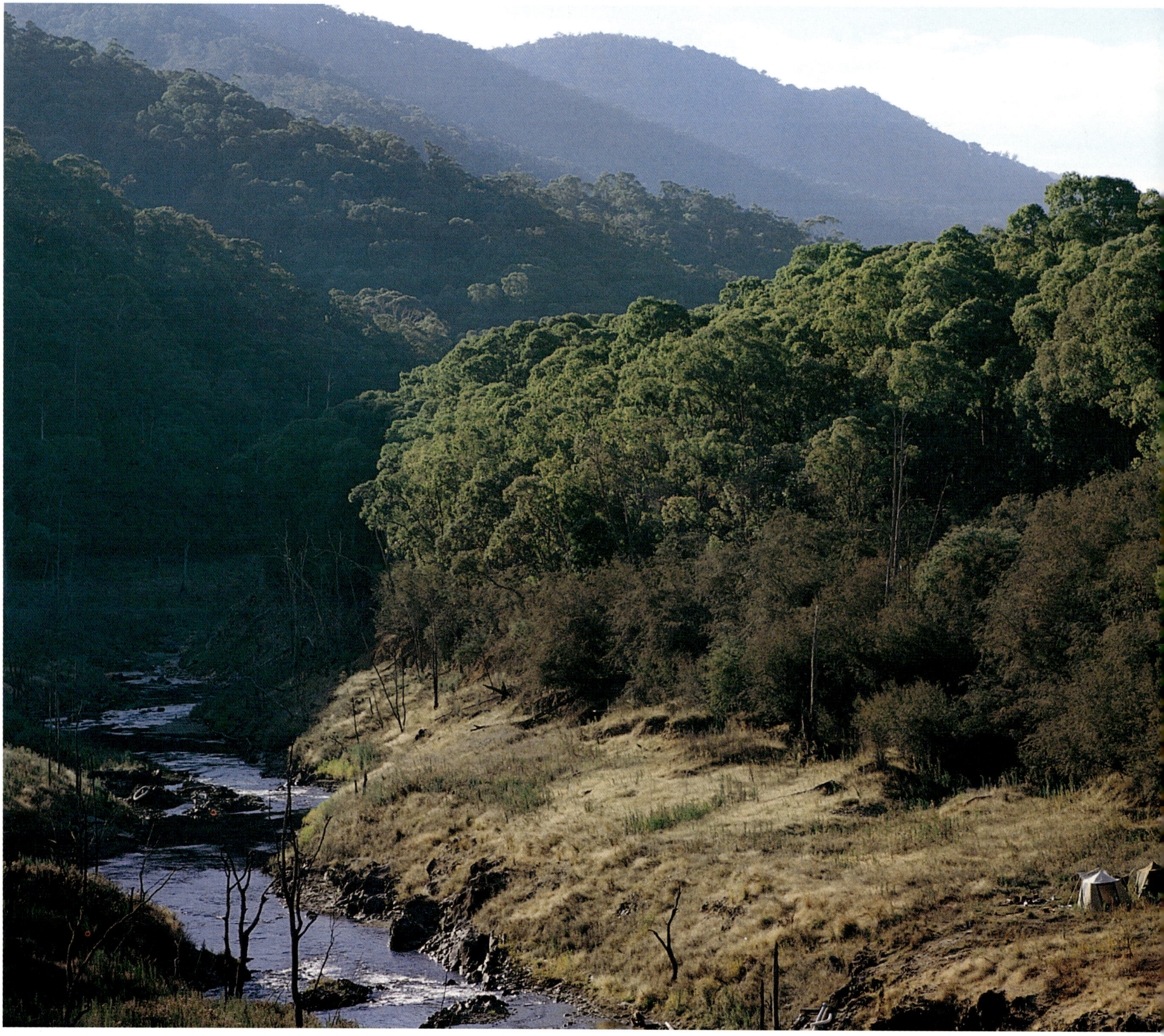

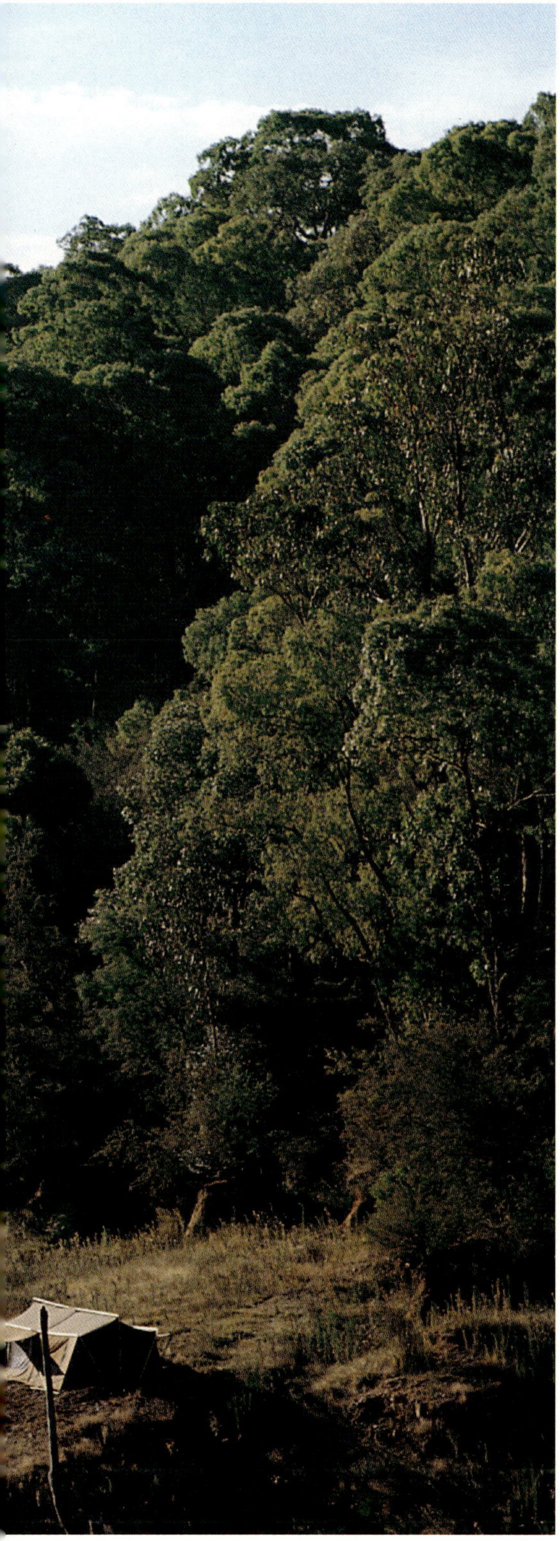

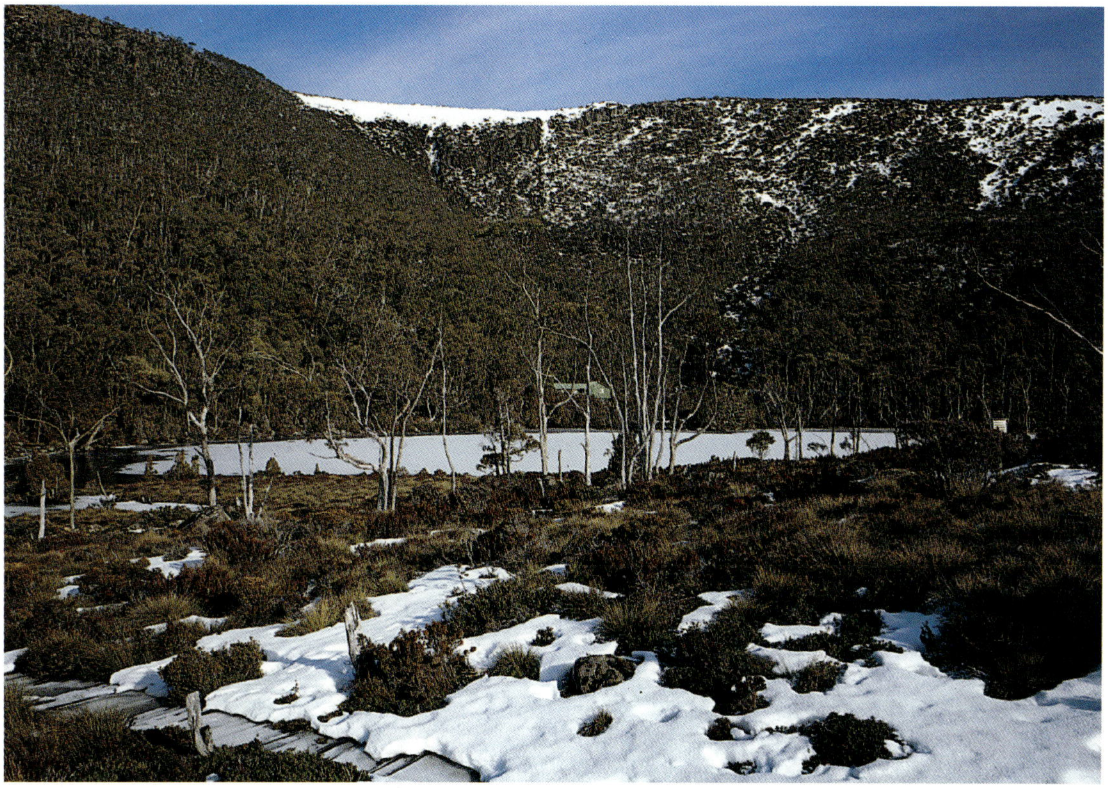

Left: Eildon State Park, a reserve in central Victoria, is a region of lakes, rivers, densely-forested hills and rocky peaks. These eucalypt-clad hillsides and grassy river banks offer a relaxing away-from-it-all atmosphere, created by the diffuse muted blues, olives and shades of tan.

Above: Winter sends a different light onto the landscape of Tasmania's Mount Field National Park. This large highland plateau reaches a peak of over 1400 metres and when the area is covered in blankets of snow and ice, it overpowers the warmer tones of the summer scenes.

RIGHT: The delightfully-named Bridal Veil Falls at the superb Blue Mountains National Park spills over the plateau into the forested Grose Valley. The plateaux is composed of Australia's most predominant rock, the sandstone, which dresses the cliff face in tones of warm red, gold and brown.

BELOW: In the far north the sandstone rugged cliffs at the Litchfield National Park guides a descending stream of white. This distinctive reddish-brown rock also protrudes from many plains on the continent to form peaks, hills and high plateaux.

FAR RIGHT: In the Buneroo Valley in South Australia the craggy Flinders Ranges soars majestically above the vast open spaces of the national park, creating a panorama of many tones of blues, greens and brown that beg to be caught by a landscape artist.

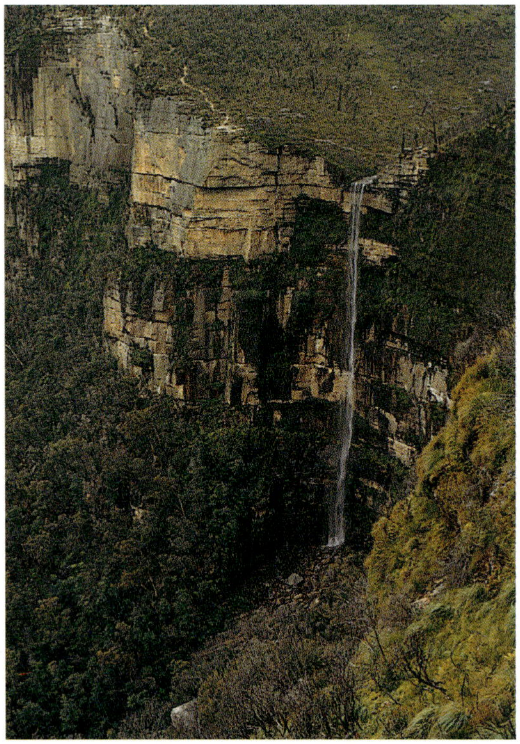

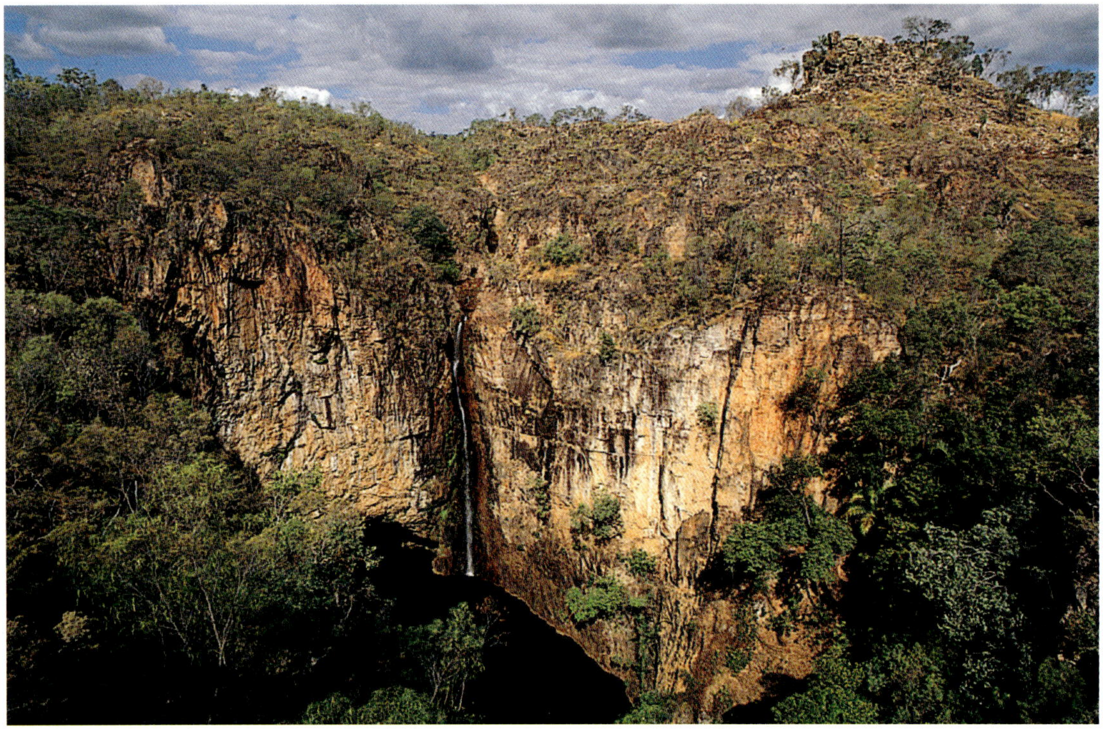

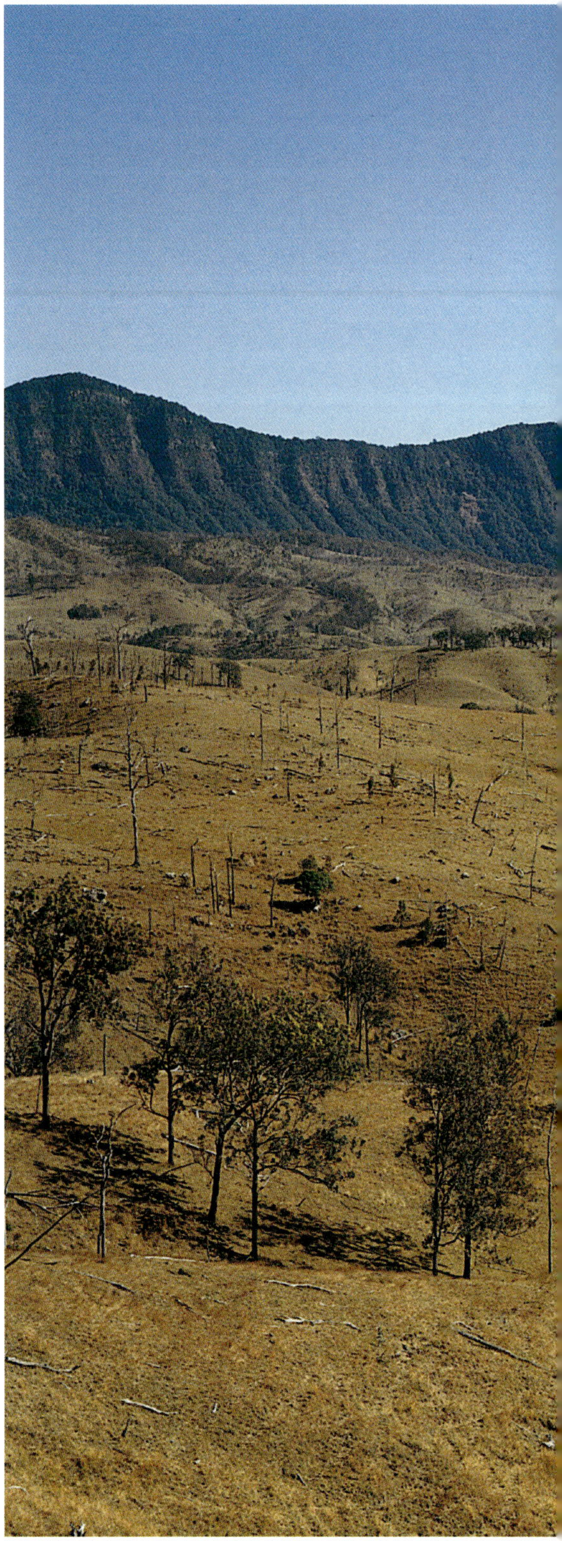

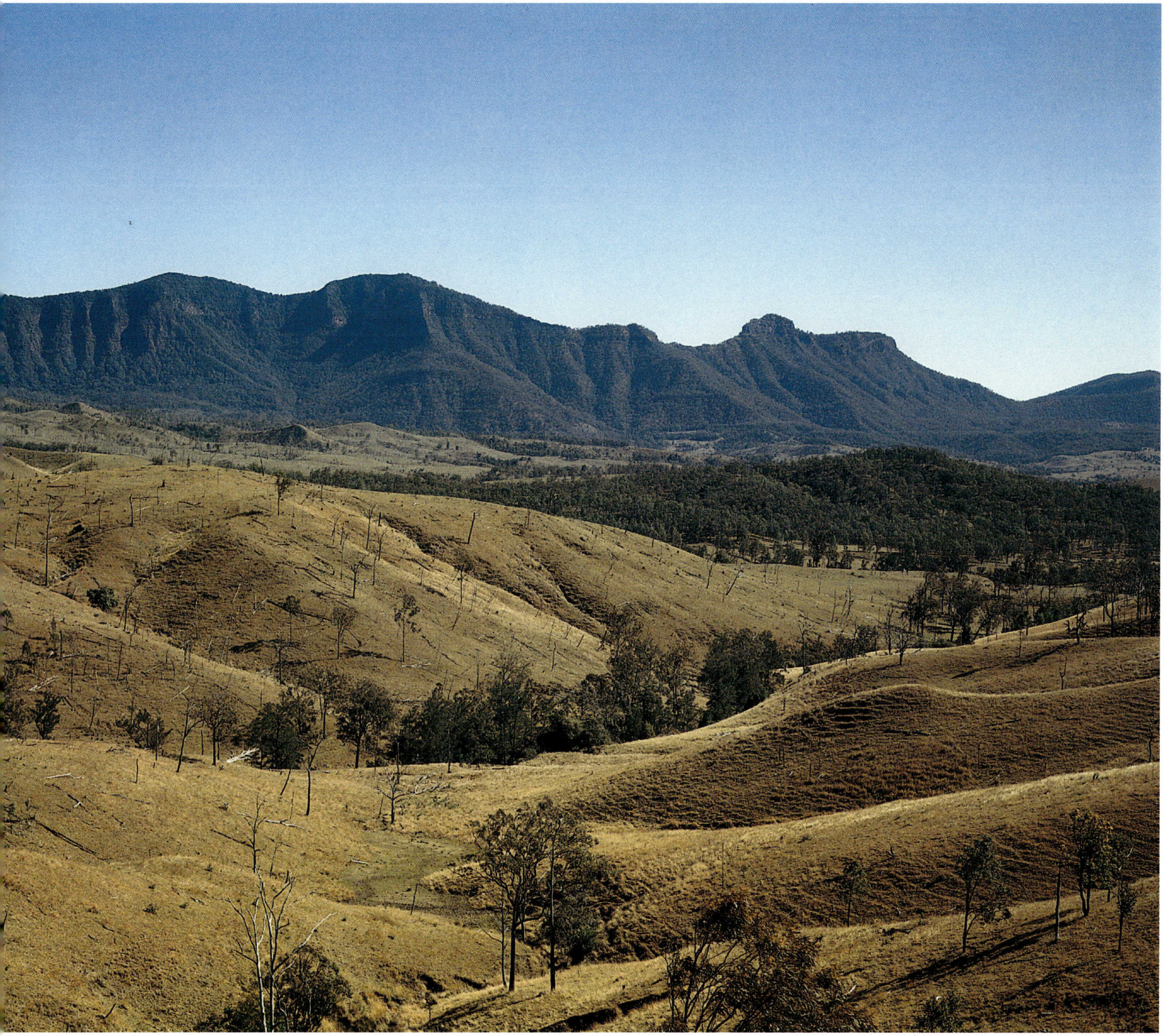

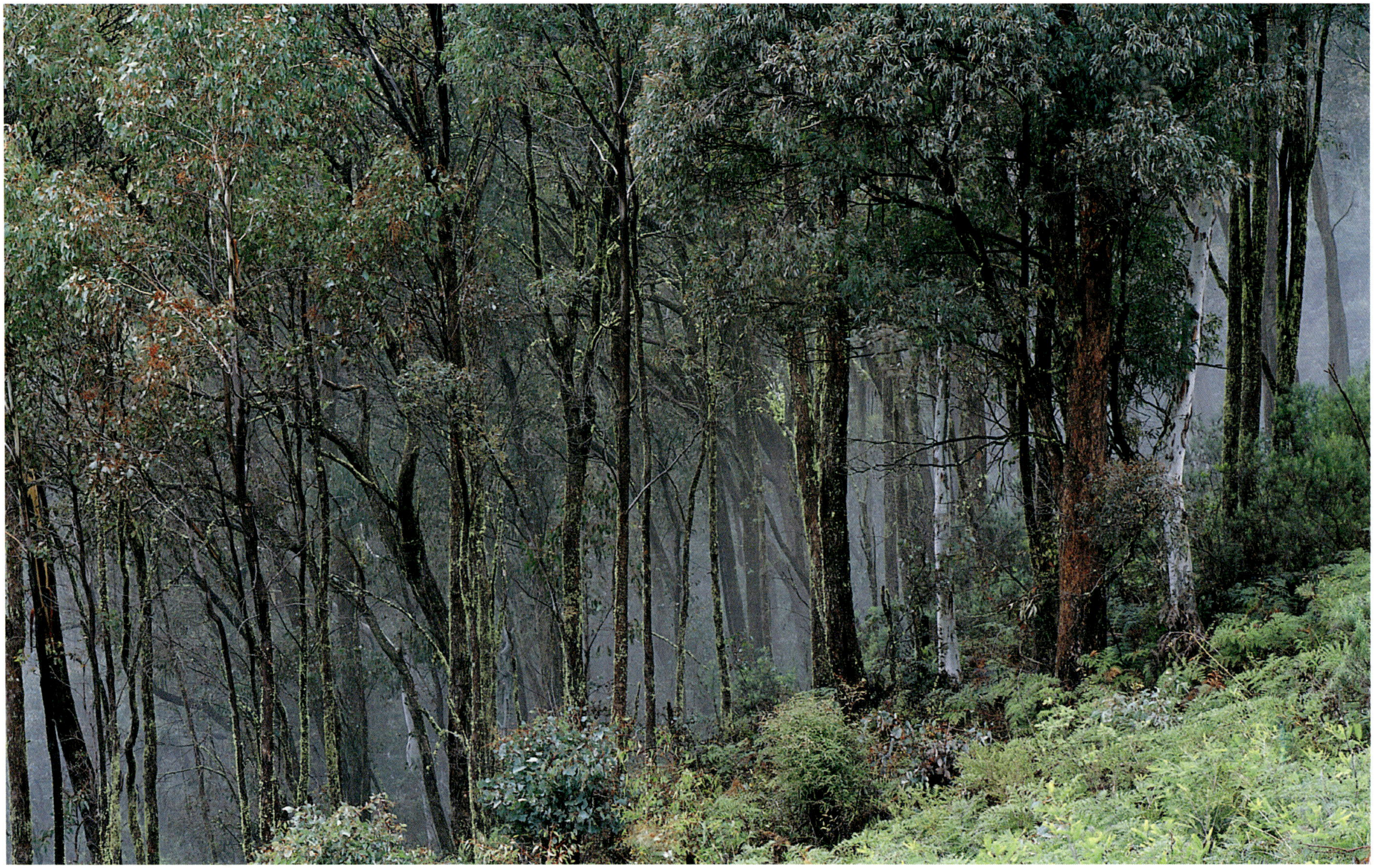

ABOVE: On the road heading up to the Victorian ski fields, the forest is often cloaked in fine blue mist in the winter months. Sometimes, when the season sets in, the road becomes impassable and snow ploughs are called in to clear the path. For diehard ski fans, this means the runs at the top will be excellent.

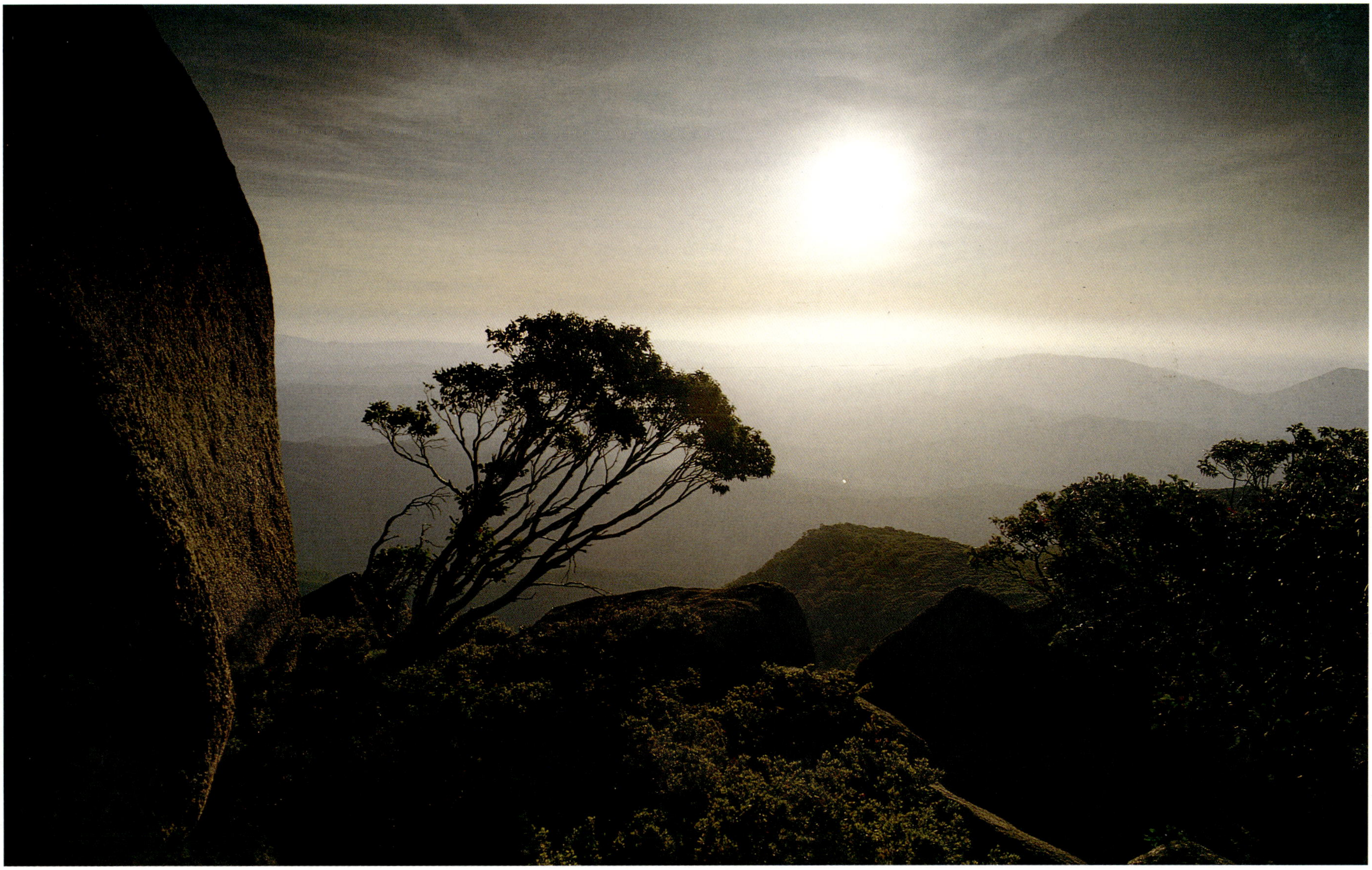

Above: Bathed in a misty highland light, this view from The Horn, the highest point of Victoria's Mount Buffalo, reveals a succession of slate-blue hills and ridge tops that stretch towards the horizon. This scene dispels the widely-held notion that Australia is a flat and featureless continent.

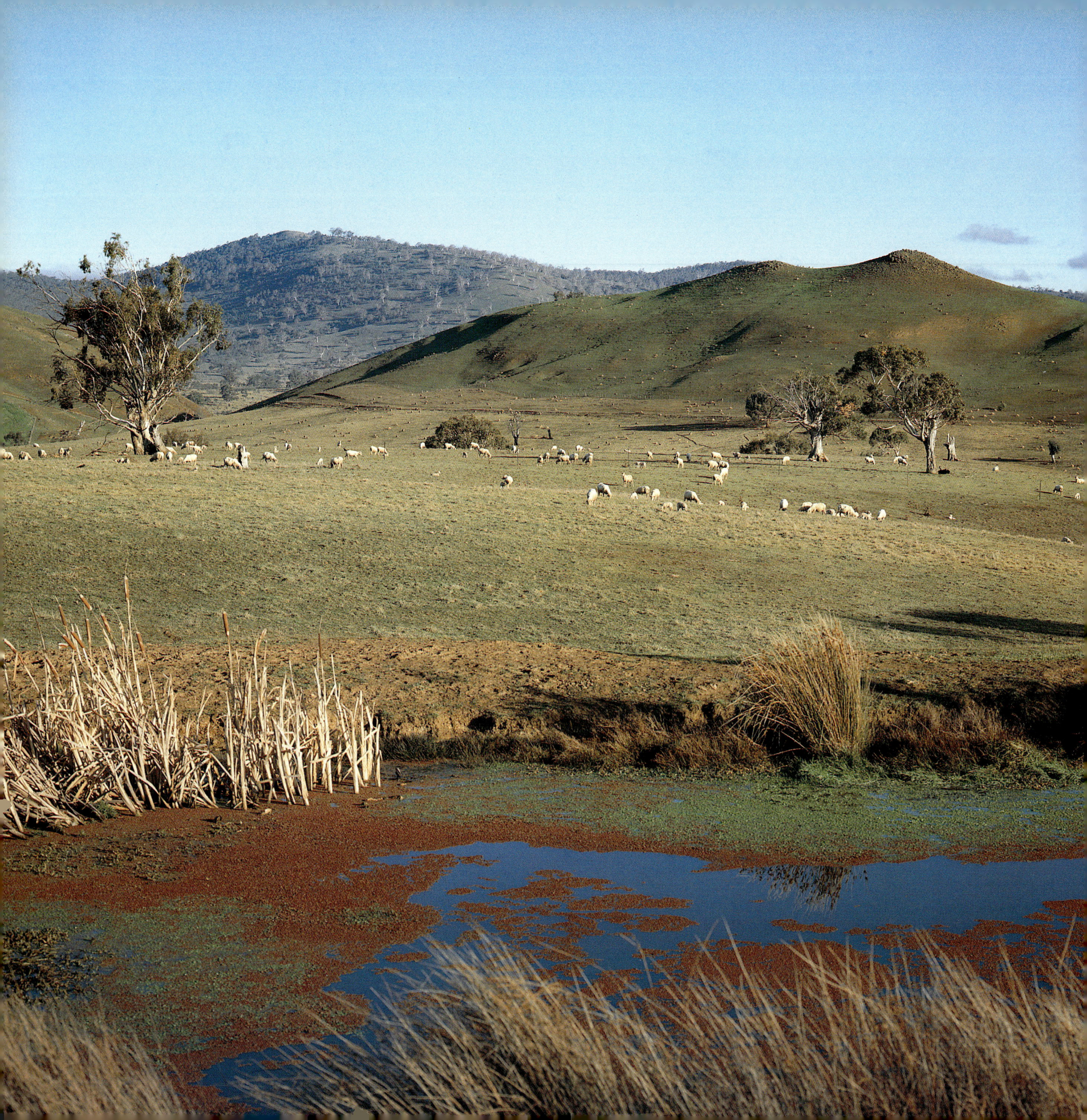

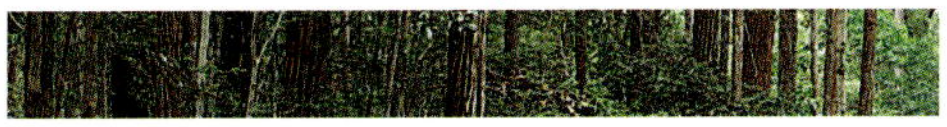

GREEN FORESTS AND GOLDEN PASTURES

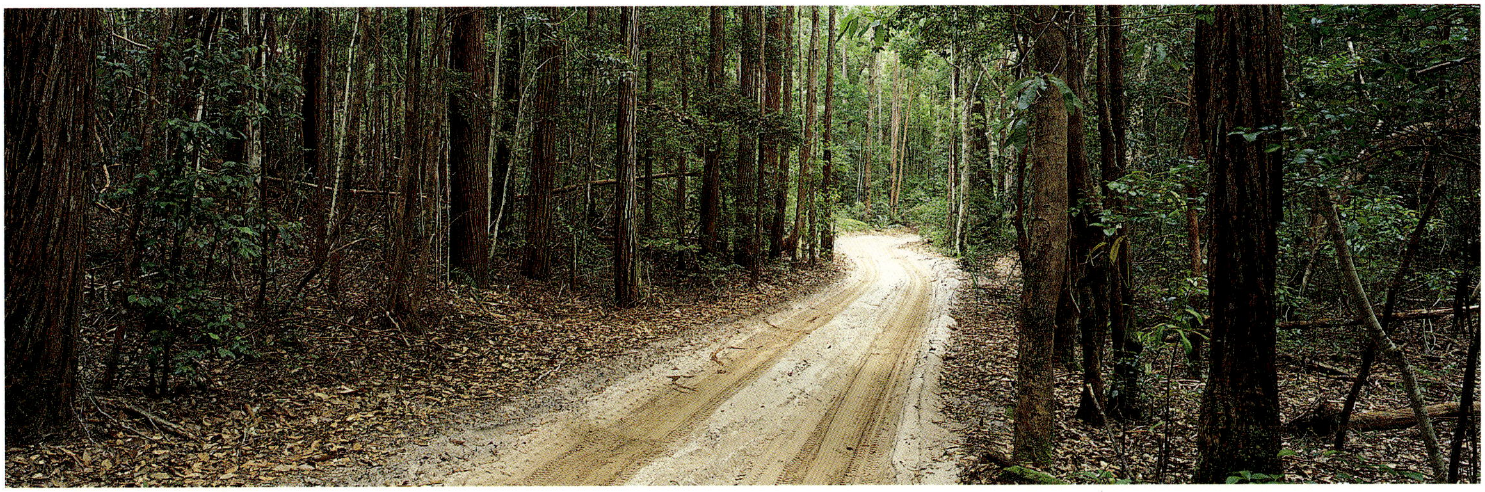

OPPOSITE: Ouse is not quite in the centre of Tasmania, yet its pastoral setting, once a woodland, seems miles from care.
ABOVE: The verdant forests on Queensland's World Heritage-listed Fraser Island are an extraordinary feature, not just because of their lush green foliage, but because these woodlands have taken root on an island composed only of sand.

Australia was once a heavily-forested continent, but as the climate changed and the interior became drier and drier vast tracts began to reveal the red geological formations that give the land its stable base. Oases of these ancient green belts still exist in places like Palm Valley in Finke Gorge National Park, but most of the country's forests and woodlands have become confined to country's fertile coastal fringes.

When Europeans arrived a number of these verdant areas were cleared for crops and grazing. These pastures also transformed the landscape, adding open fields of sweeping gold and bright green alongside the natural Australian bush.

The continent's most flourishing woodlands are the rainforests that still cling to life in various pockets of land from northern Queensland to the land's very south. In the far north these rich moist environments receive heavy monsoonal rains and provide habitat for colourful and exotic tropical plants, birds and animals. Further south, in Tasmania for example, the rainforest becomes more temperate with vibrant yet soothing tones emanating from the moss, ferns, brackens, figs, palms, vines and tall-growing trees. Rainforests create a sense of serenity and fecundity wherever they appear on the landscape.

The continent has an enormous variety of soil conditions and this has meant that an extraordinary range of crops can be grown. In South Australia and Western Australia vast tracts of cultivated land grow wheat and other cereal crops, creating seas of gold that stretch as far as the eye can see. Small farms nurture fruit trees, vegetables, and grapes for wine making and dot the temperate south. Pastoral lands of the damp tropical north are likely to feature the intense emerald tones of harvests like tea, sugar cane, bananas and macadamia trees. The fertile pastures along with the lush green forests add further levels of texture and tone to a seemingly endless array of Australian scenes.

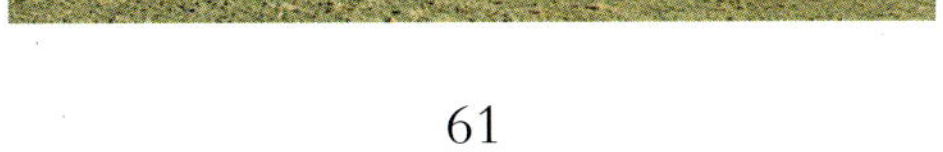

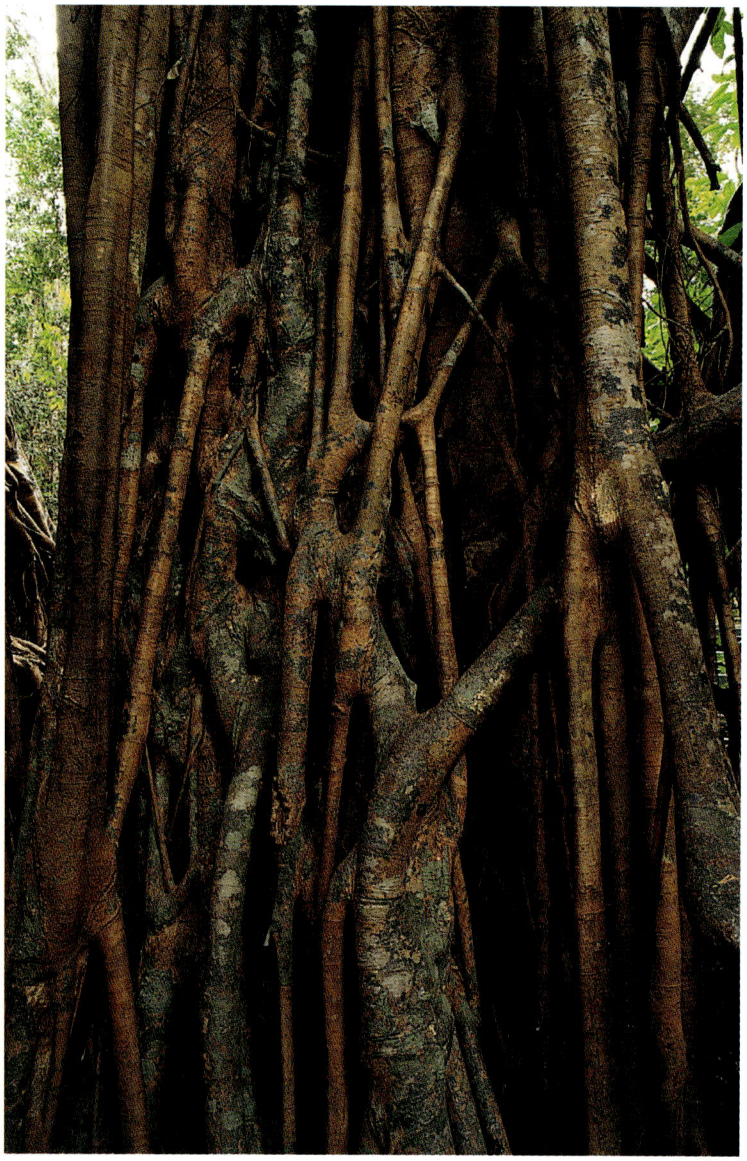

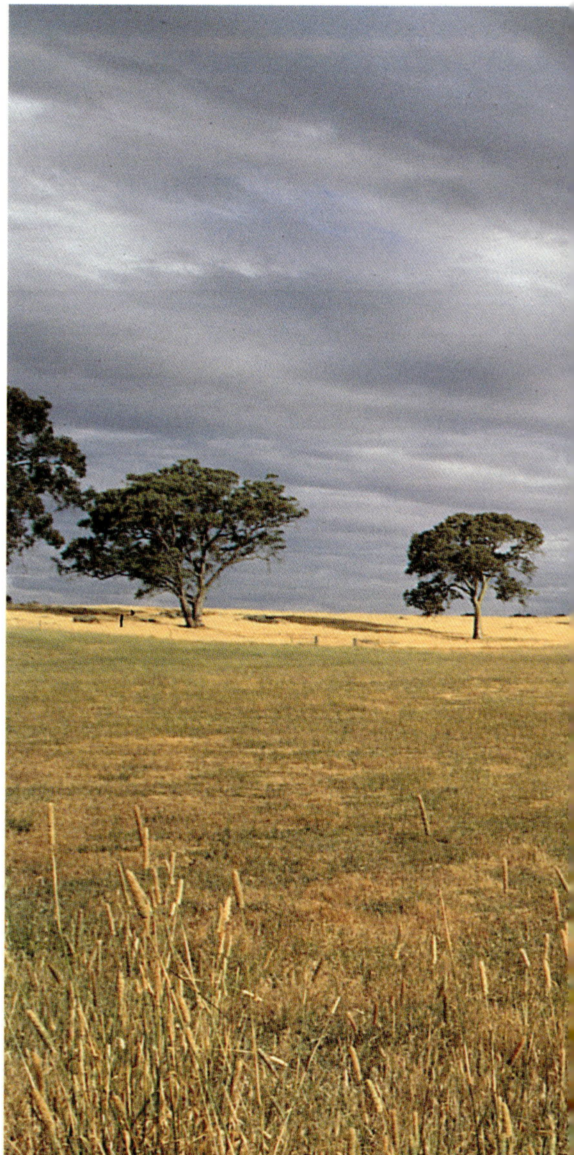

ABOVE: The Cathedral fig tree on the Atherton Tableland in Queensland is 500 years old, and the subtle tones of its warm mahogany and olive green roots reside restfully amongst the lush greens of an east-coast rainforest.

RIGHT: The wheat fields of Springton near the Barossa Valley in South Australia present a contrasting picture to Australia's woodlands as it throws gold and pale green up towards the pastel clouds of the southern sky.

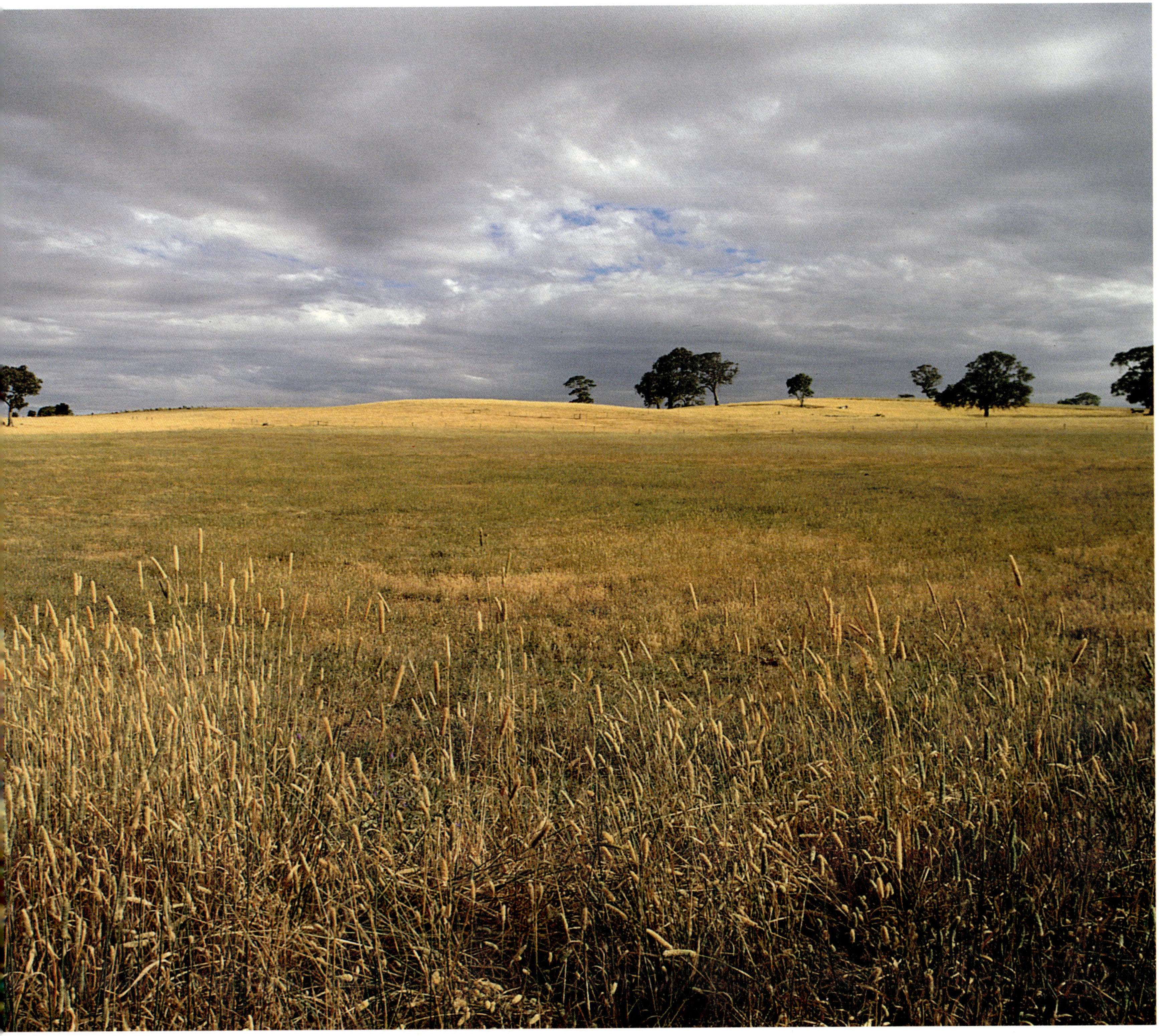

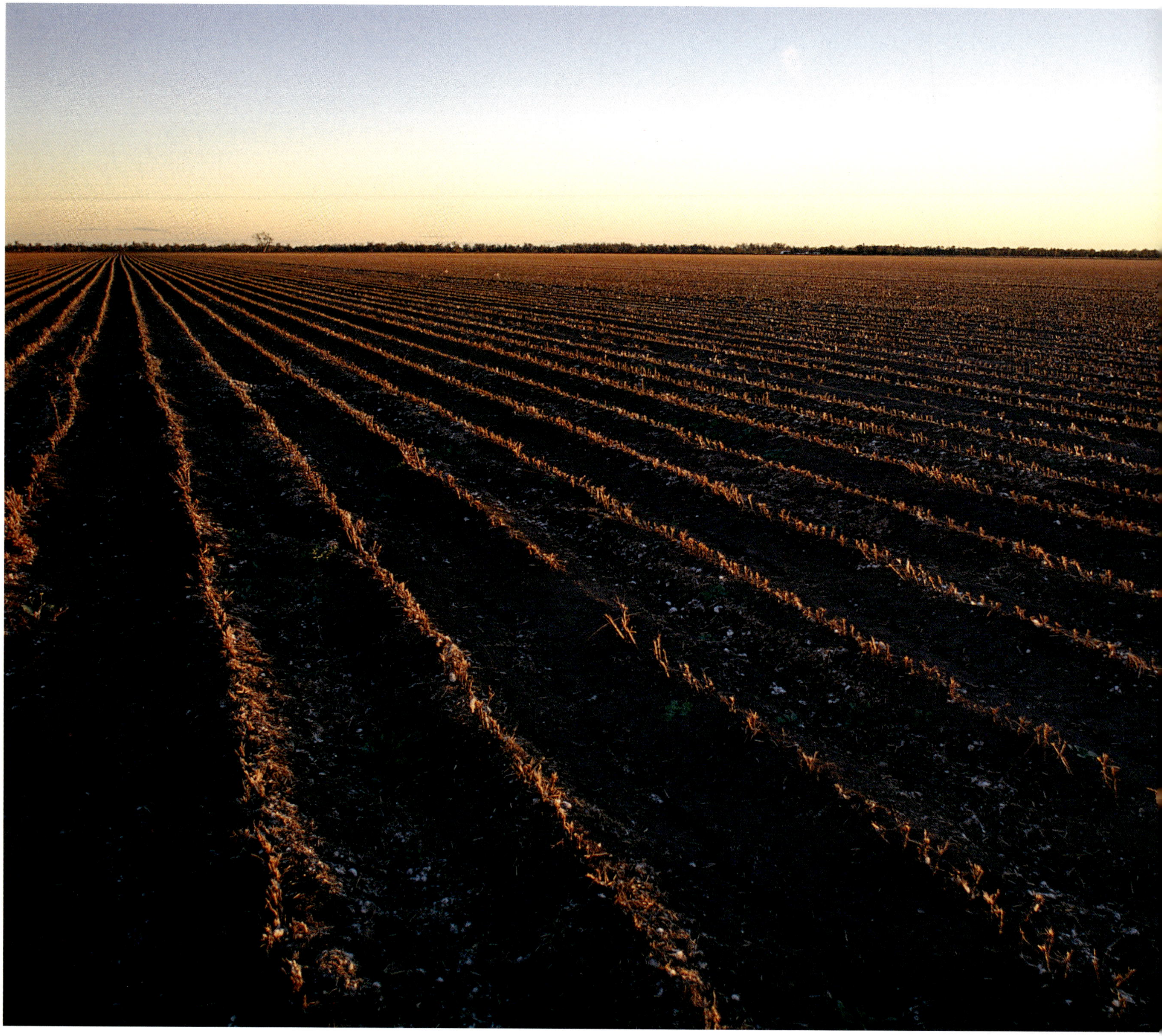

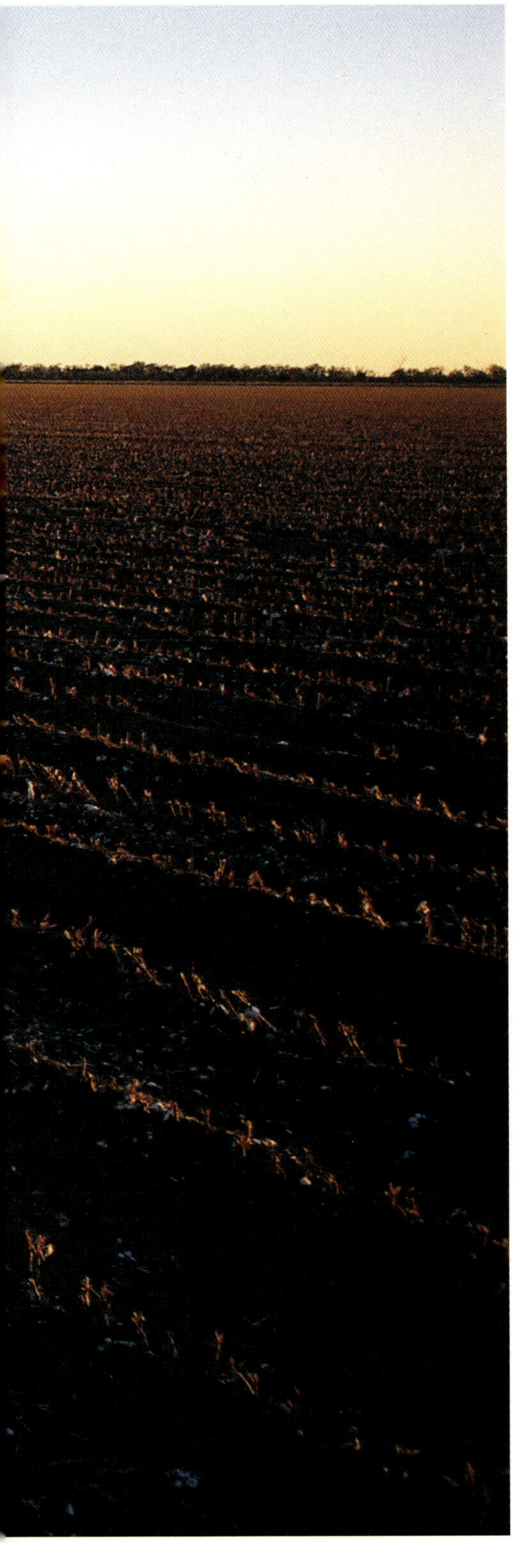

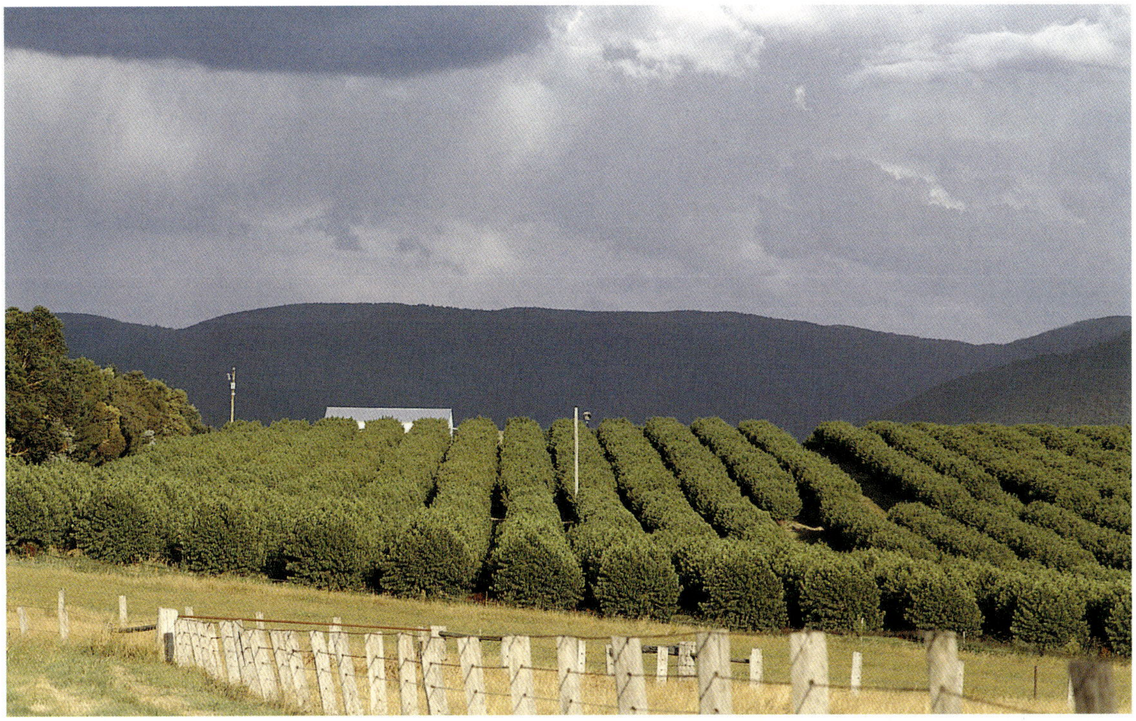

Left: The sun casts a rich garnet glow over ploughed fields in Dalby, Queensland. The green crops are just beginning to peak through the dark fertile soil. These fields will soon come alive with lighter gold, green and white crops, like wheat, millet, maize and cotton.

Above: Growing in well-tended rows, fruit trees form a orderly pattern in Victoria's Healesville region. The light shed upon the landscape gives an ethereal glow to the crops under the slate-grey sky and with distant hills forming a background.

Right: A bright sun spot on ferns growing on Kangaroo Island off South Australia highlights the delicate leaves of one of the continent's most charming native plants.

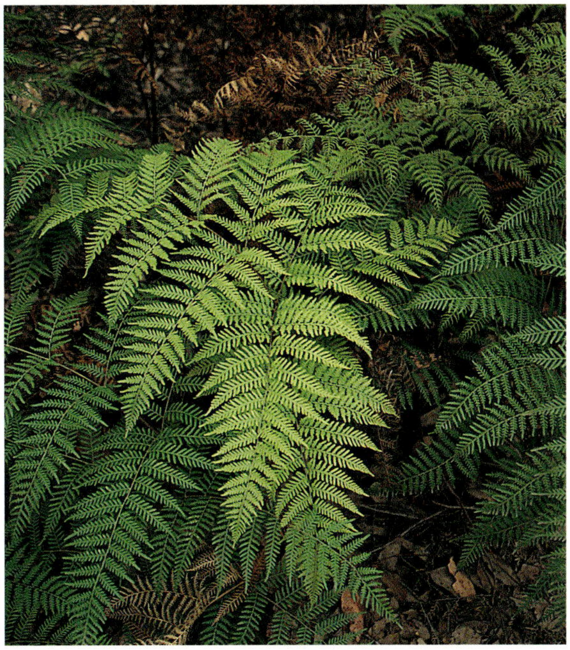

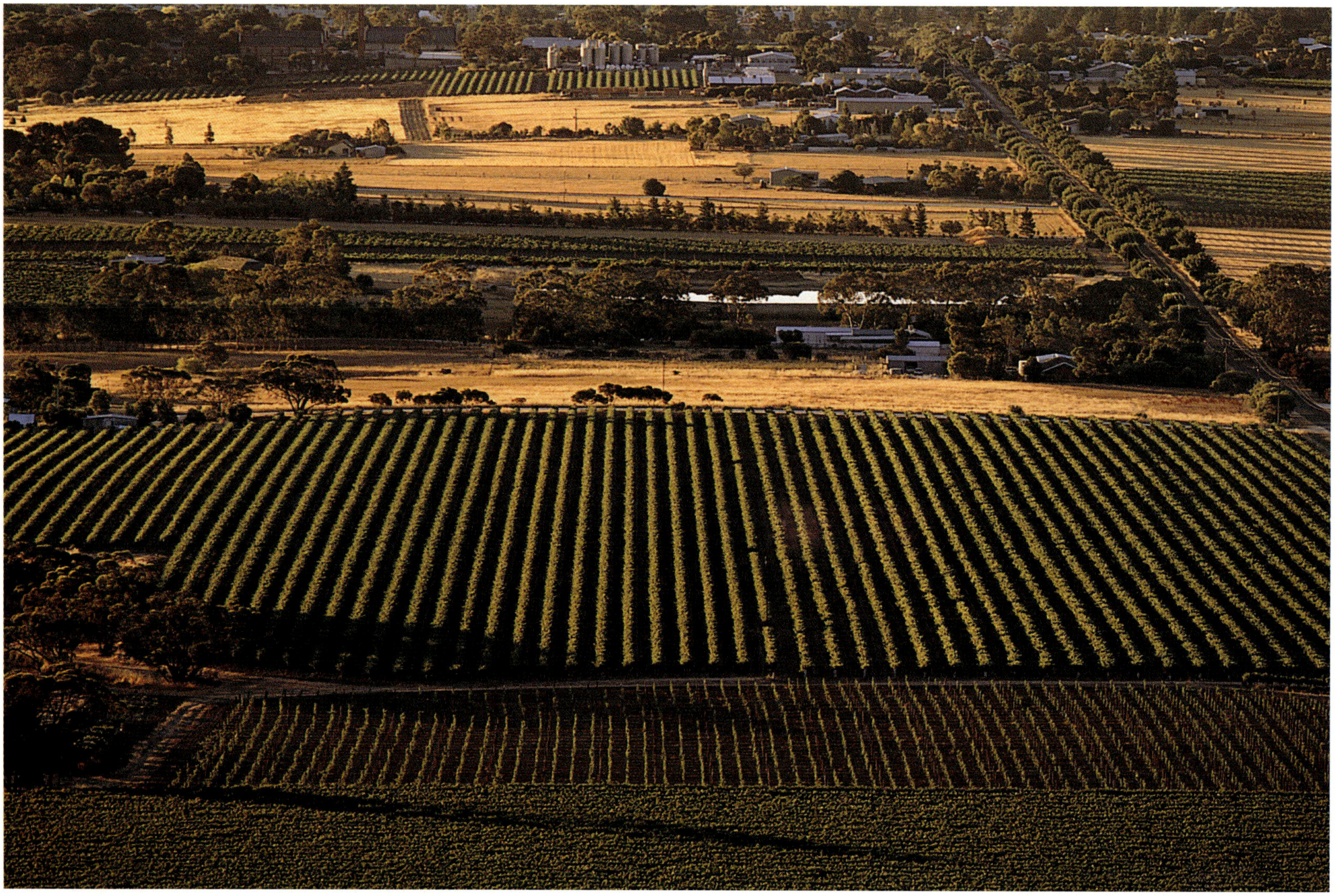

Above: South Australia's Barossa Valley is one of the nation's most important wine-growing regions. Around 60 per cent of Australia's wine comes from vines cultivated in regular lines. The different stages of vine maturity creates the boxes of green, gold and rich brown, which dot the valley's landscape.

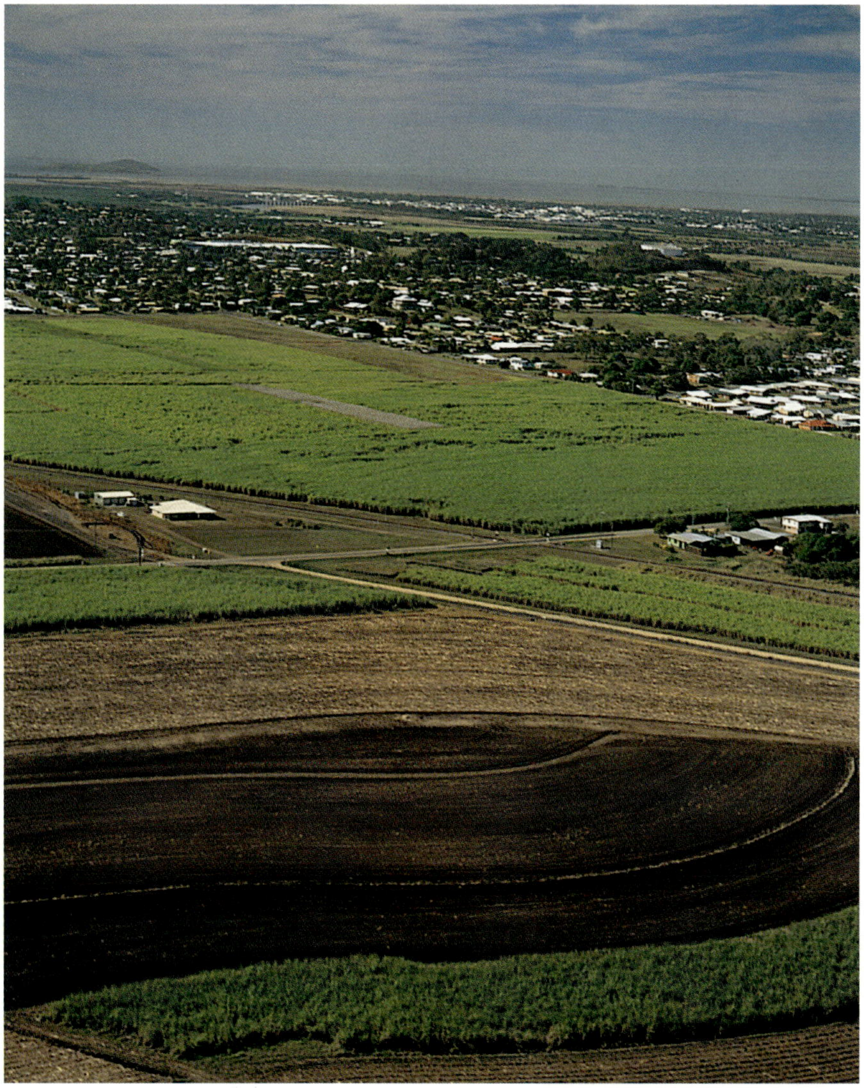

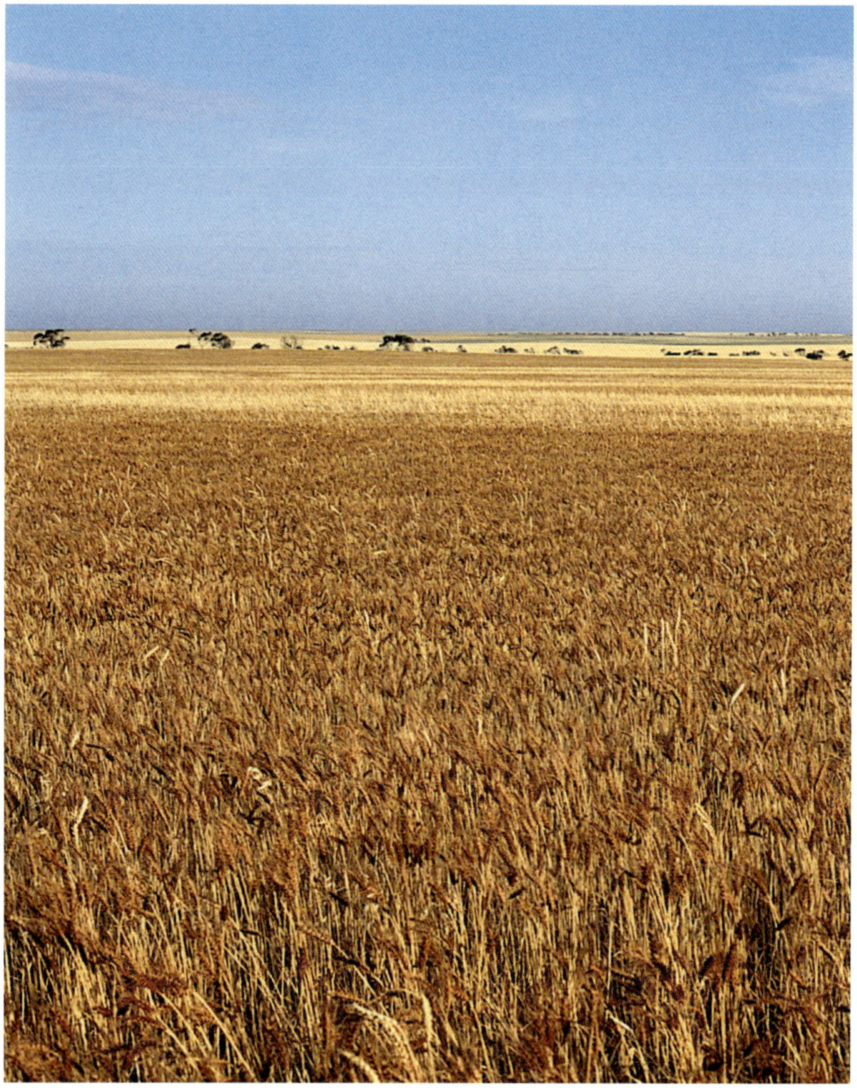

ABOVE LEFT: In Mackay, Queensland, sugar cane is an important crop and large patches of lush fields surround the town. Like a number of other tropical crops, sugar cane is grown along coastal Queensland and northern New South Wales.

ABOVE RIGHT: Wheat fields near Tumby Bay in South Australia create expanses of warm gold and ochre. Vistas of vast wheatbelts overlooked by an almost cloudless sky are just one of the country's wide range of agricultural shades.

RIGHT: Berry in the Southern Highlands region of New South Wales looks like much of the continent during summer, dry, sun-bleached, and painted in hues of pale gold. After heavy rain, however, the land comes alive and a fresh shade of dense green grass adds new life to the landscape.

BELOW: The gentle pastoral terrain around the Barossa Valley is transformed at sunset. What is a verdant vineyard countryside during the day becomes bathed in a magical golden light with trees silhouetted on the horizon at dusk.

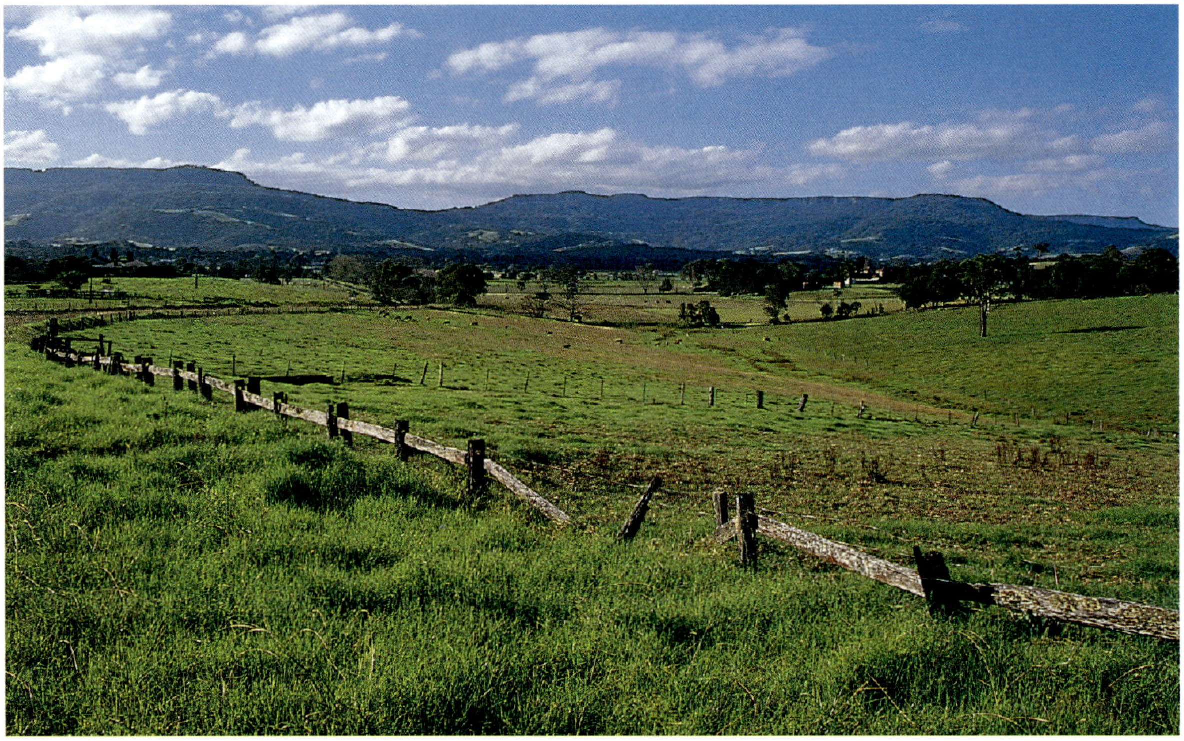

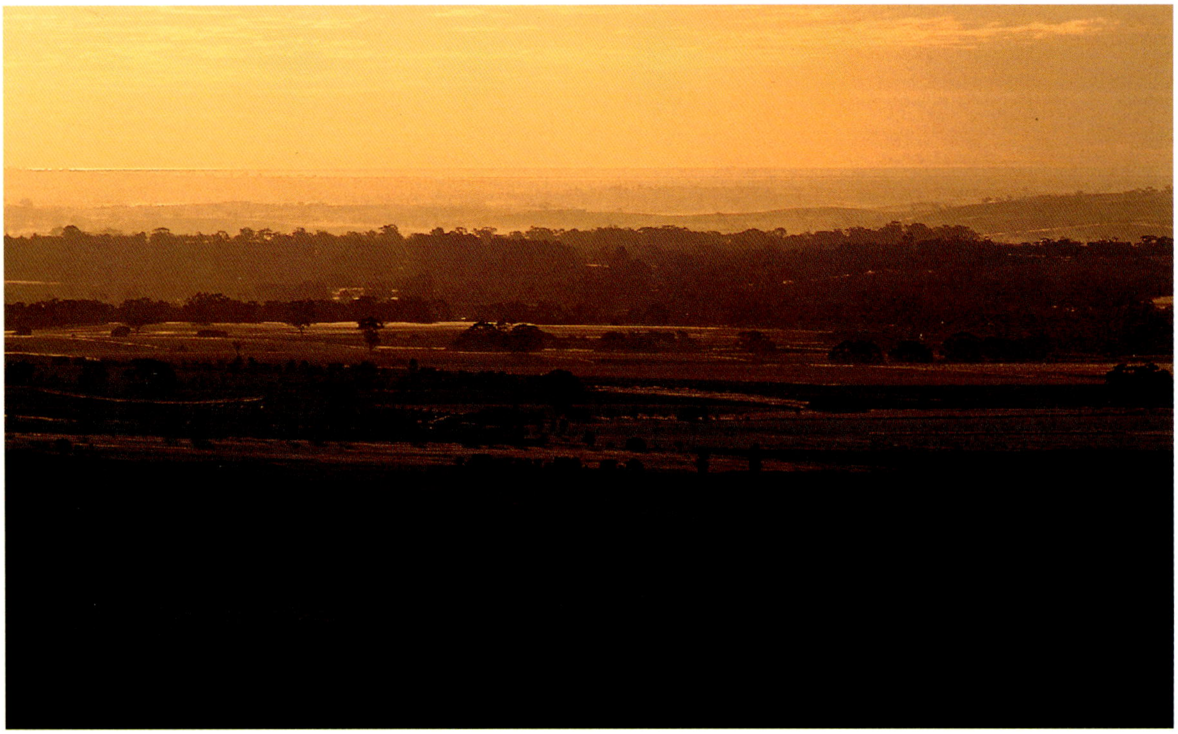

OPPOSITE: The tree-cleared and cultivated land of the southern Victorian coastline possesses its own delightful flecks of colour. The rolling hills and fields are a study in gold, brown, green and olive—and all their accompanying shades and tones.

FOLLOWING PAGES: In the wide agricultural lands of Lyndoch in South Australia, crop fields stretch broadly toward the horizon. Acres of golden wheat, fringed by green fields and trees, thrive under an azure, cloud-dotted sky.

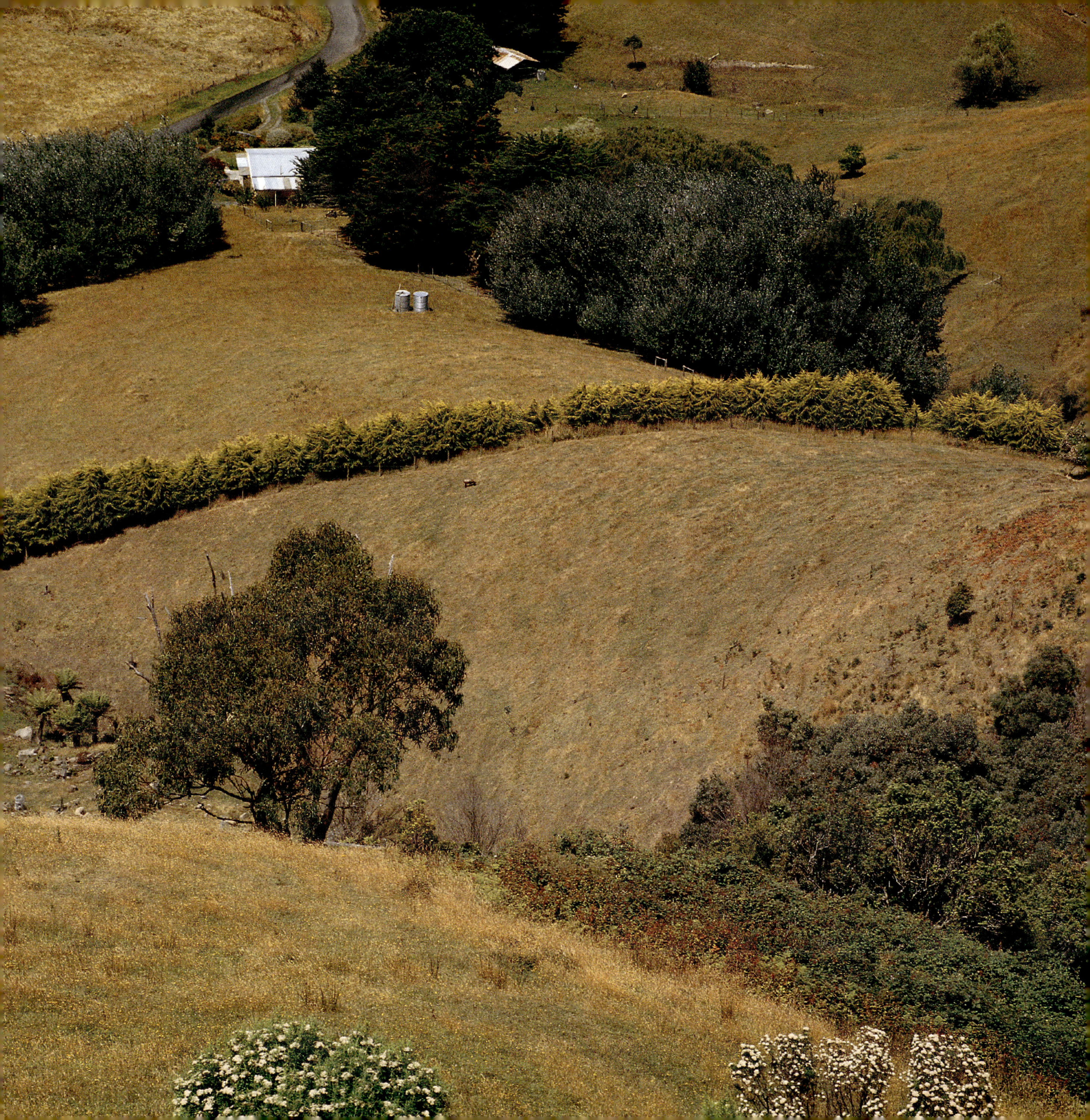

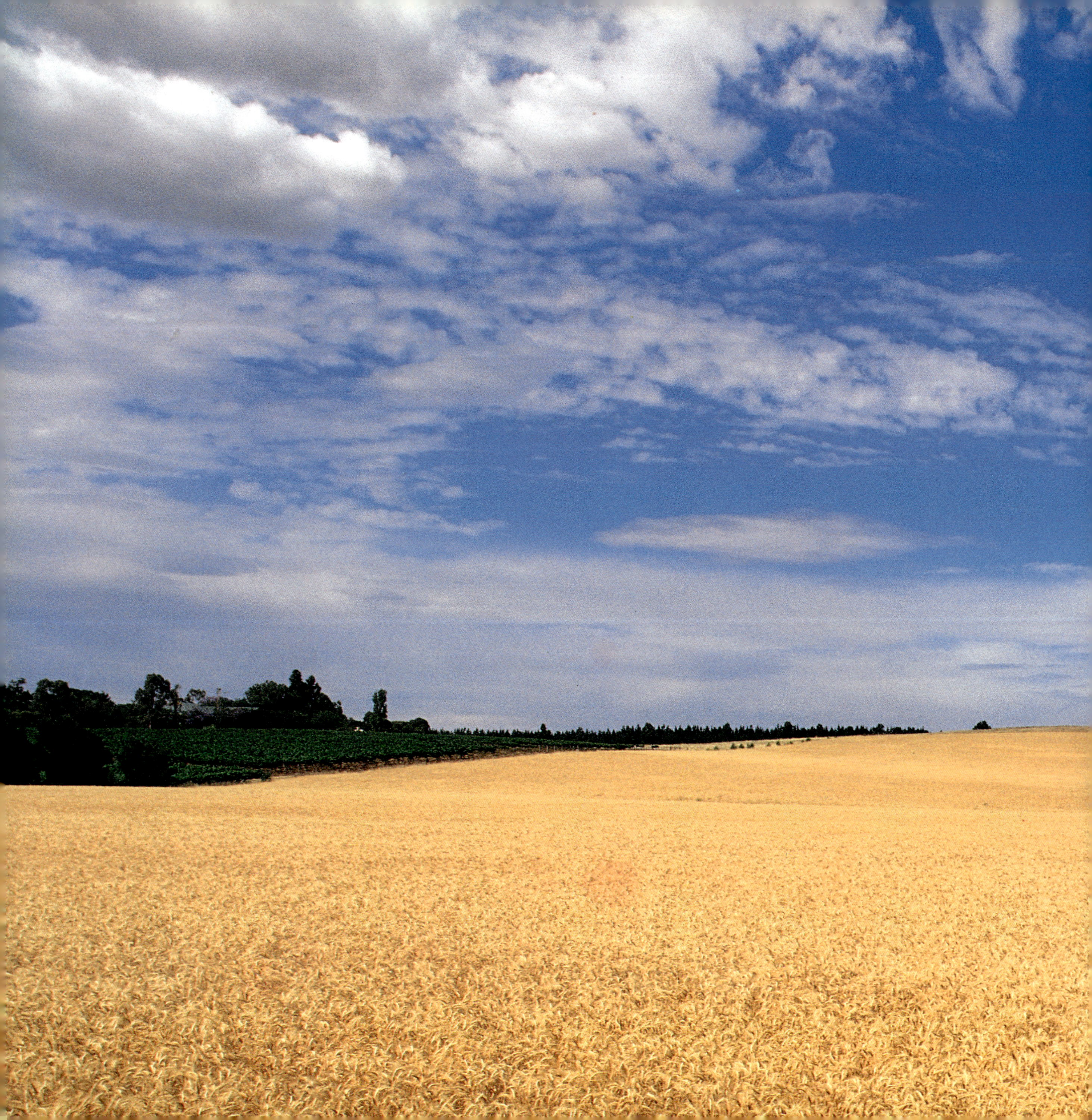

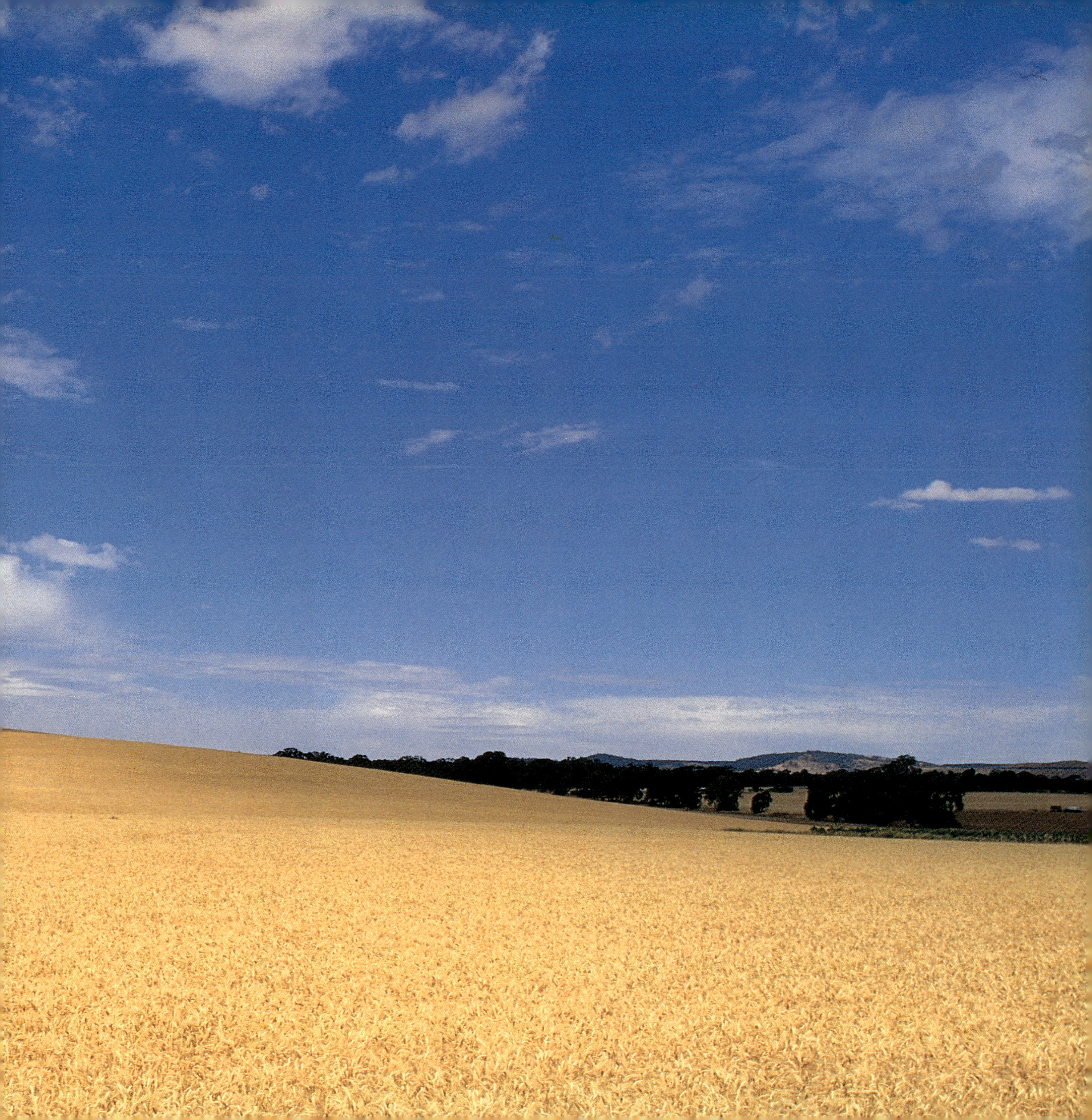

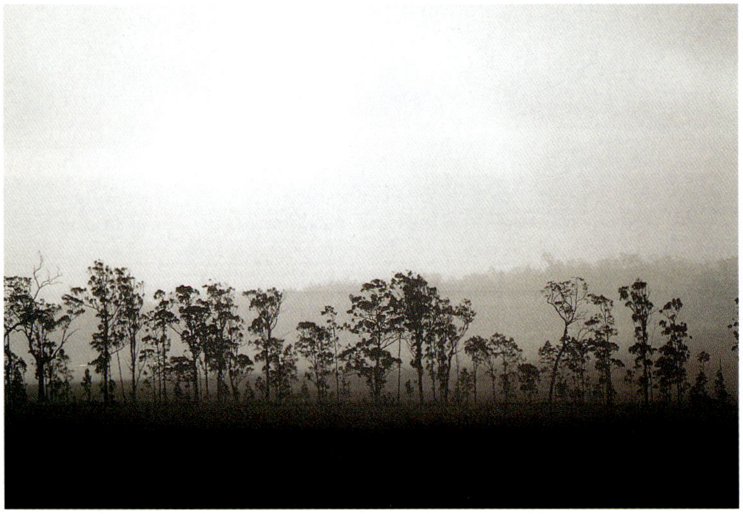

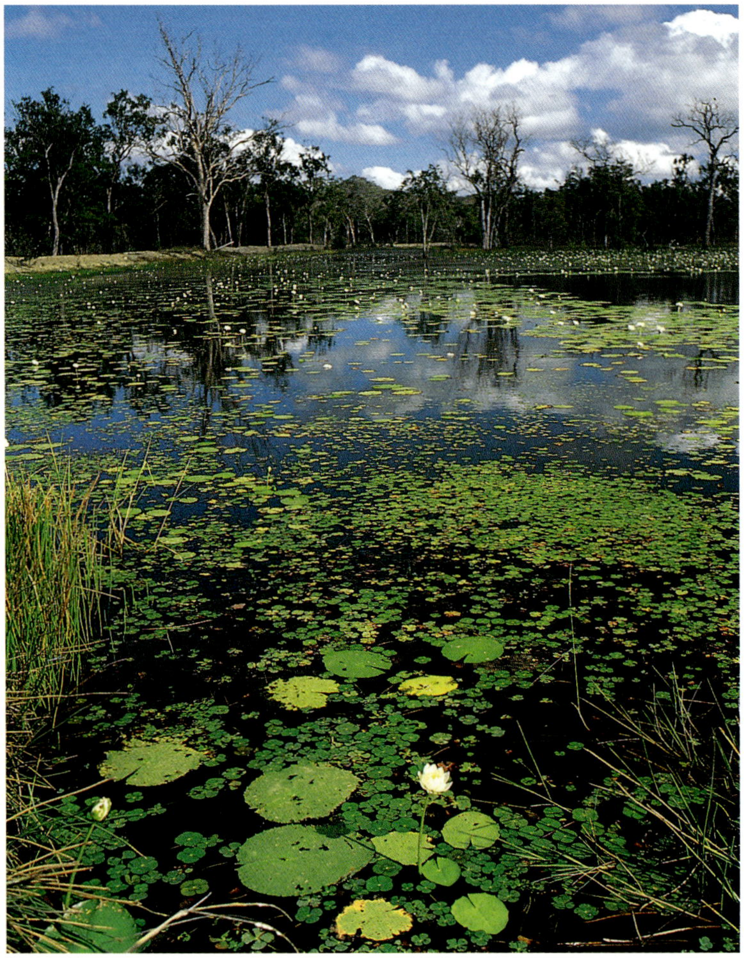

Left: Mist cloaks the landscape of the upland regions in North Queensland's Atherton Tableland region during the cooler seasons. This creates a moody scene of stark greys and black. The area contains many dairy farms, and also a number of plantations producing such crops as tobacco, maize and macadamia nuts.

Left below: Green floods the surface of a dam near Lakeland in far north Queensland. The flowering water lilies thrive in waterways, built to irrigate the nearby farmland and create new habitats for a number of wildlife species.

Right: The Murrumbidgee River is an important tributary of one of the country's major river systems. These golden willows, that cuddle to the side of the bank where the river passes through the Australian Capital Territory, create a striking stance against the indigo water.

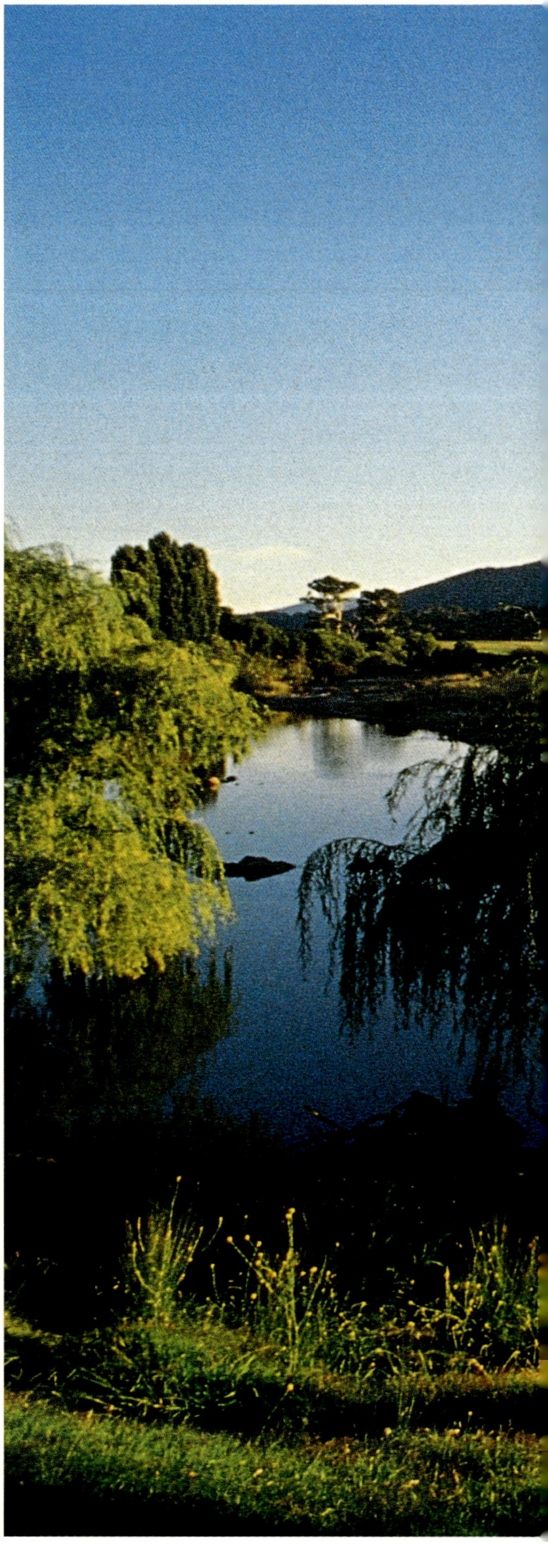

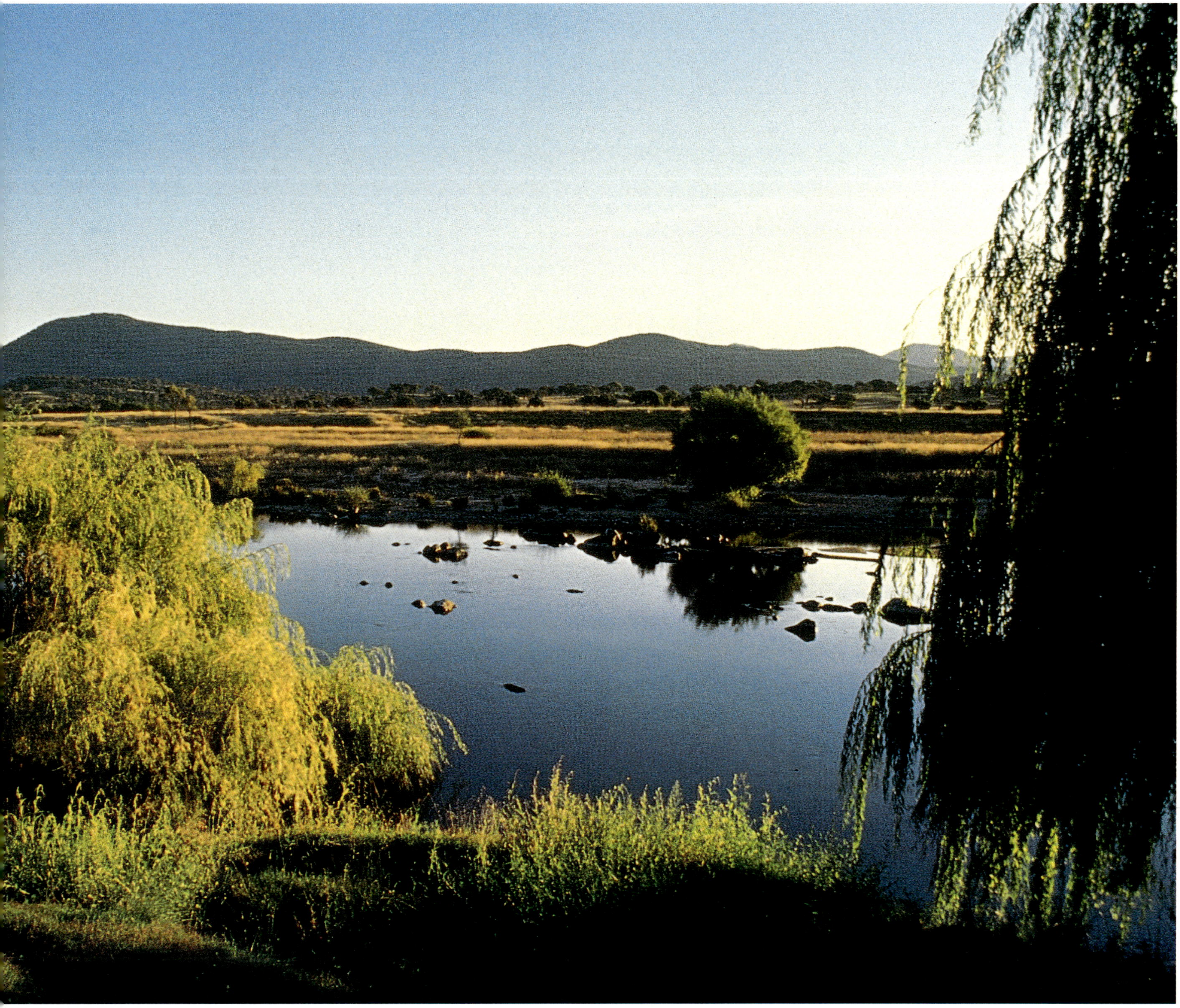

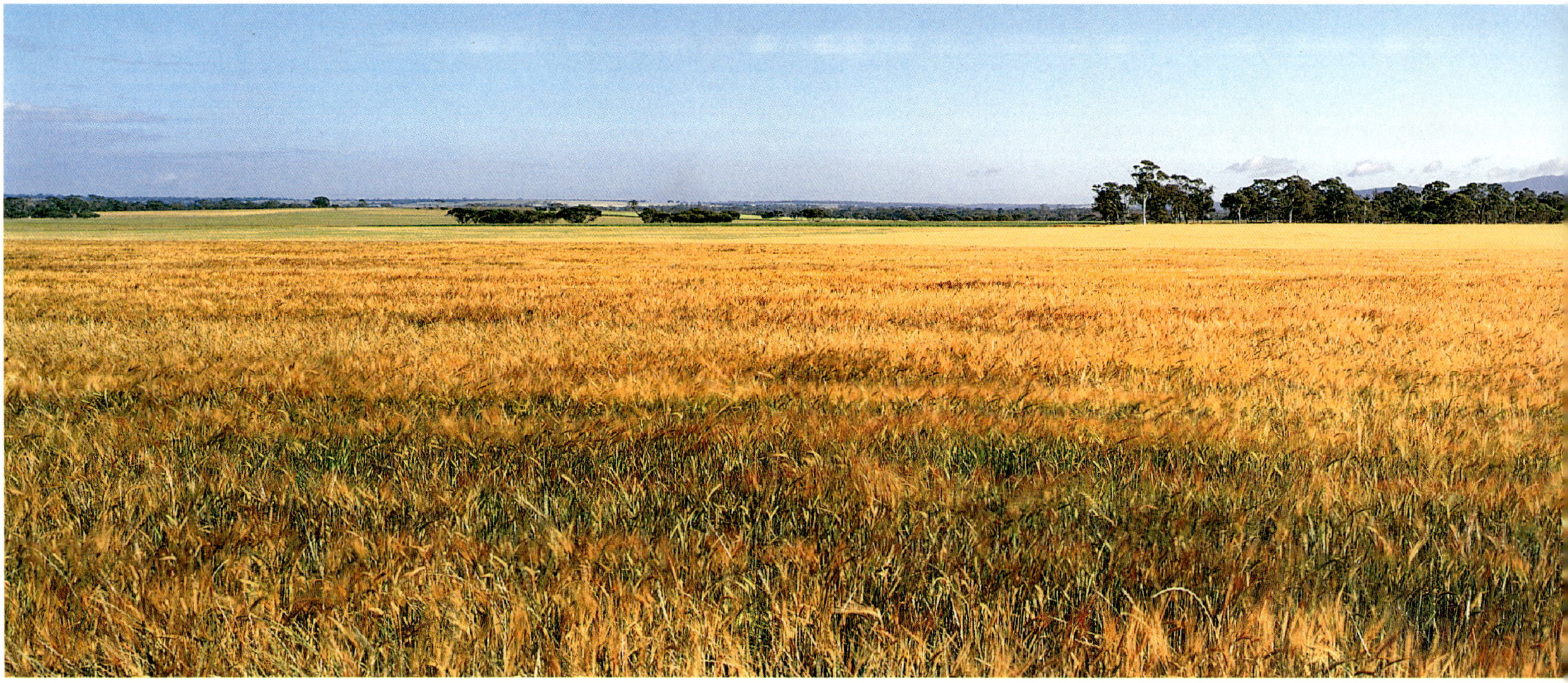

Above: Large areas near the Stirling Ranges in southern Western Australia are cultivated for intensive wheat growing. These crop belts create broad panoramas of gold and green-tipped harvest, more often than not, capped by cloudless pale blue skies.

Right: Although the southern fringes of South Australia's vast outback receive erratic rainfall, the area bordering the Flinders Ranges somehow manages to support crops. This marginal farming country presents a myriad of contrasts in its variety of produce, trees, sky and rugged rocky outcrops.

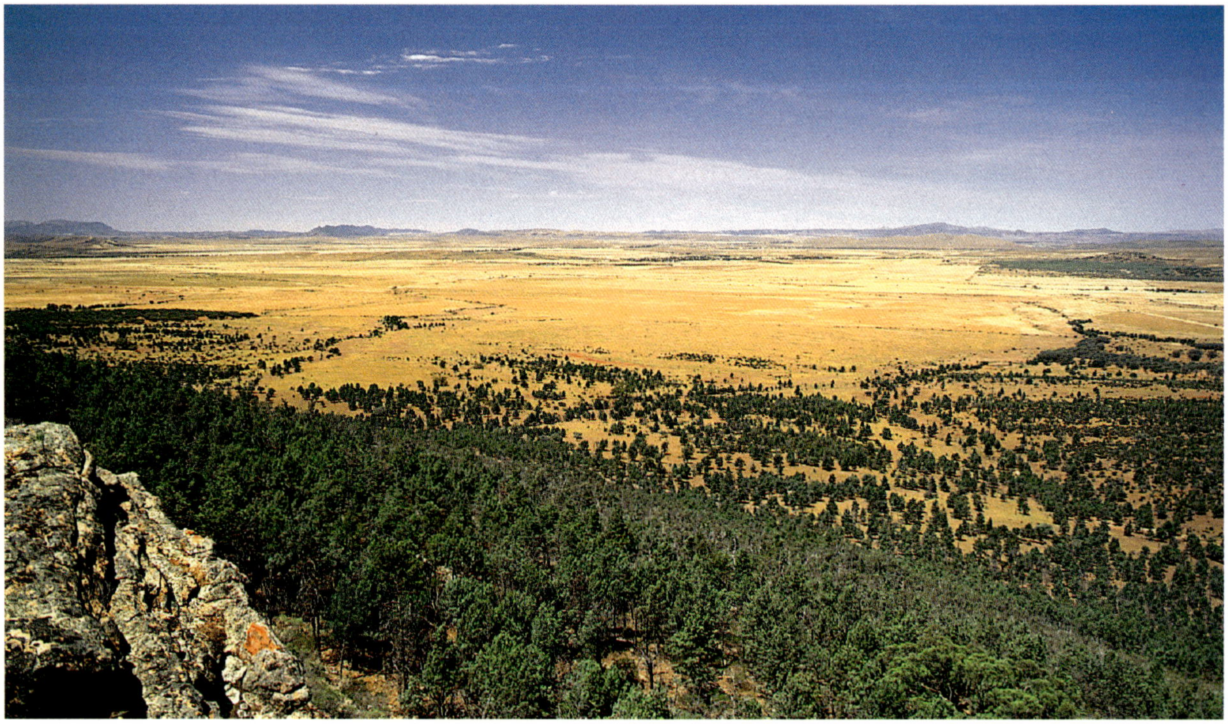

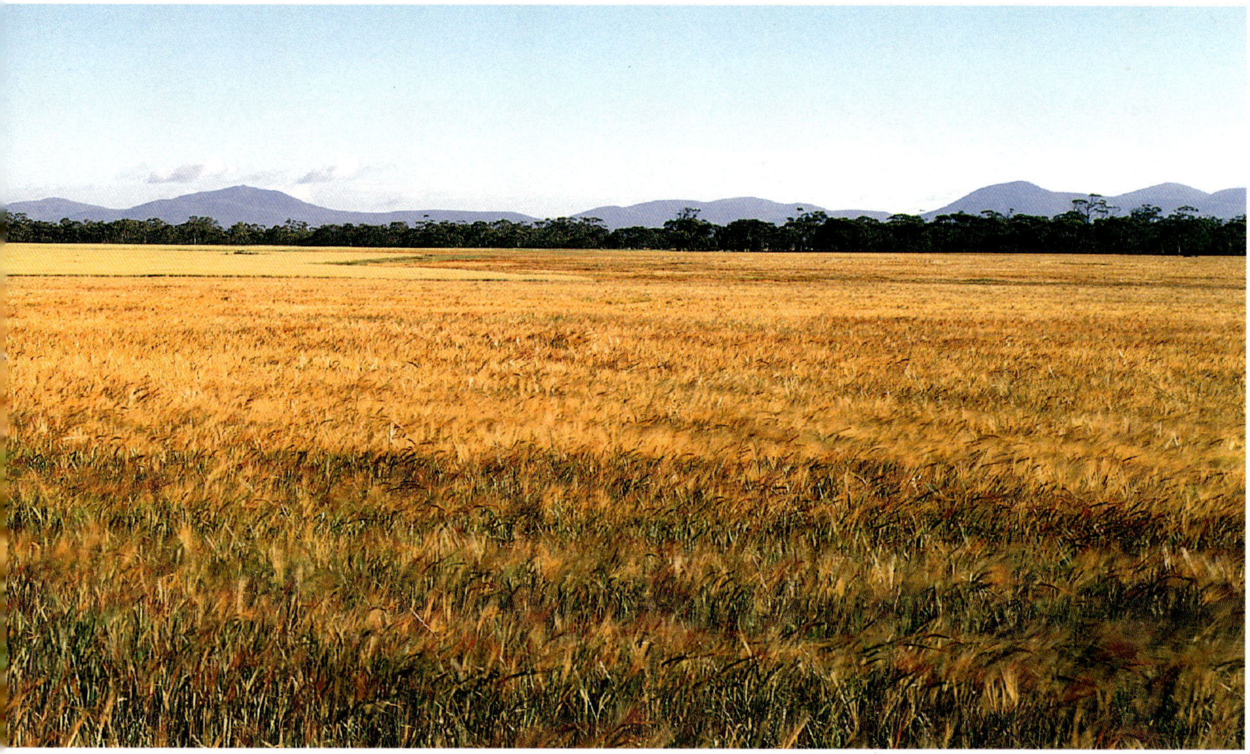

Below: The dark greenery of a dense rainforest near Cooktown in far north Queensland is broken only by a large area of natural pasture. Such verdant swampy areas are not uncommon in this tropical, high-rainfall region.

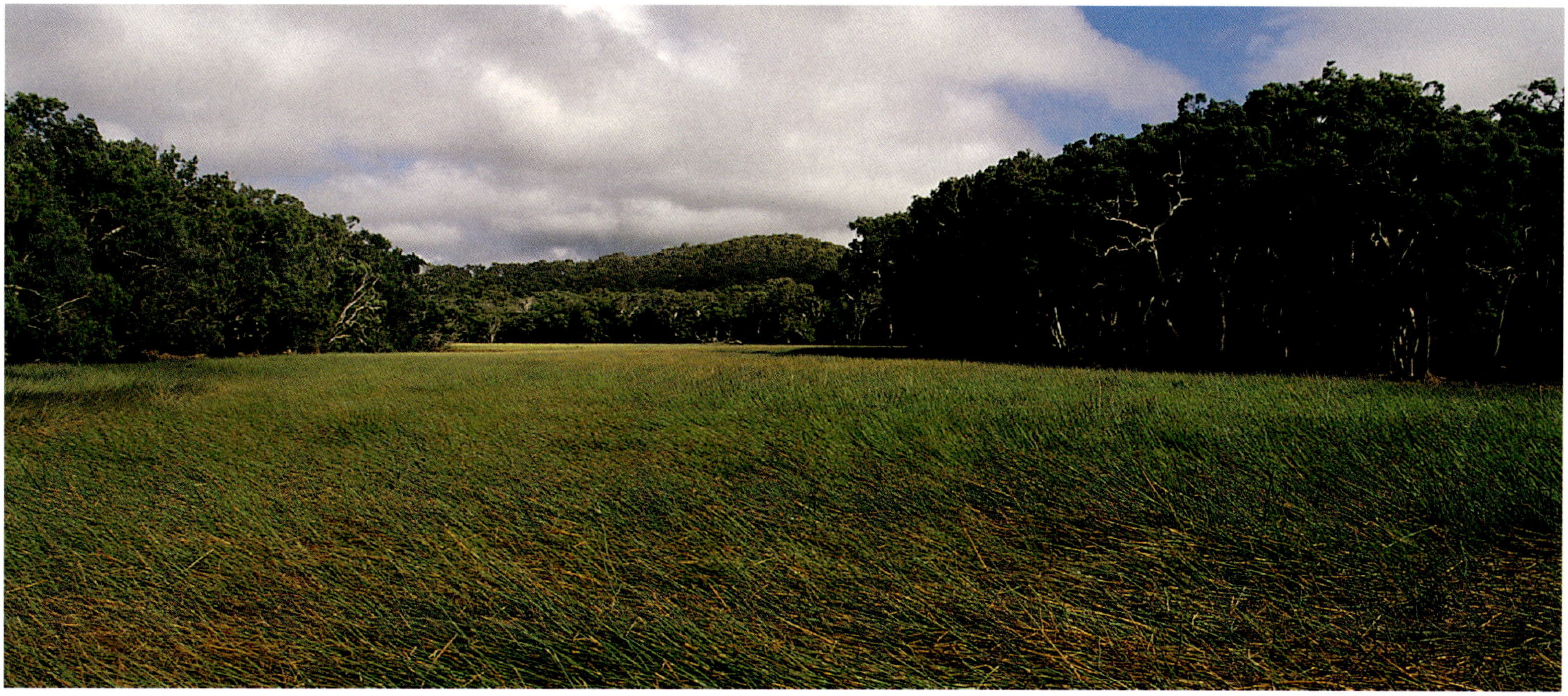

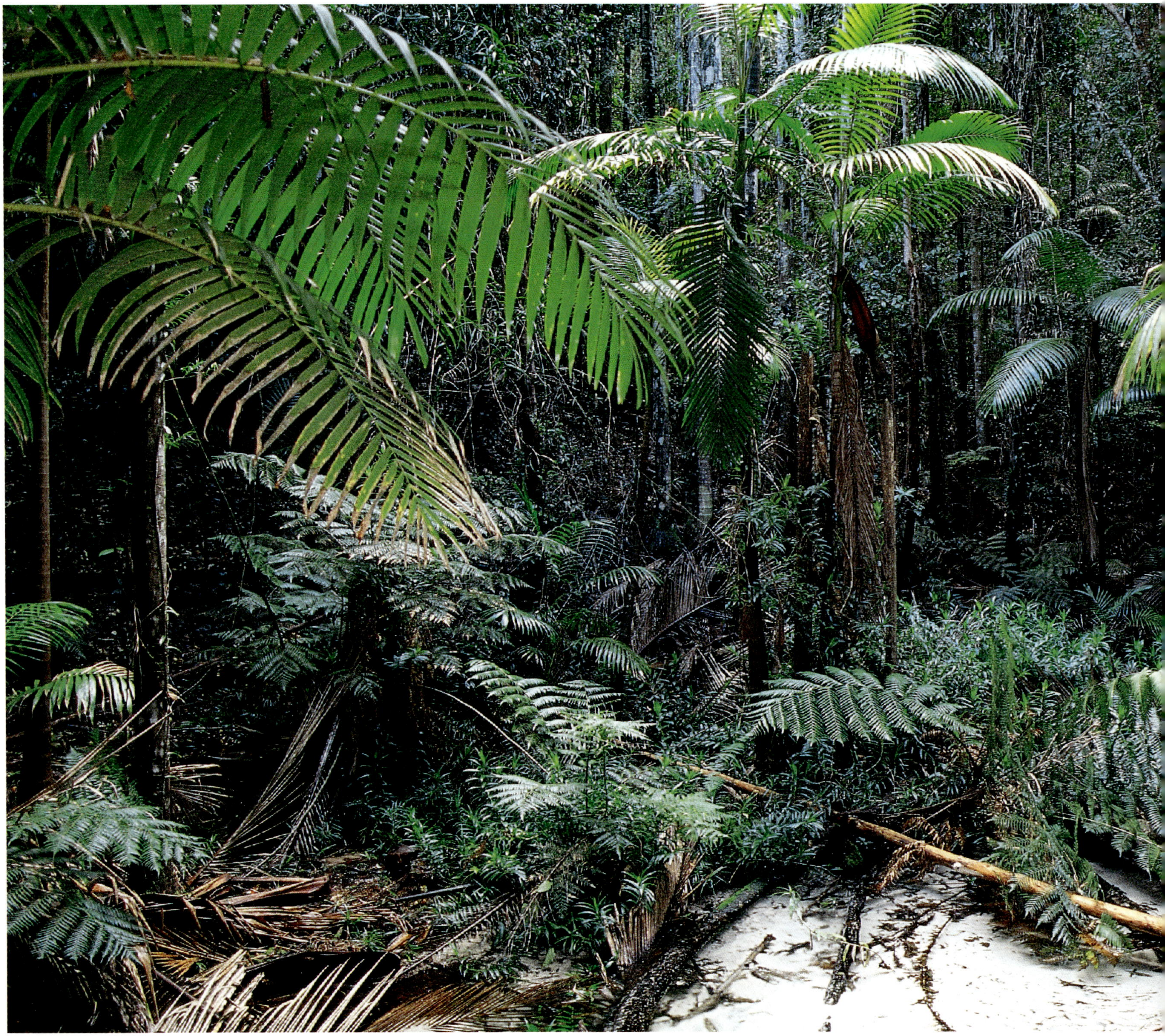

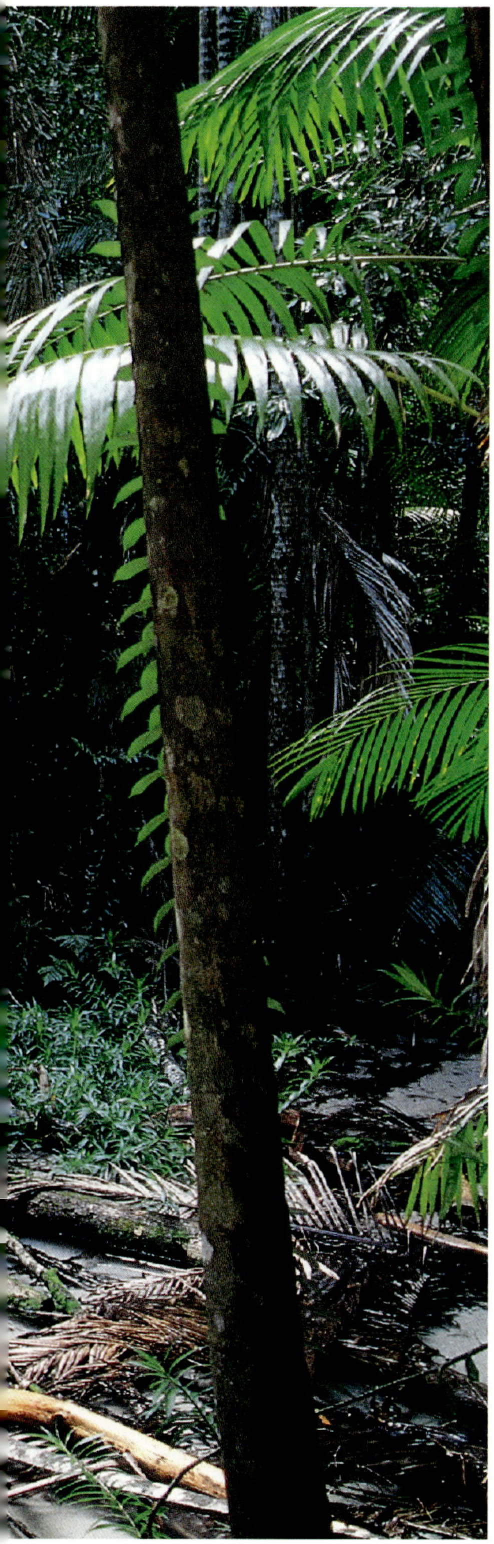

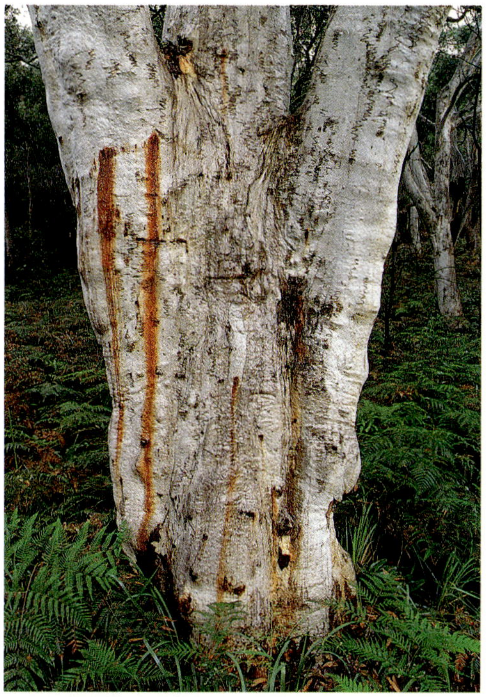

Far left: Although it is the world's largest sand island, Fraser Island off the southern Queensland coast contains a surprising abundance and variety of vegetation. Lush rainforest is found on several parts of the island.

Left: Surprisingly, eucalypts also manage to grow among Fraser's verdant domain. The sturdy, brown and rust-streaked scribbly gum, so-called because of the patterns left by insects living beneath the bark, is just one of the plants that creates the layers of the forests.

Below: The Atherton Tableland's fertile farmland turns a golden-brown under a storm-gathering clouds. Long shadows are cast across the land from the resilient trees that cling to the landscape.

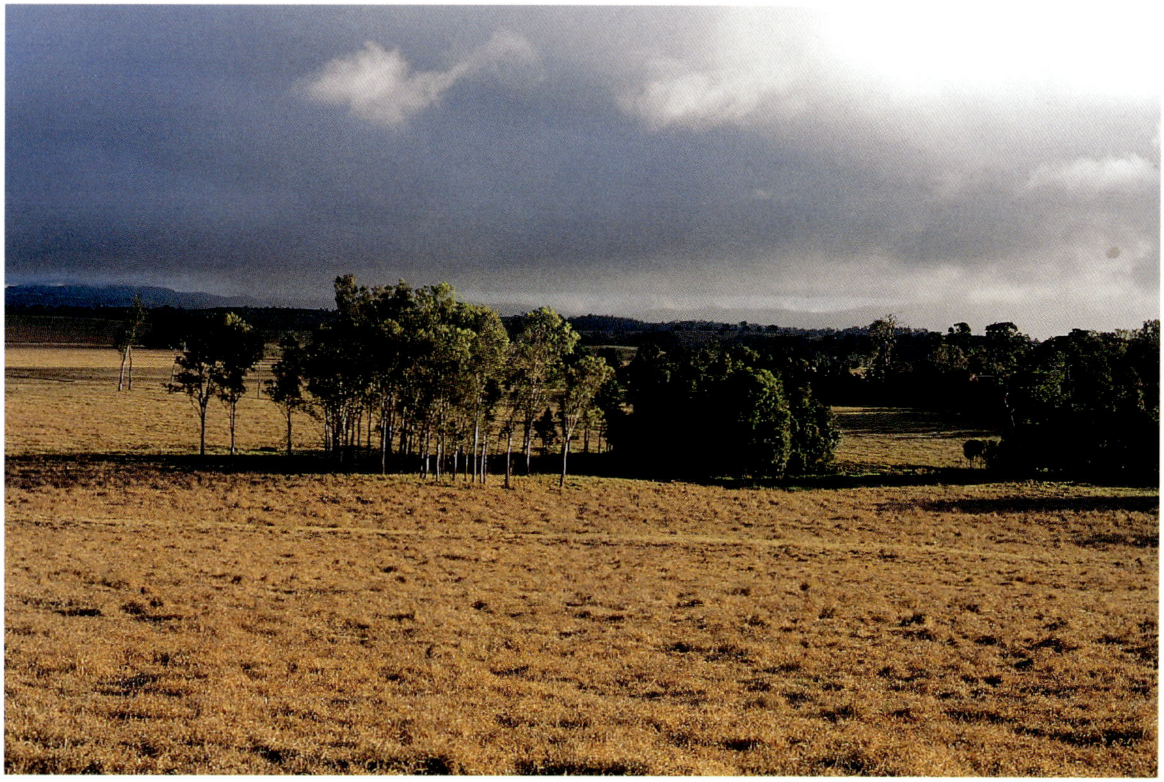

RIGHT: Colourful wildflowers in Nambung National Park in Western Australia attract many visitors, including kangaroos. This mother is venturing out with a Joey in her pouch. She is heading towards marginal pasture lands to feed on the gold and green feasts provided by nature and industrialisation.

BELOW: Kangaroo Island features an extraordinary range of scenery, from rugged cliffs and sandy bays to grassland and forests. Much of its environment lends an air of peacefulness, with rough-barked eucalypts softened by an understorey of ferns and bracken.

FAR RIGHT: A farm at Burnie on Tasmania's north coast presents a pastoral study in restful shades of blue, brown and green. It is framed by a cloud-streaked sky, with the Bass Strait looking unusually calm in the background.

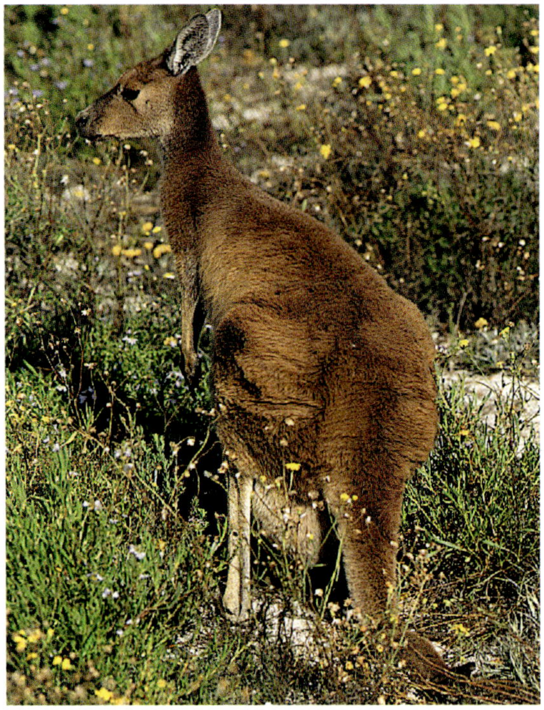

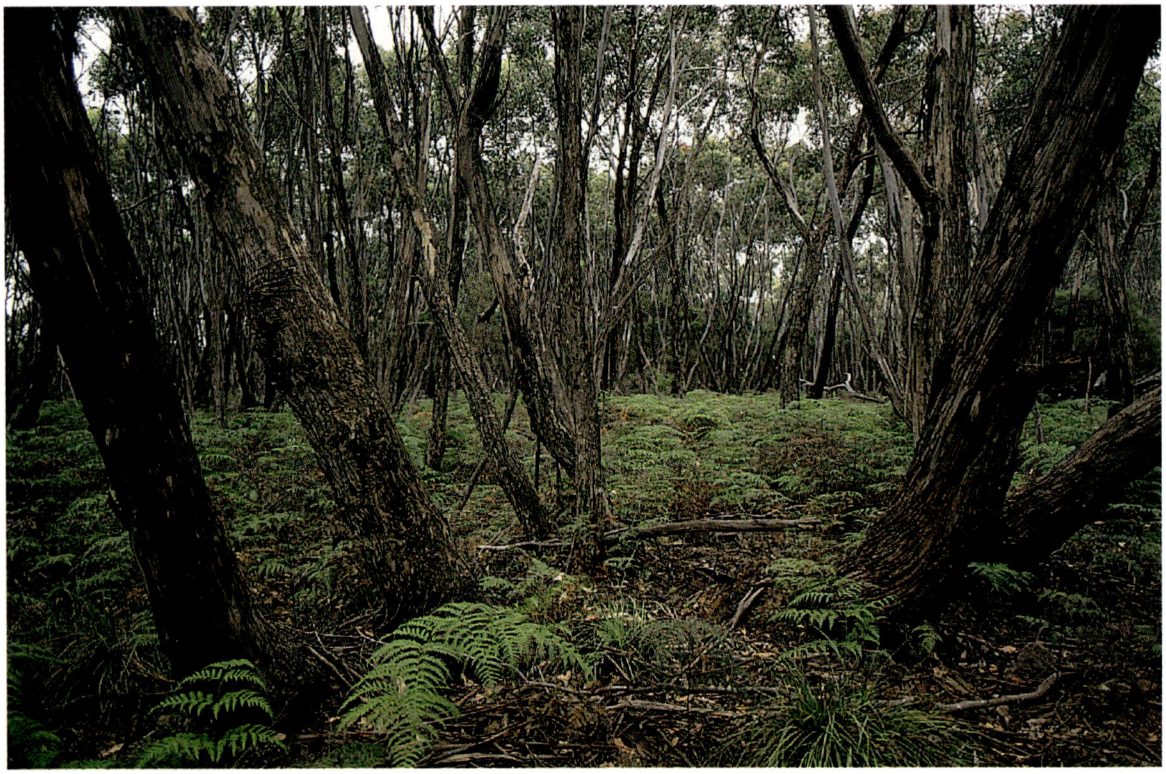

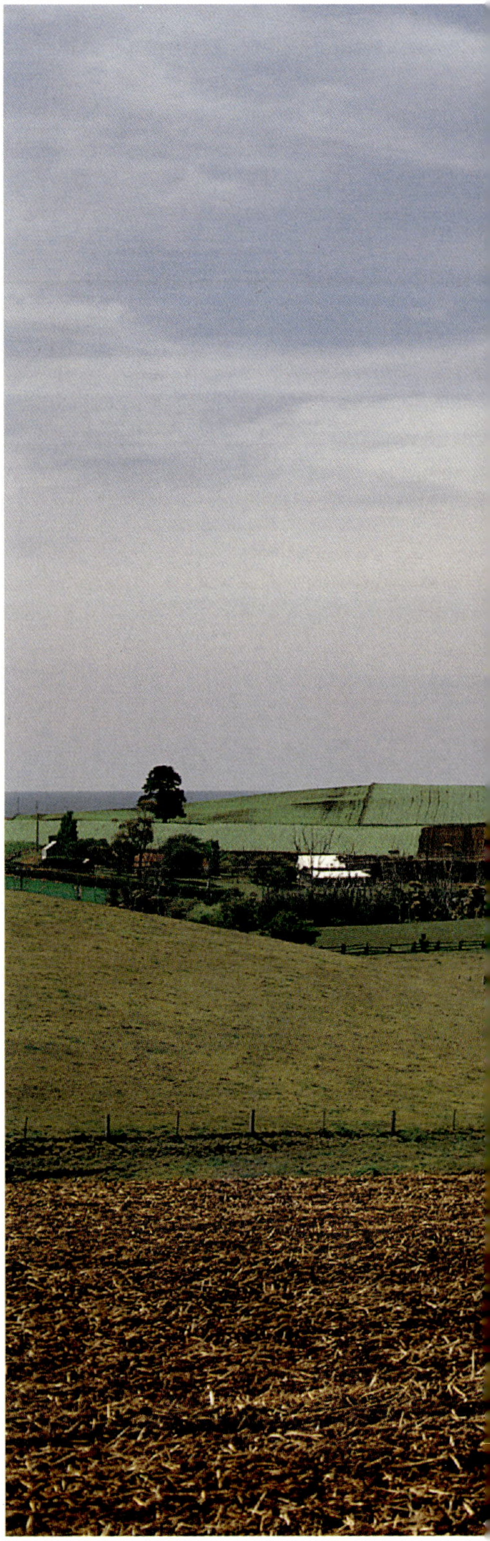

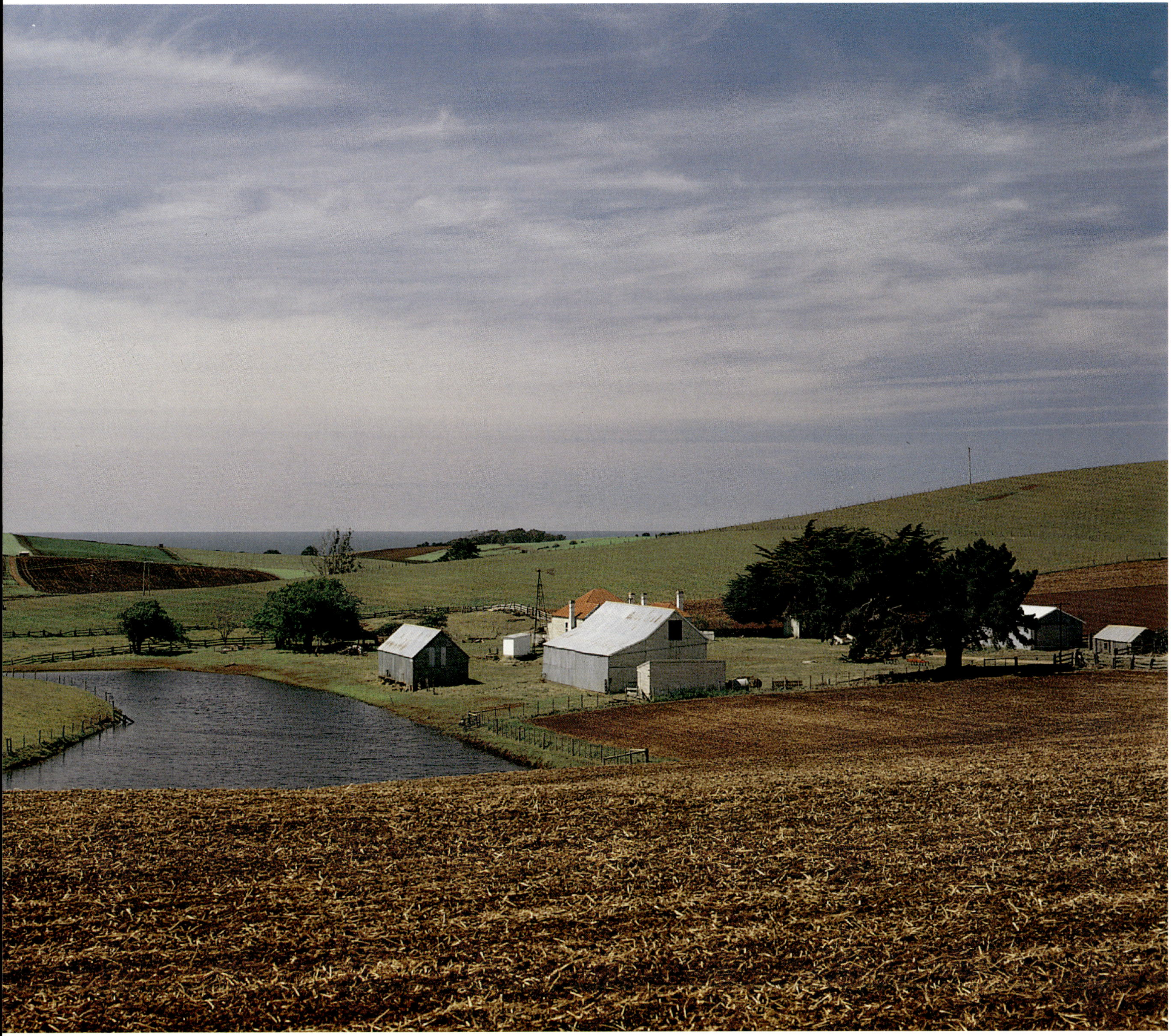

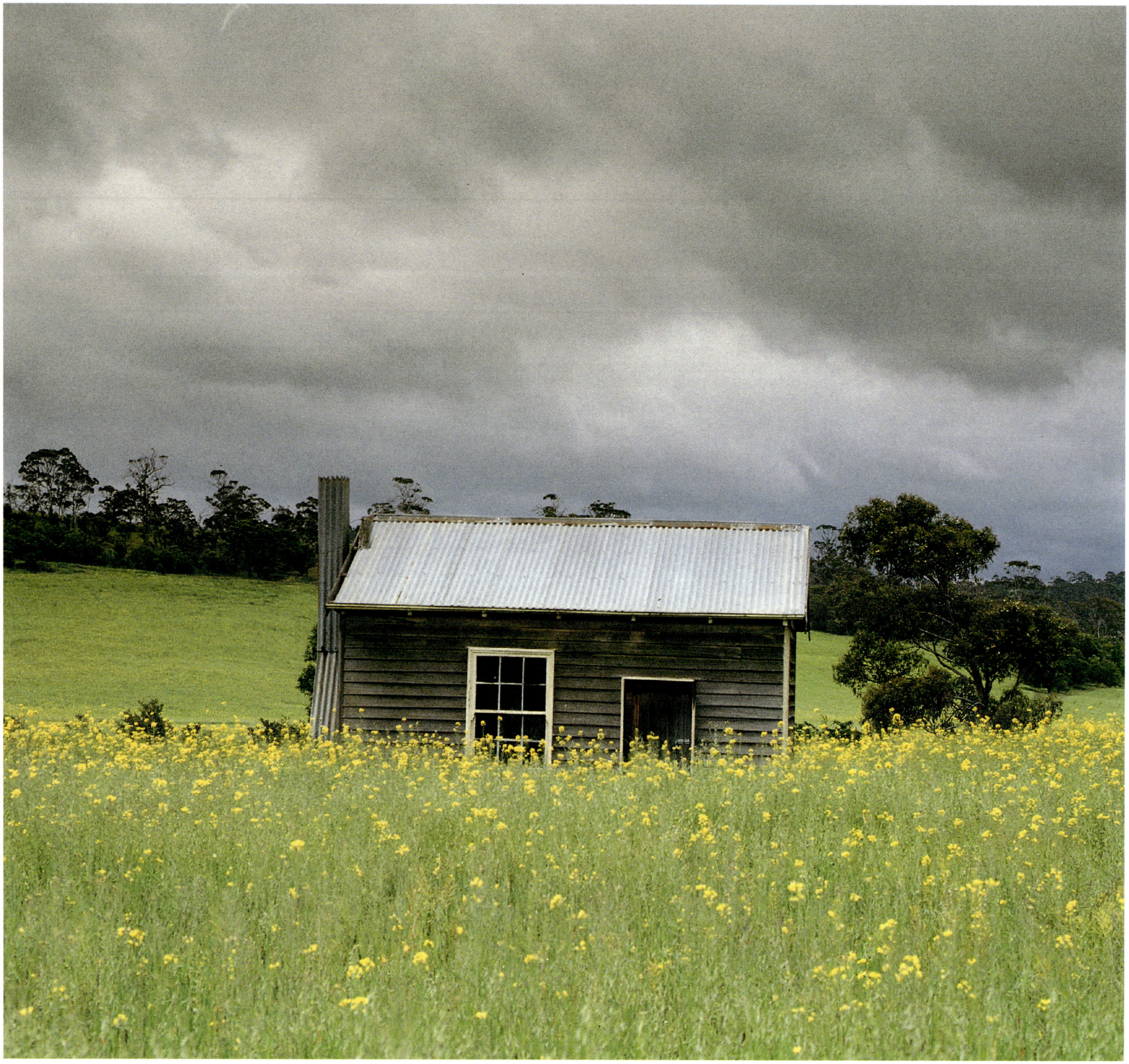

Opposite: Under a heavy grey sky, bright yellow rape flowers atop tall slender stems brighten a field, near Sorell in Tasmania. A rustic shack remains as a reminder of the Europeans pioneers who forged a life in the remote regions of the country.

Below: Sugar cane is a major produce for the state of Queensland, and it thrives and grows tall beneath a dazzling sapphire sky over Bundaberg.

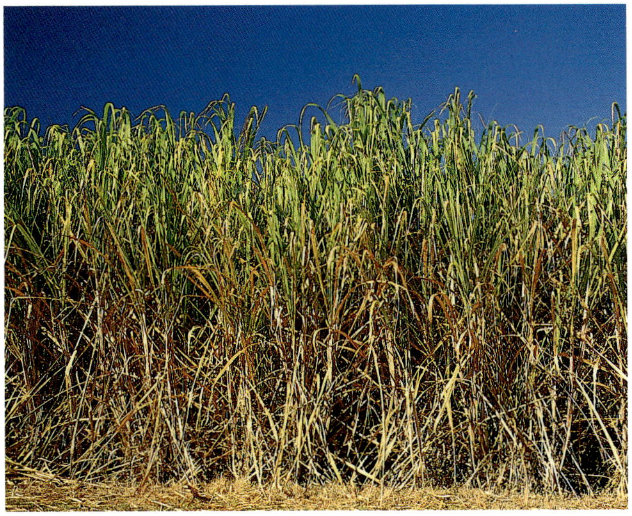

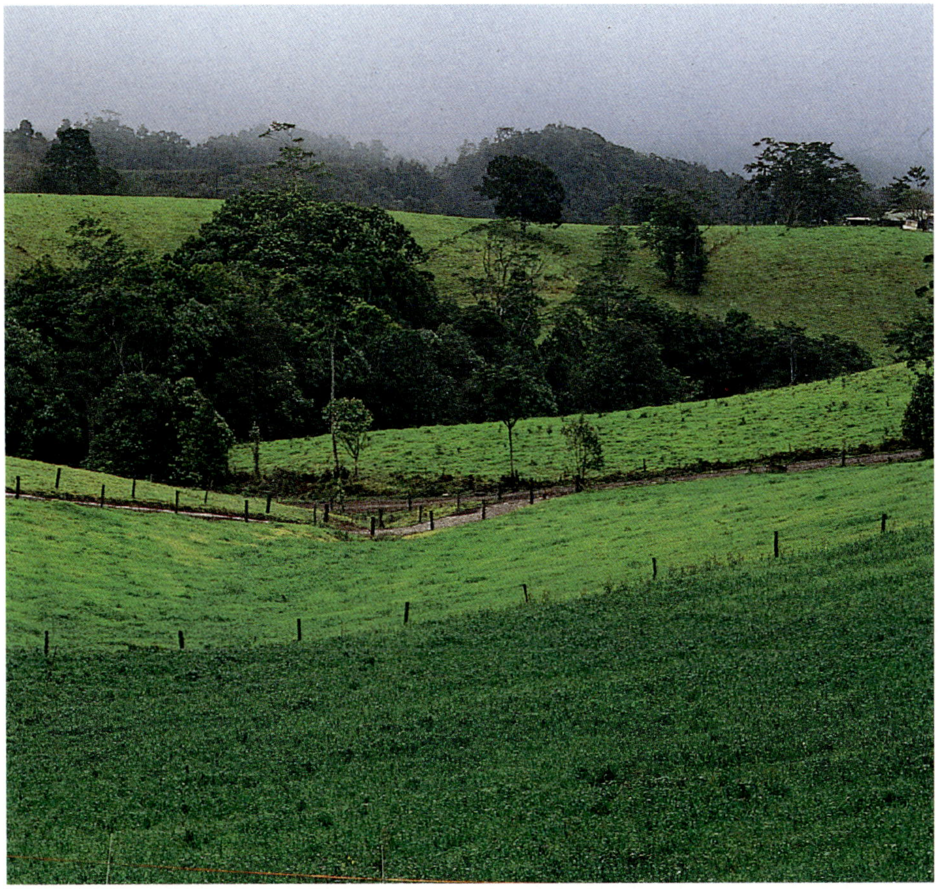

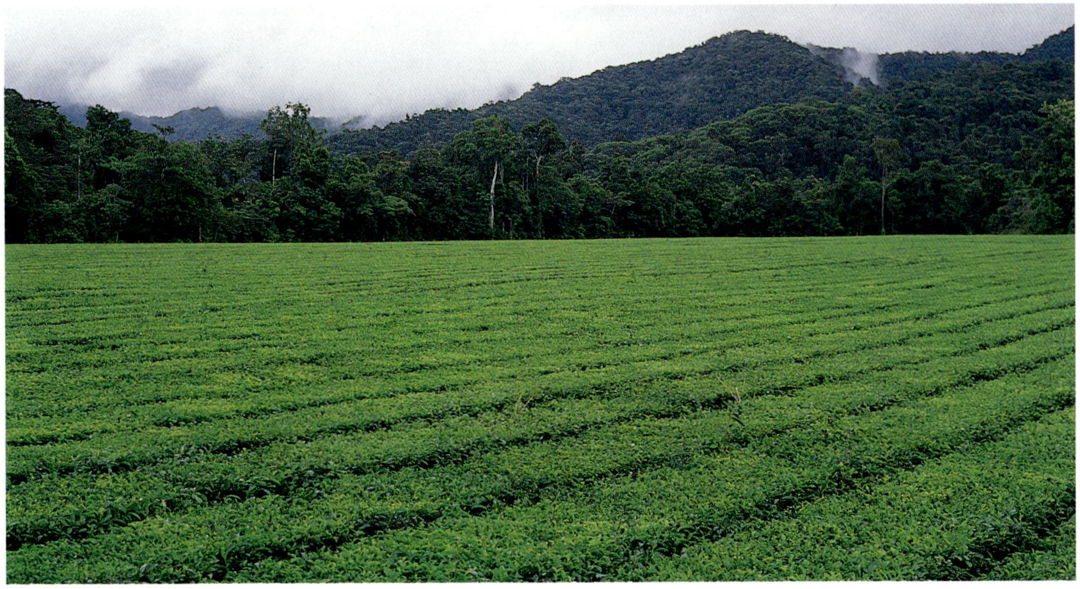

Above: Emerald predominates the colour of Millaa Millaa farmlands on the Atherton Tableland. These tones quell the many perceptions about Australia, particularly the notion that it is mostly a dry and barren land. The vivid green makes the scene look more like rural England than a farm in the tropic zone.

Left: The bright intense colour of a tea plantation at Cape Tribulation in north Queensland is also the result of the region's high rainfall and rich soils. The rainforested hills bordering the farm reveal the darker shades of green that are found in tropical woodland.

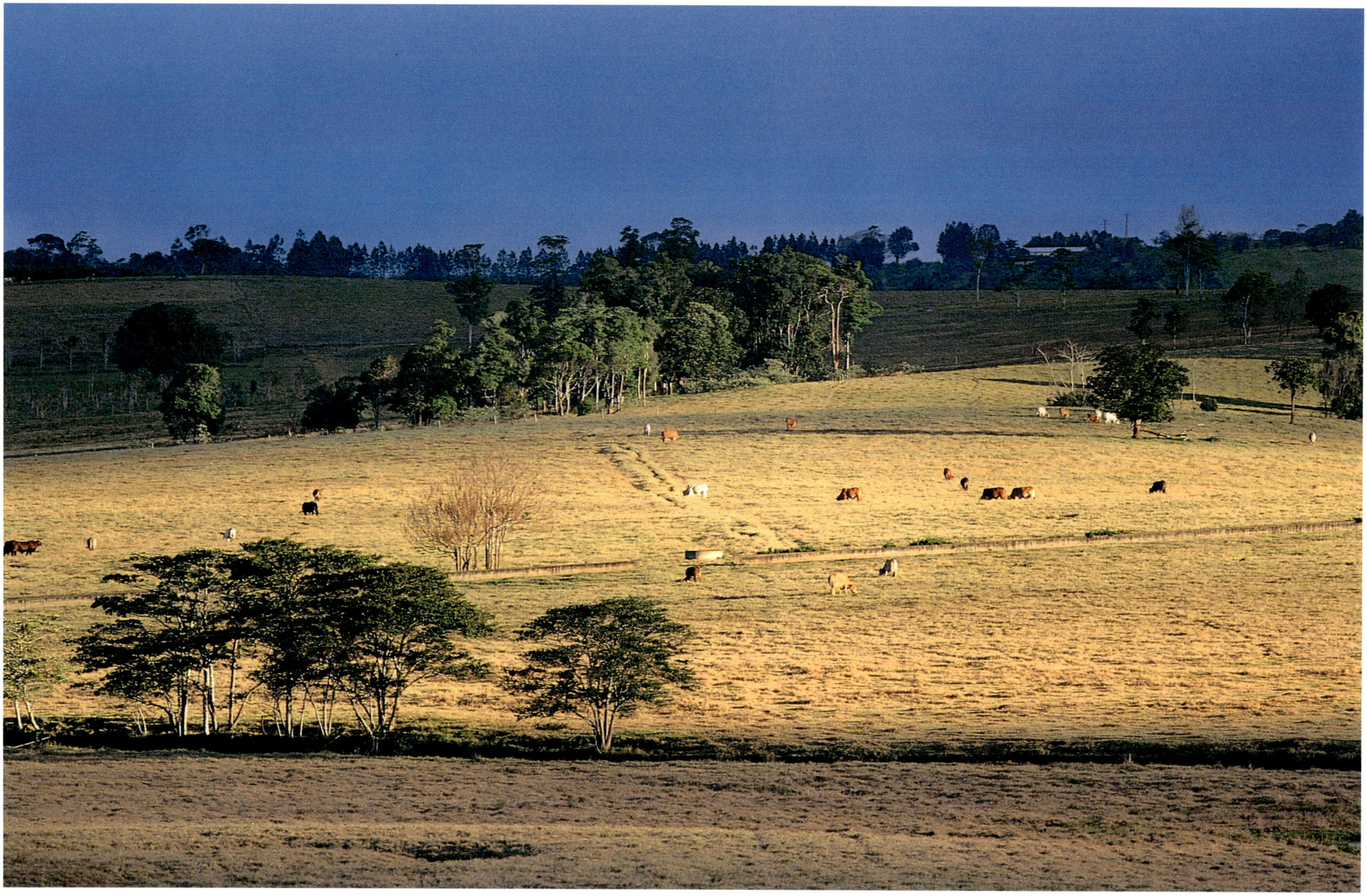

ABOVE: A splash of sun highlights the many colours of pasture lands on the Atherton Tablelands. This area is one of the continent's most productive agricultural regions. Famous for its beef and dairying industries, maize and coffee are also grown.

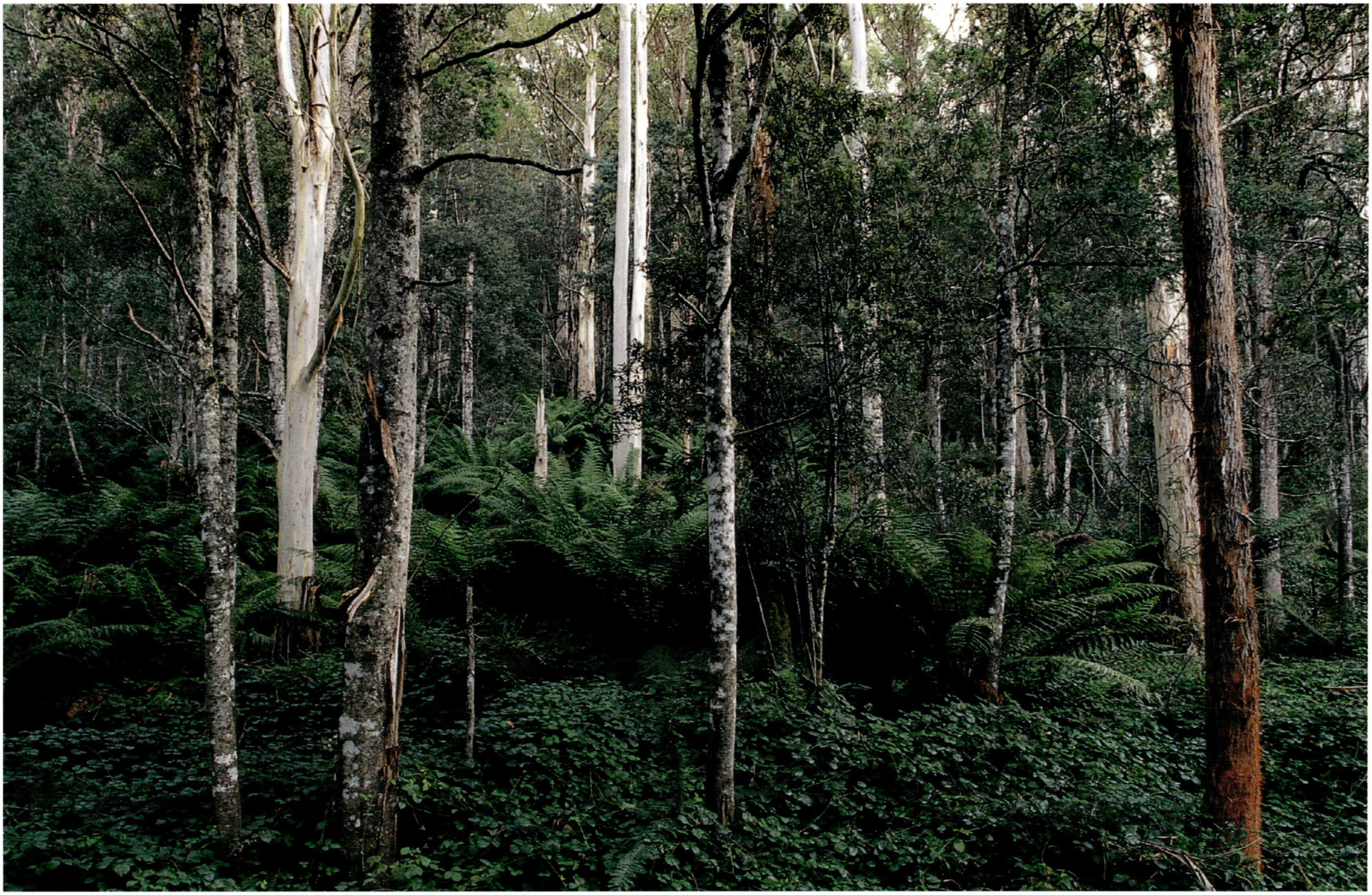

Above: Tasmania contains a large proportion of Australia's flourishing green forest lands. Temperate rainforests are abundant in the island state's wilderness areas, such as Cradle Mountain and the Southwest National Park.

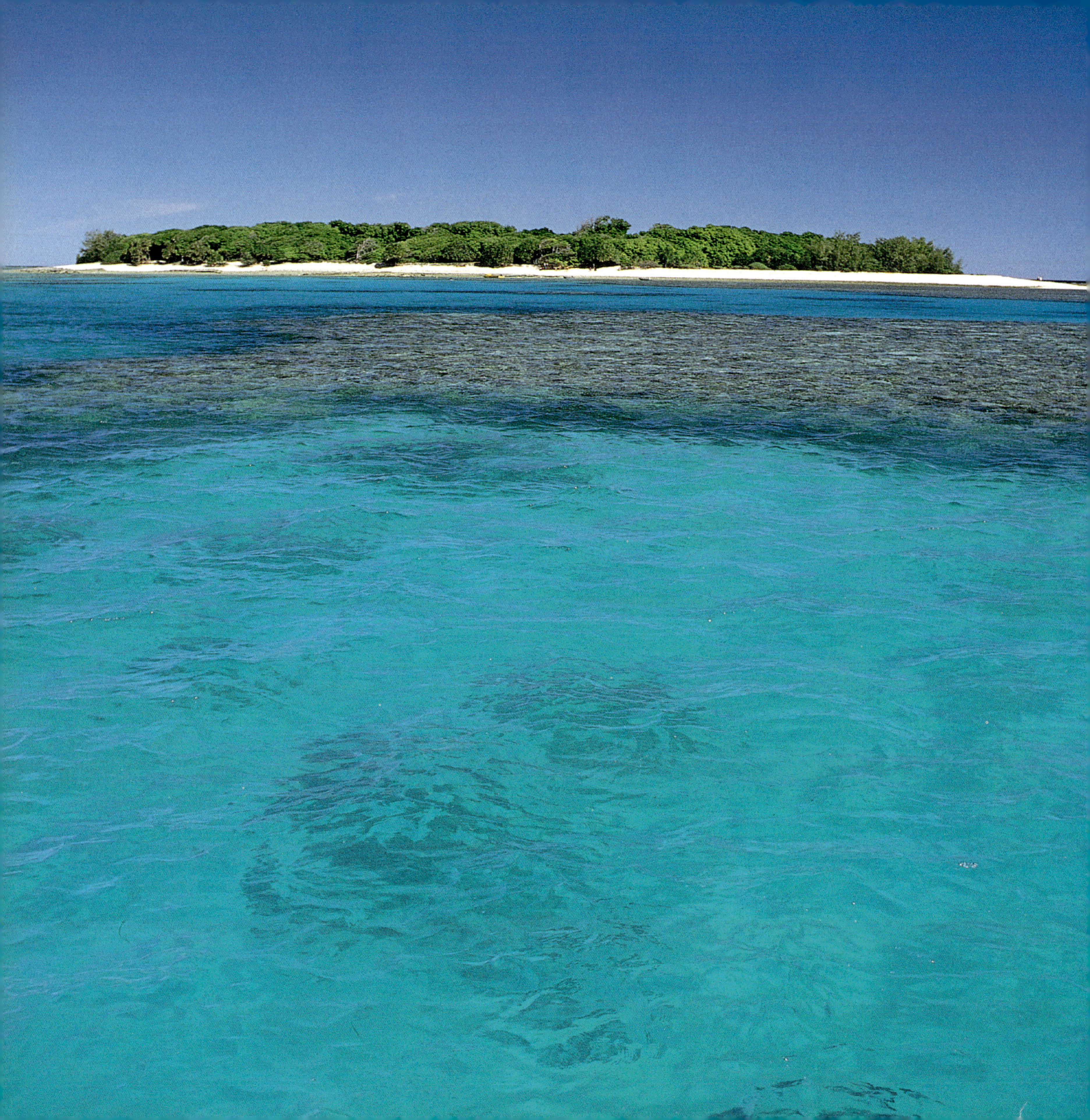

Yellow Sands and Sapphire Seas

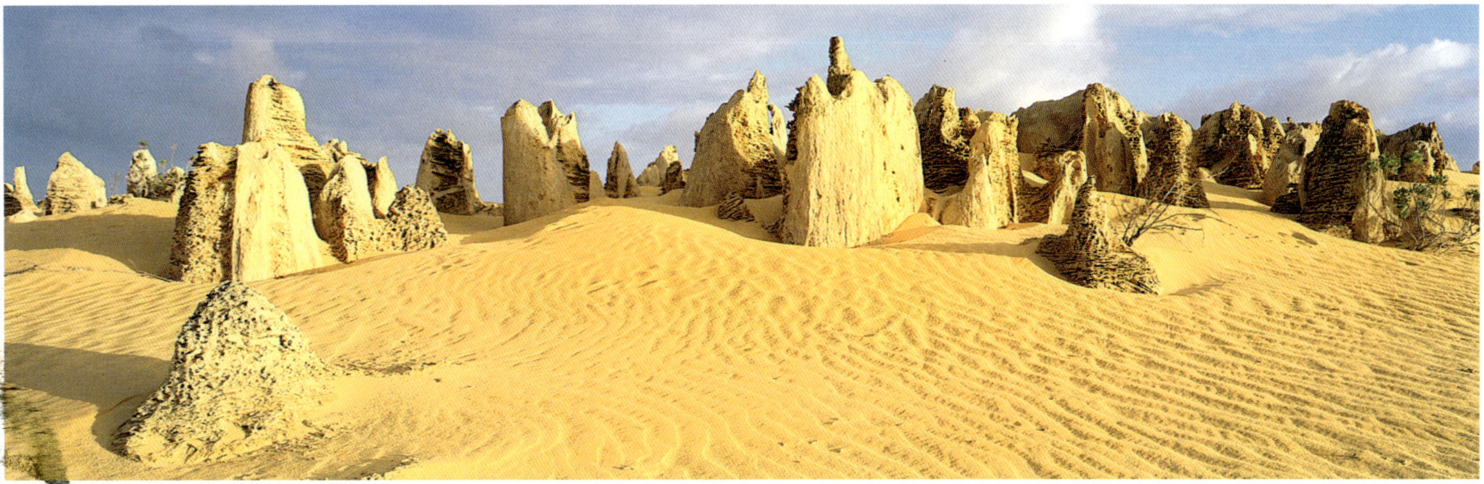

Opposite: Australia's golden beaches and blue seas are best exemplified by Lady Musgrave Island, an idyllic coral cay. Above: Western Australia's famous rock formations, The Pinnacles, present a striking contrast to ocean dunes. These curiously-shaped limestone needles and wedges protrude chaotically from the shifting sands of a coastal desert.

Australia is surrounded by a remarkable 36 700 kilometres of coastline. Within this almost inconceivable length is an amazing range of terrain—everything from sheer wave pounded cliffs on the south coast through long sandy beaches that stretch for up to 100 kilometres to tranquil coves, inlets and estuaries.

Offshore, over 1200 islands lie within Australia's boundaries. Many of these belong to what might be considered the world's most impressive natural wonder, the Great Barrier Reef. The reef runs for an incredible 2300 kilometres from beyond the tip of Cape York to just off the coast south of central Queensland.

Australia's coasts, islands and reefs are washed by the waters of many seas and oceans. The Coral Sea and Pacific Ocean are to the east, the wild and unpredictable Southern Ocean and Bass Strait to the south, the Indian Ocean to the west, and the warm tropical Arafura Sea laps the continent's northern edge. This ever-changing coastline is a quixotic mix of colours, shades, shapes and forms, yet the seemingly disparate elements come together in a magnificent, complementary natural blend.

The water of the oceans that surround the continent can be described in the most amazing superlatives; sapphire, turquoise, deep indigo and stormy-grey among them. The surf can also seem cliché in that it does roll and is capped with boiling white tips. The shoreline is tinged with a kaleidoscope of hues with sandy bays and beaches and dunes, which sometimes shift inland covering everything in their path, appearing from an almost blinding white through to a deep, mellow gold.

The wave and wind lashed cliffs, their boulders and strangely sculpted rock formations, feature colours that vary from the rich rusty-red of sandstone to pale creams, greys and browns. And the coastal vegetation displays innumerable examples of softening green, olive and khaki to an environment that predominantly radiates brilliant blue and gold.

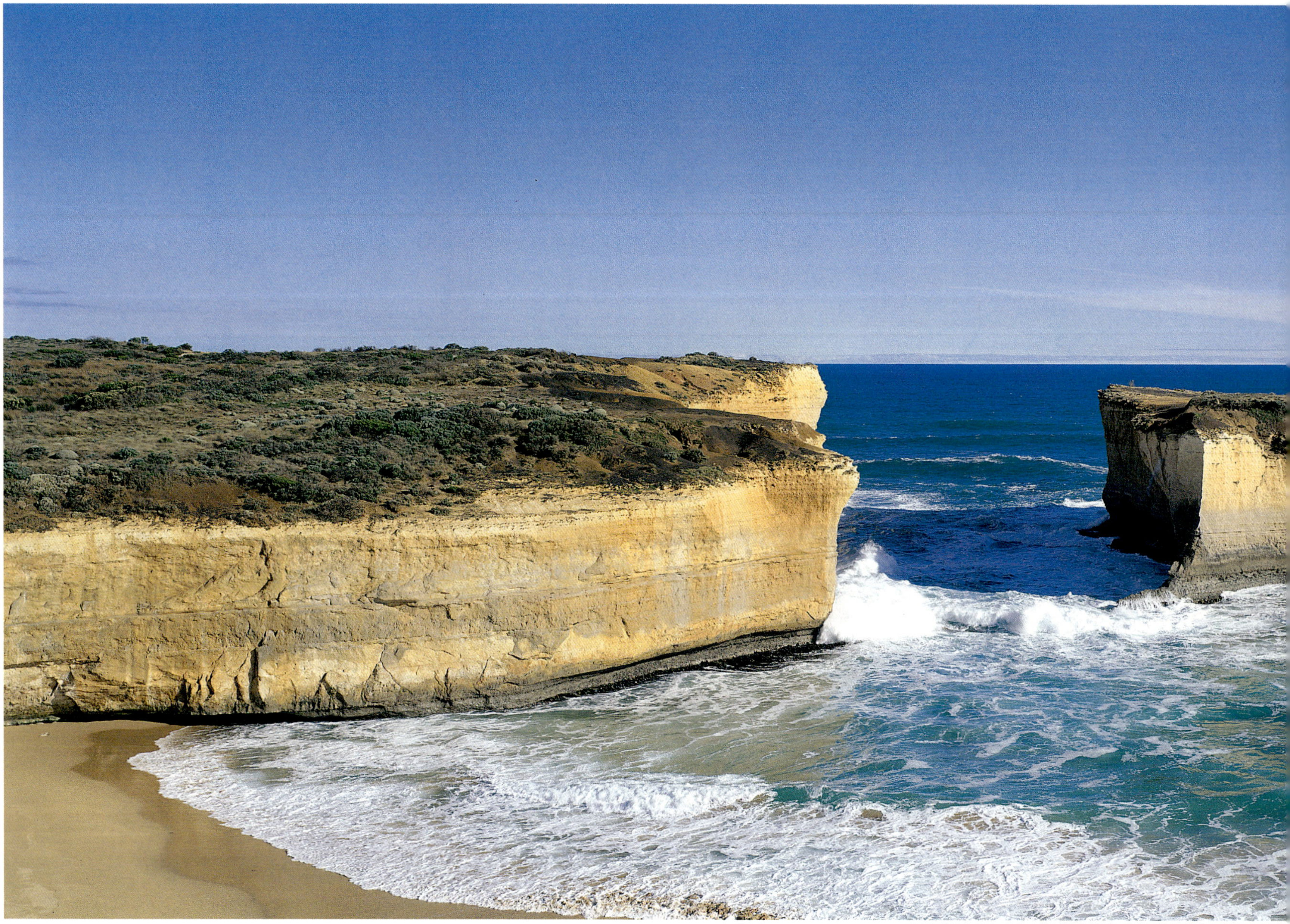

Above: Some of Australia's most dramatic coastal scenery is located in southern Victoria, where the limestone cliffs have been battered and eroded by the wild waves and surf of the Southern Ocean.

Opposite top: Muted coloured fossils can be found on the sands at Hinchinbrook Island.

Opposite bottom: Coral cays present unique coastal texture. They form a brilliant contrast of stark white lying within dark patches of coral and the turquoise northern sea.

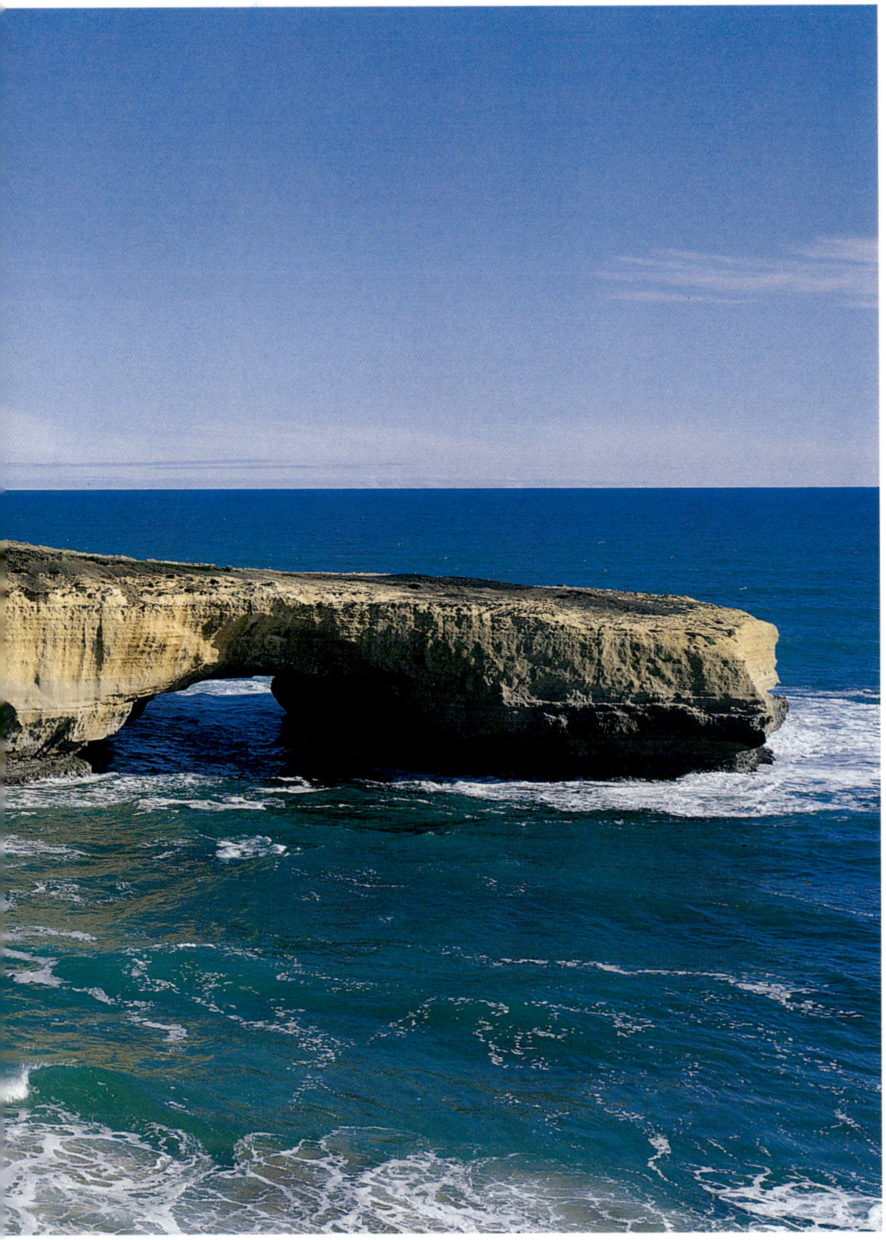

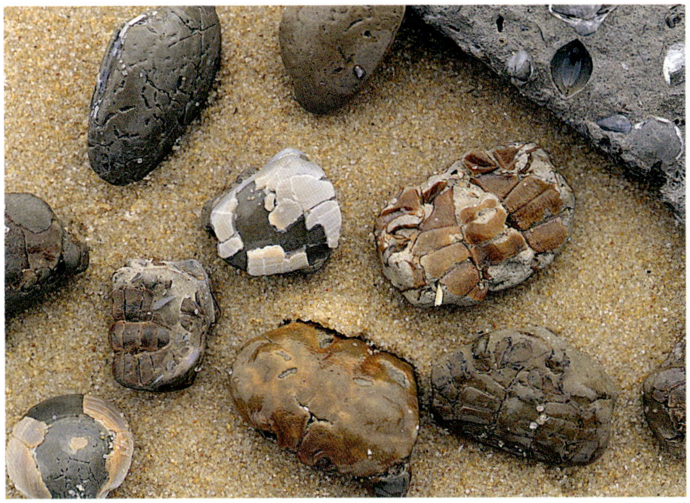

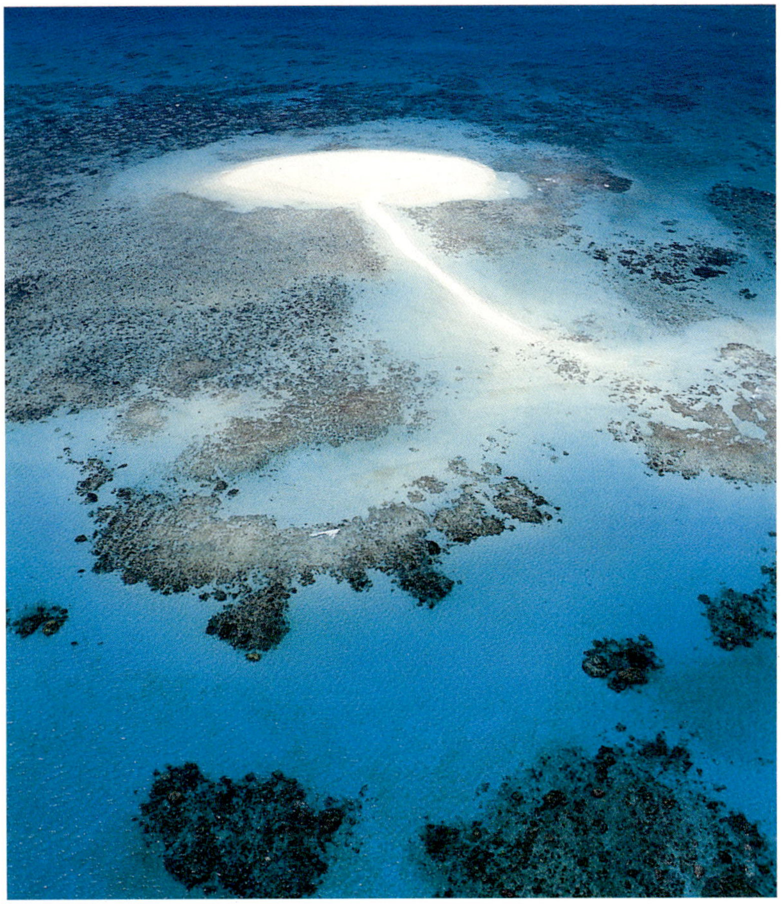

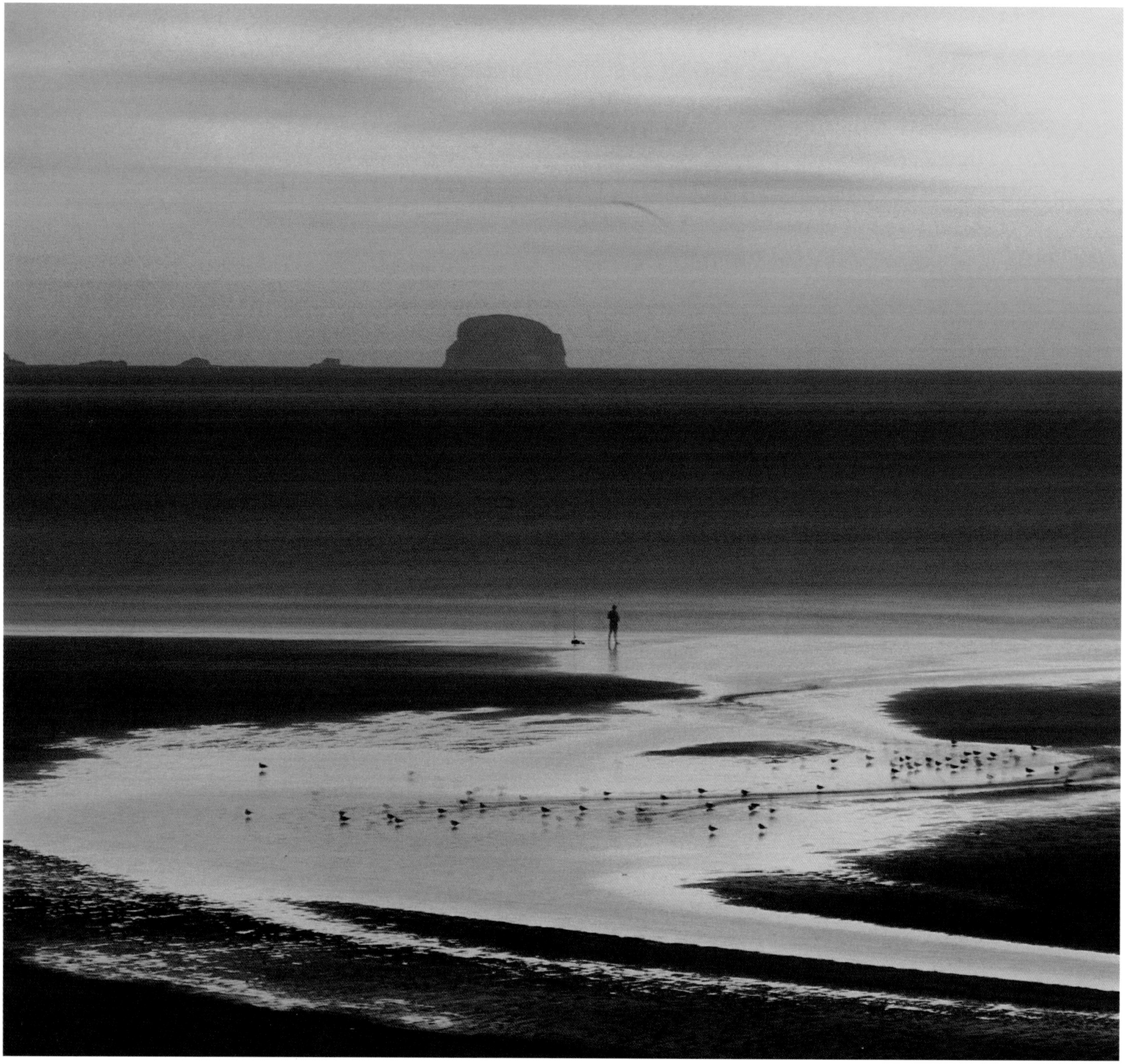

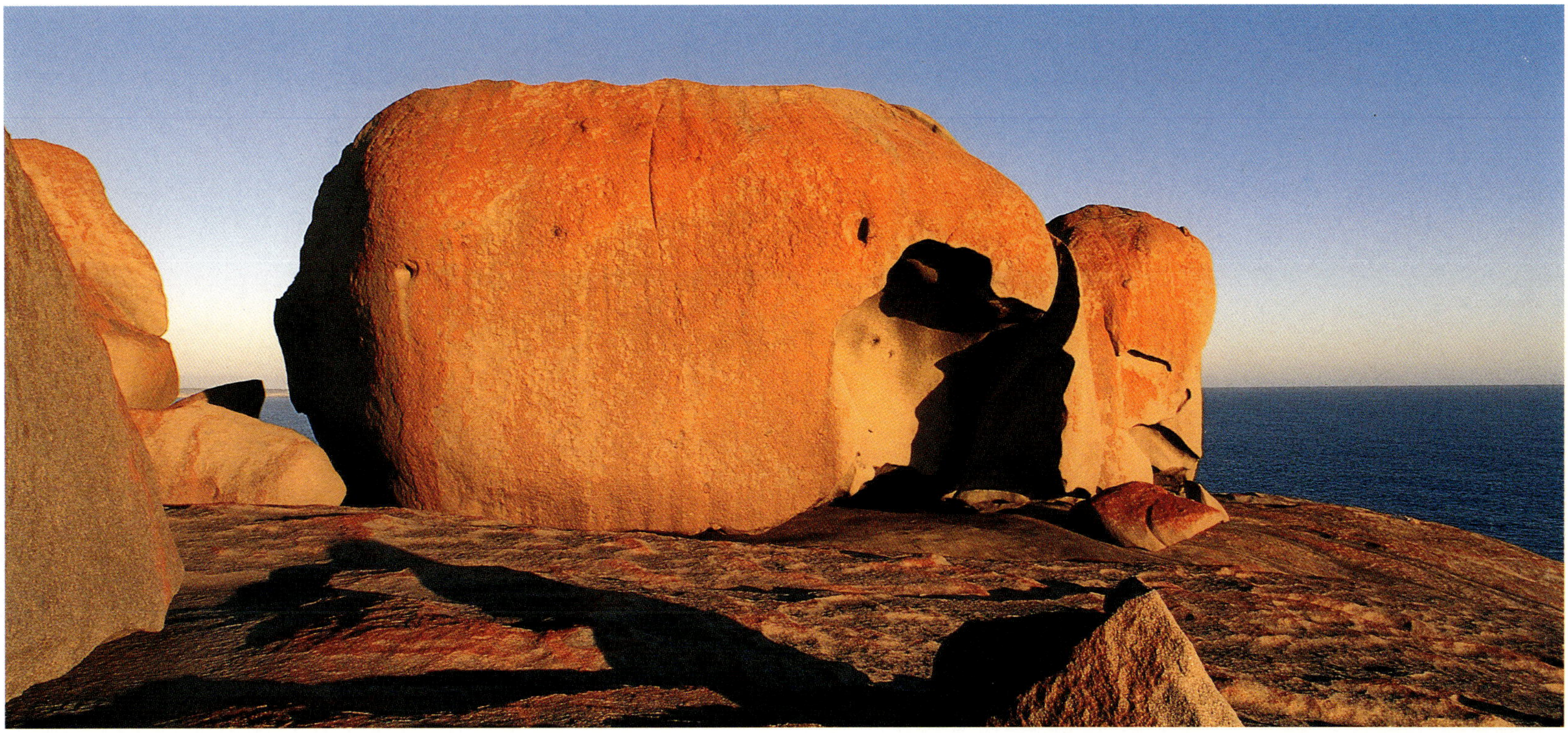

OPPOSITE: A tranquil light over Wilsons Promontory National Park on the Victorian coastline reveals a serene patch of calm, soft-toned images in amongst a coastline often seen as tempestuous. The area is lashed by surges from the Bass Strait.

ABOVE: The solid red Remarkable Rocks on Kangaroo Island in South Australia are a result of the never-ending process of erosion. The wave pounded southern coastline of the continent is made up of numerable rocky cliffs and promontories, many of which have been weathered by the sea, rain and wind into smooth forms.

RIGHT: Australia's coastal scenery can present tranquil and placid scenes, as revealed by the mazes of dazzling white sand banks and shallow turquoise waters found in tropical Queensland.

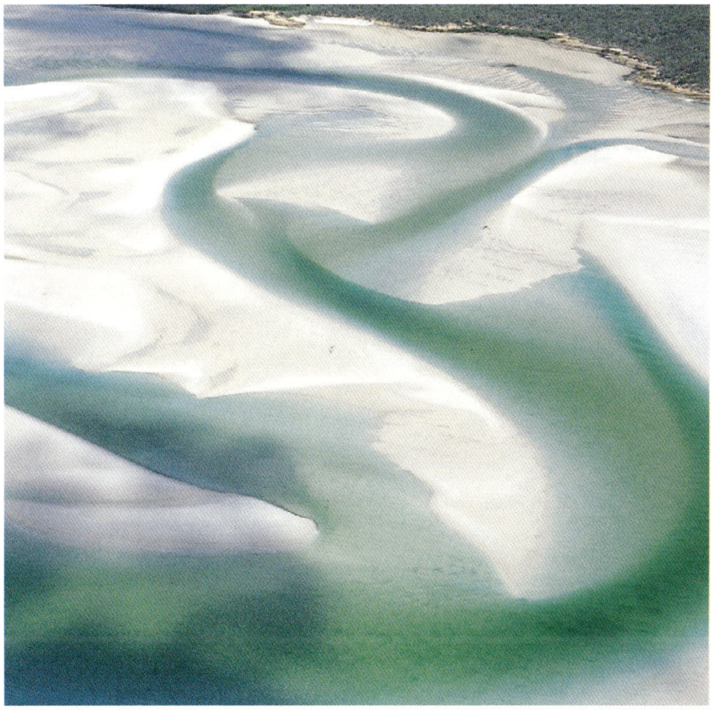

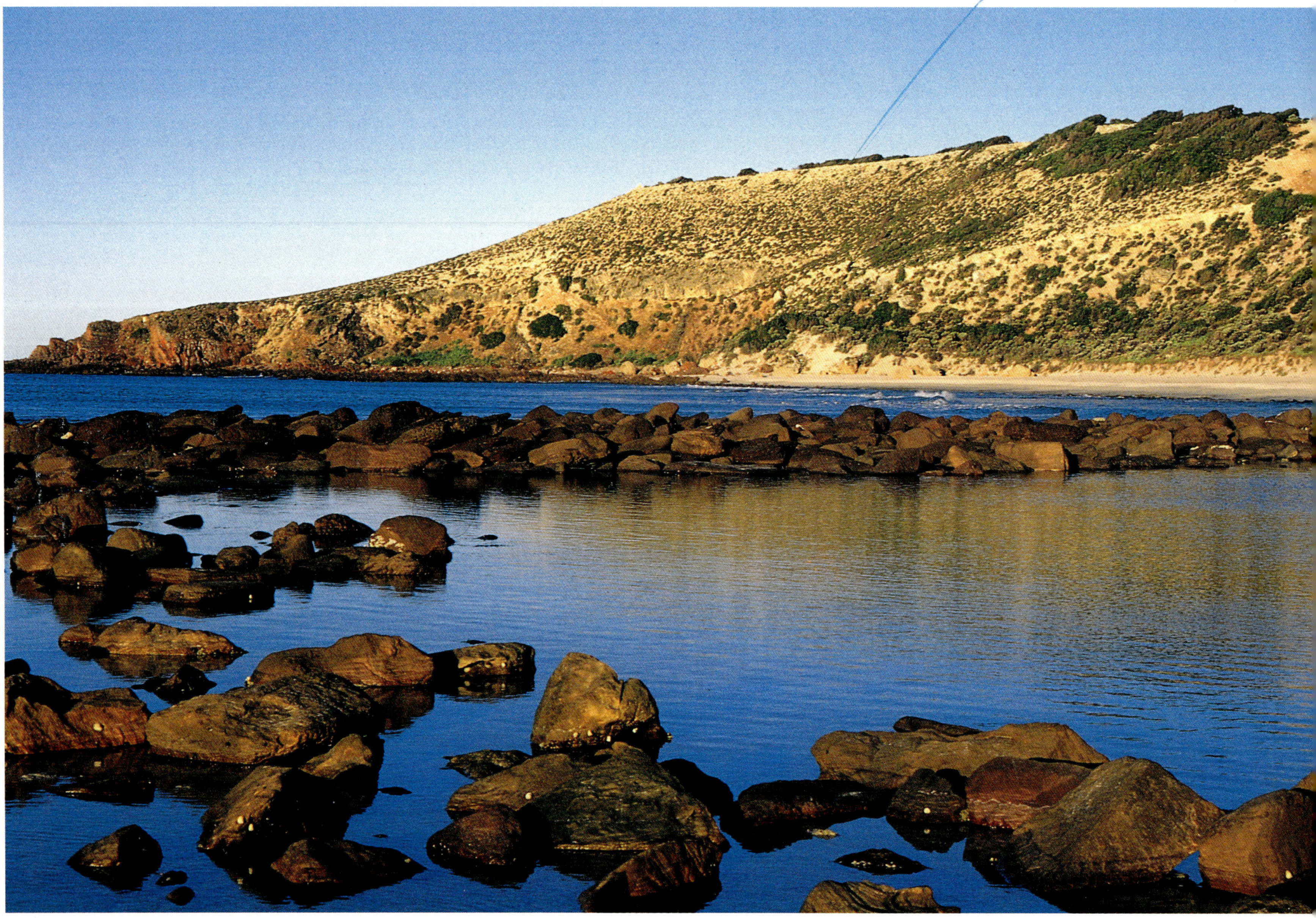

Above: Stokes Bay at Kangaroo Island is protected from the wild surf, and its peaceful tones of blue, broken only by the warm rocks, creates a scene that many landscape artist would like to capture.

Opposite top: The Twelve Apostles in Victoria are friable formations attacked by the relentless action of the wind and water, but they take on a vision of strength in a glorious evening light.

Opposite bottom: The Australian coastline is teeming with animal and bird life. Seabirds, like terns at Fraser Island, flying over above pale sands are a sight common sight in Australia.

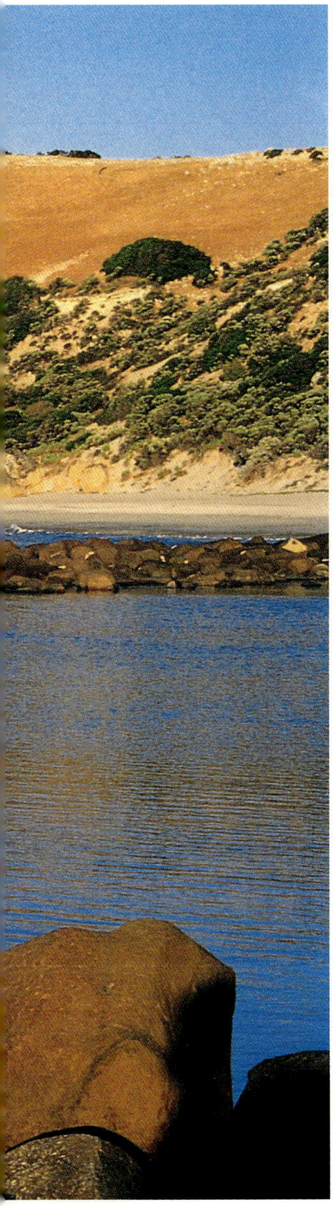

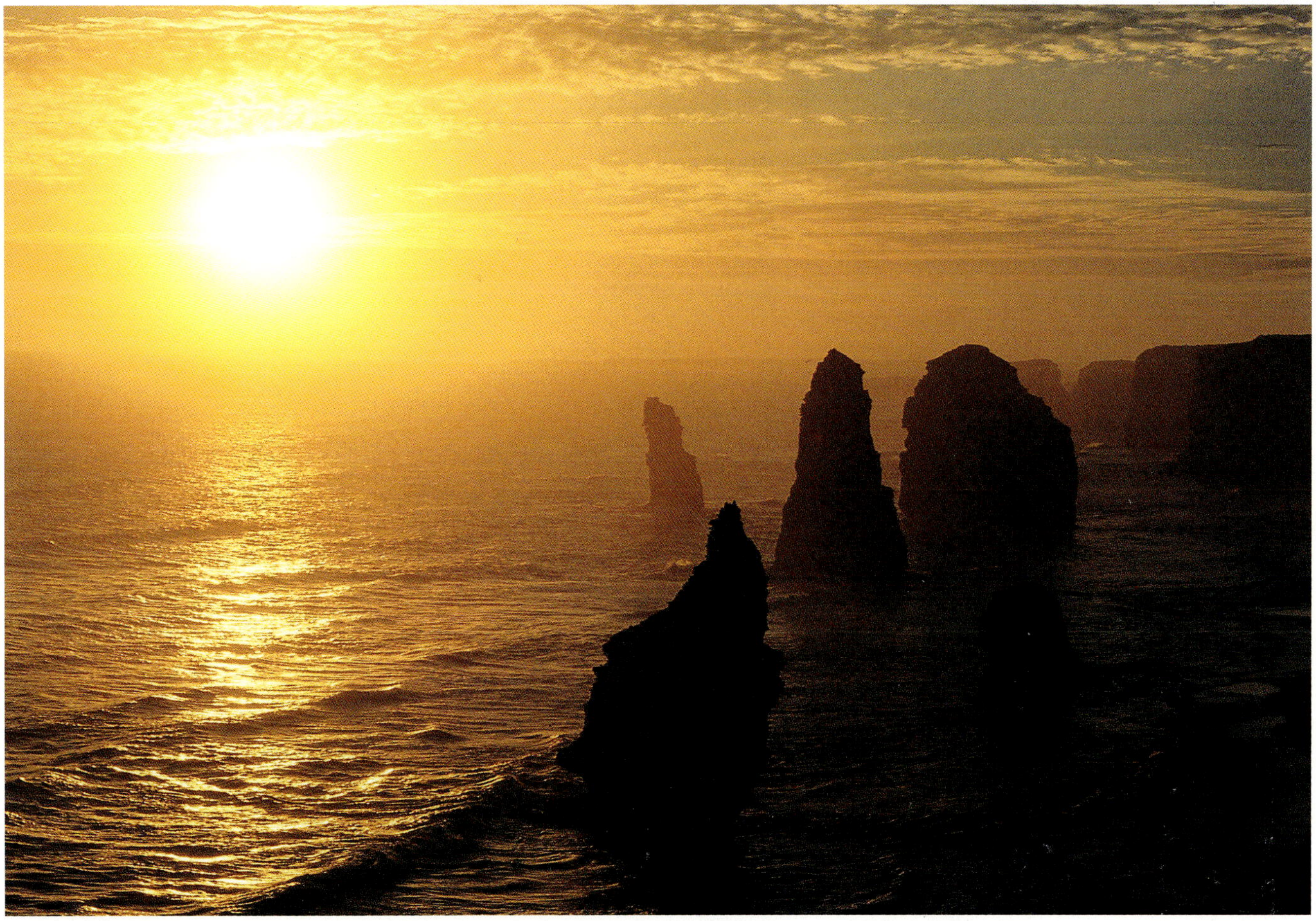

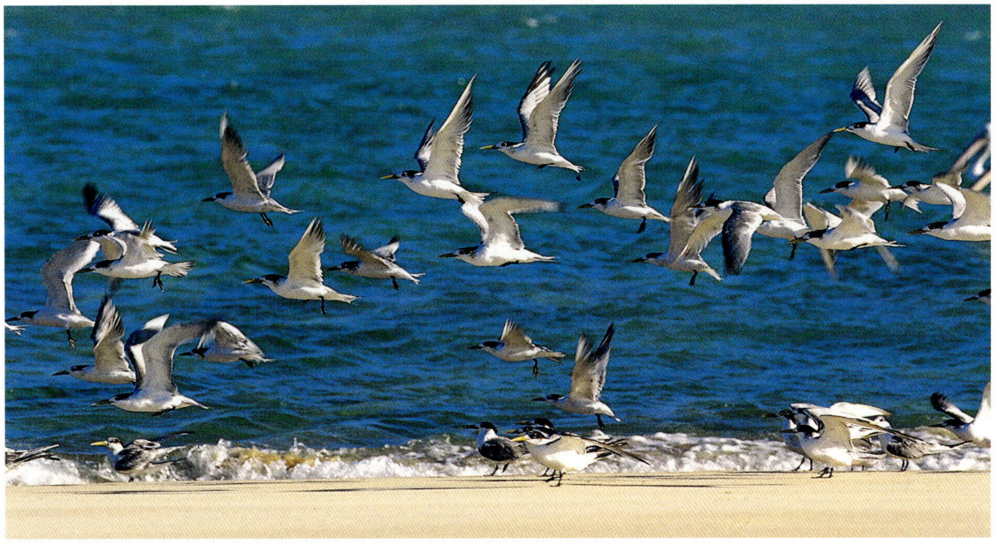

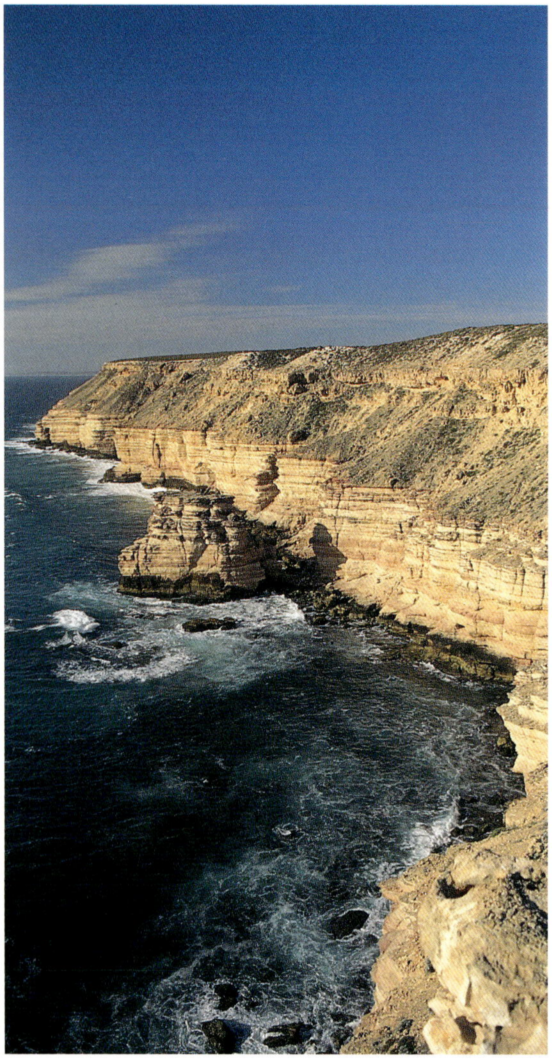 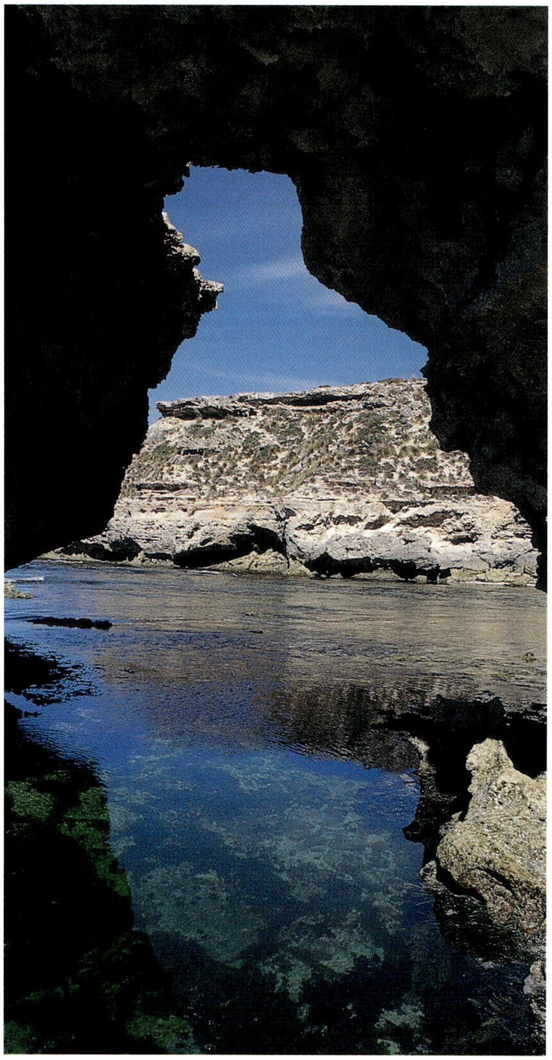 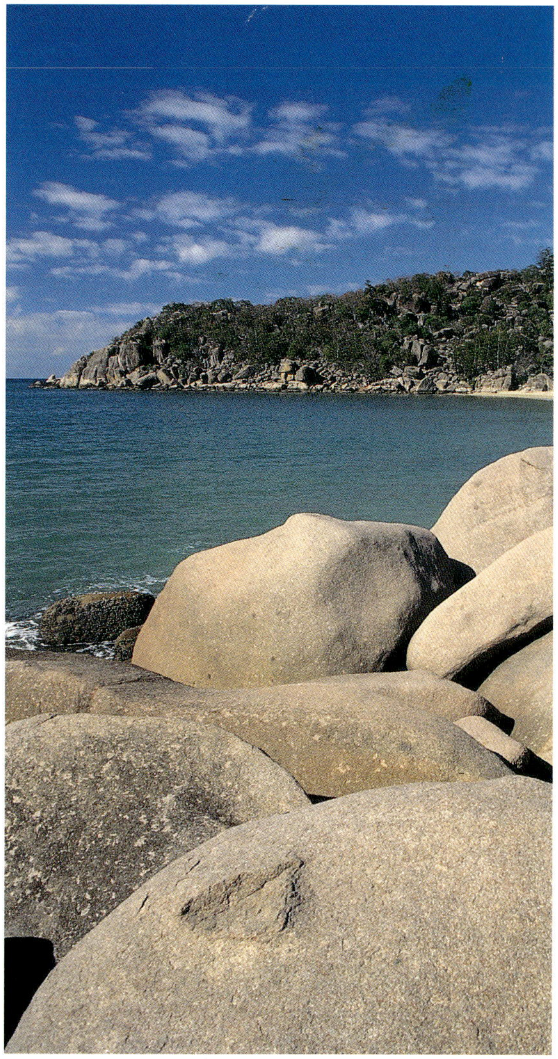

Above left: The rugged cliffs at Kalbarri National Park in Western Australia present a formidable front to a surging ocean. The limestone-capped sandstone rock face is banded in many subtle hues,

Above centre: The jagged, heavily weathered rock formations at Bales Bay on Kangaroo Island frame the cliffs and reveal an inviting blue-green water.

Above right: On Queensland's Magnetic Island the pleasing curves of smooth boulders at Radical Bay present a soft image against the golden bays, wooded headlands, brilliant sky and tranquil sea.

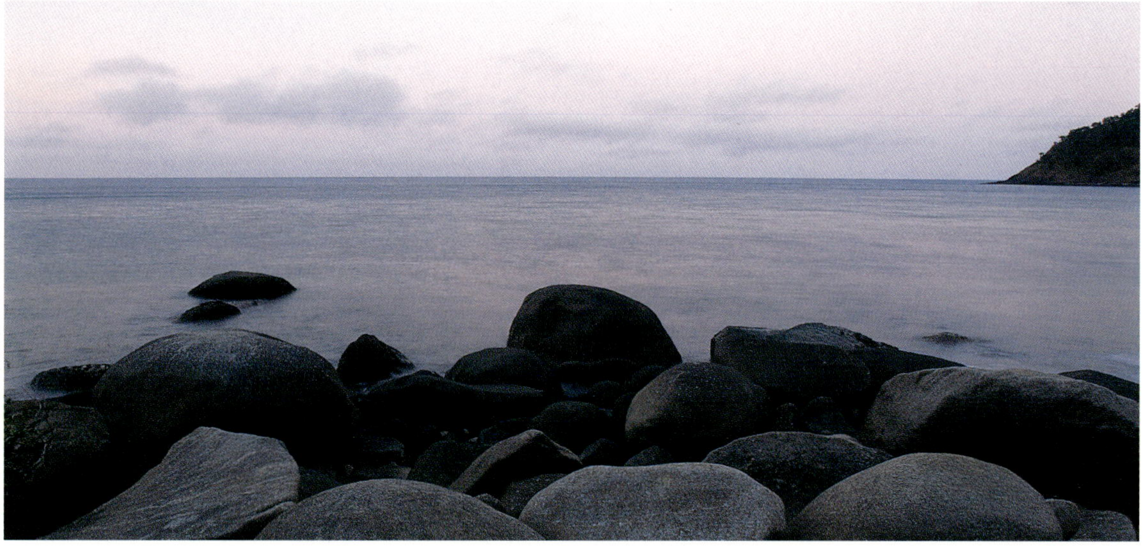

Above: A soft purplish dusk frames large boulders beside Cooktown's Quarantine Bay. The rocks have long been battered by the elements to their present round shapes.

Below: Tessellated rocks at Tasmania's Eaglehawk Neck are criss-crossed by neat regular lines. The mudstone pavement looks as though it was chiselled by a jackhammer, but it is a good example of the power of the weather.

Following pages: Surreal colours at sunrise bathe Lammermoor Beach at Yeppoon in Queensland in colours reminiscent of the liquid-metal tones of a blast furnace.

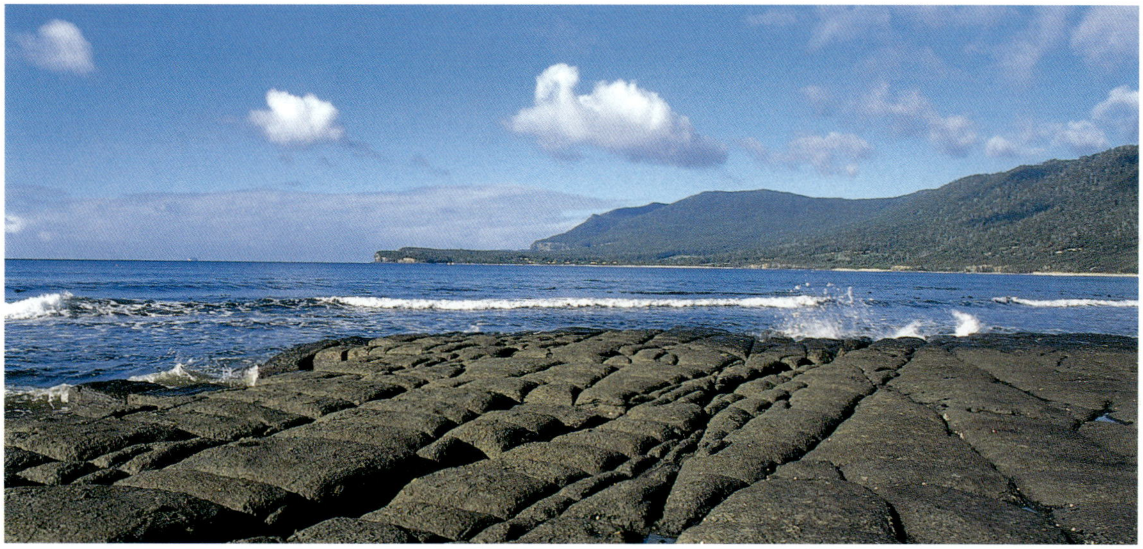

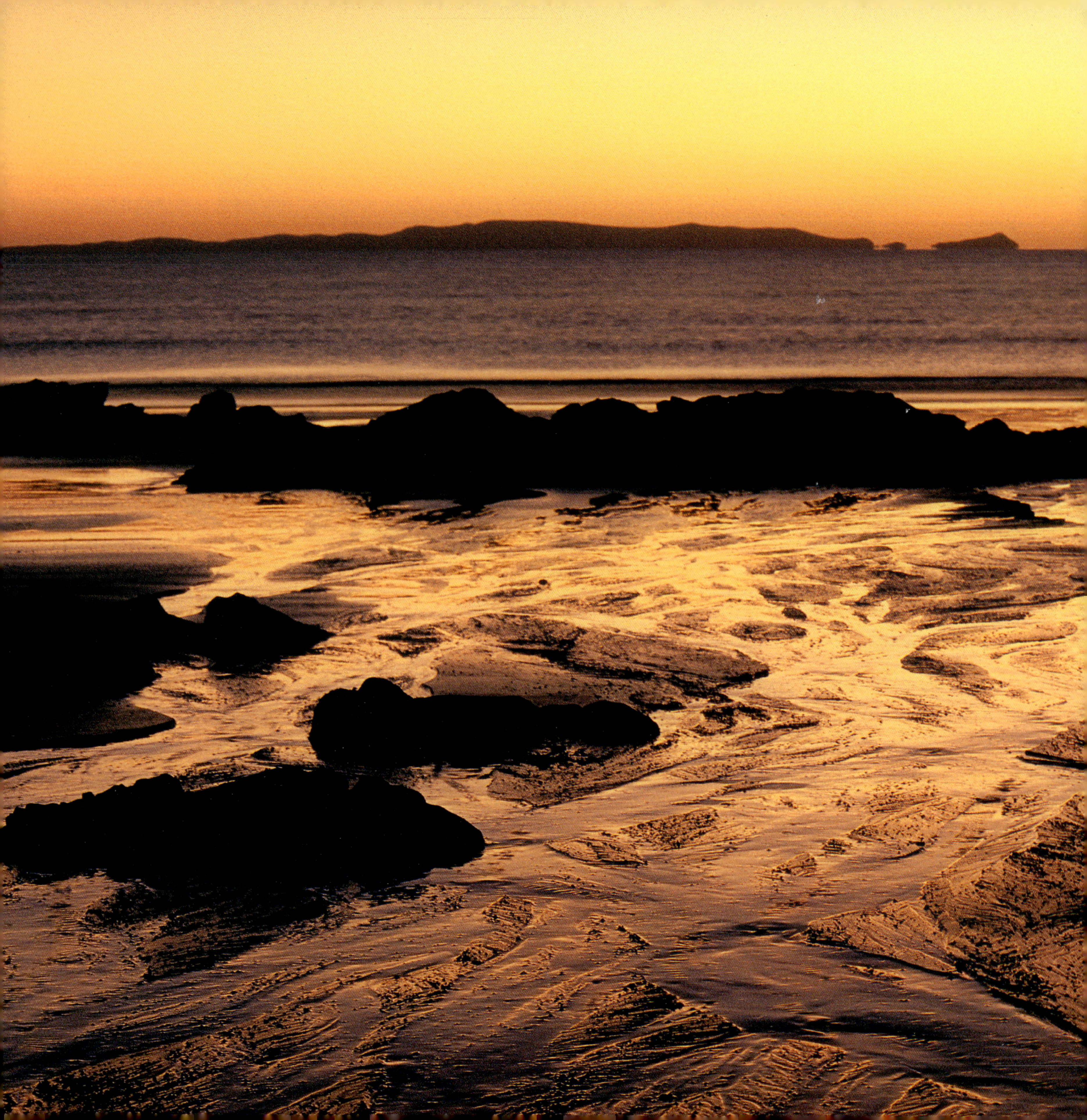

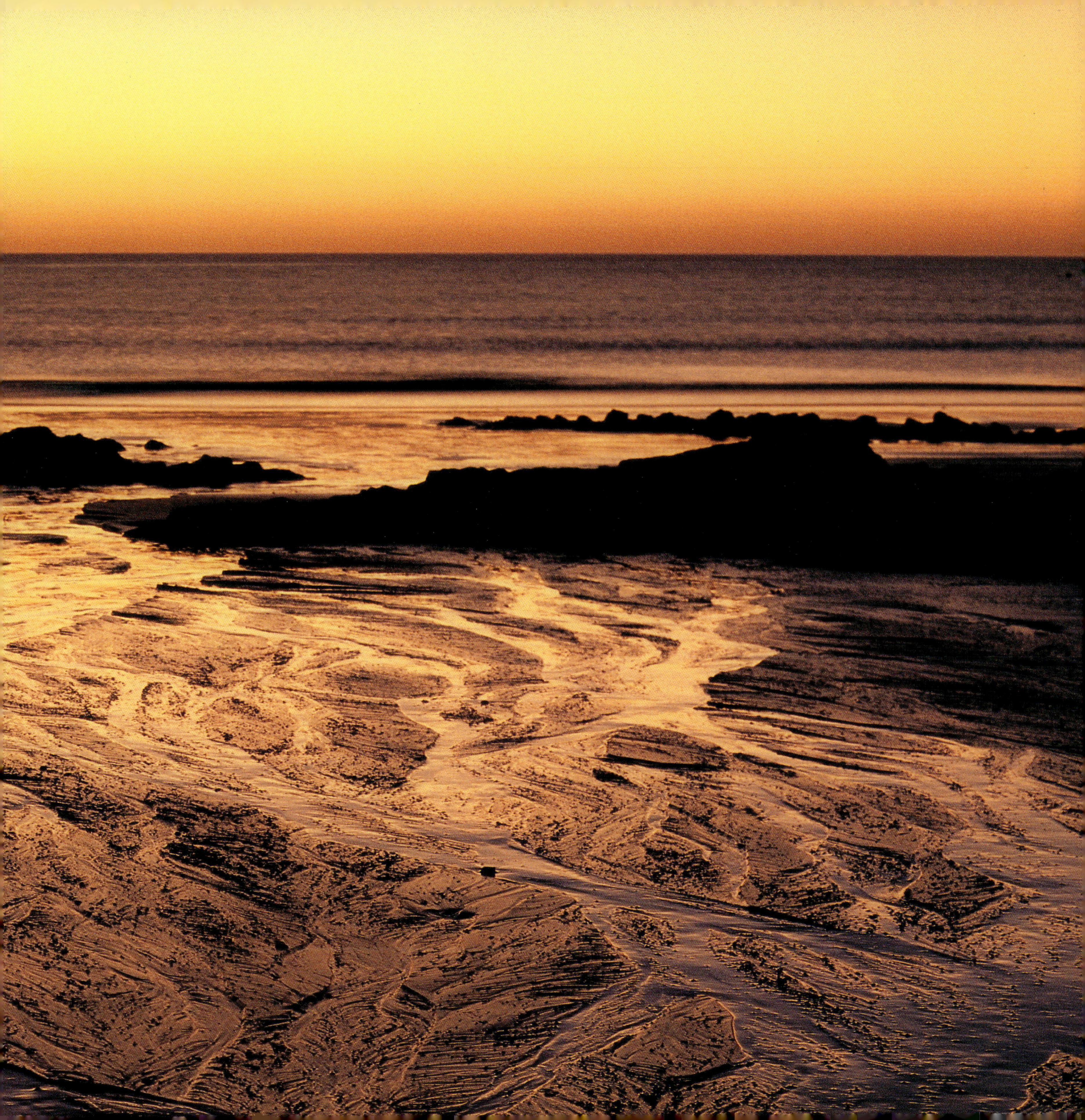

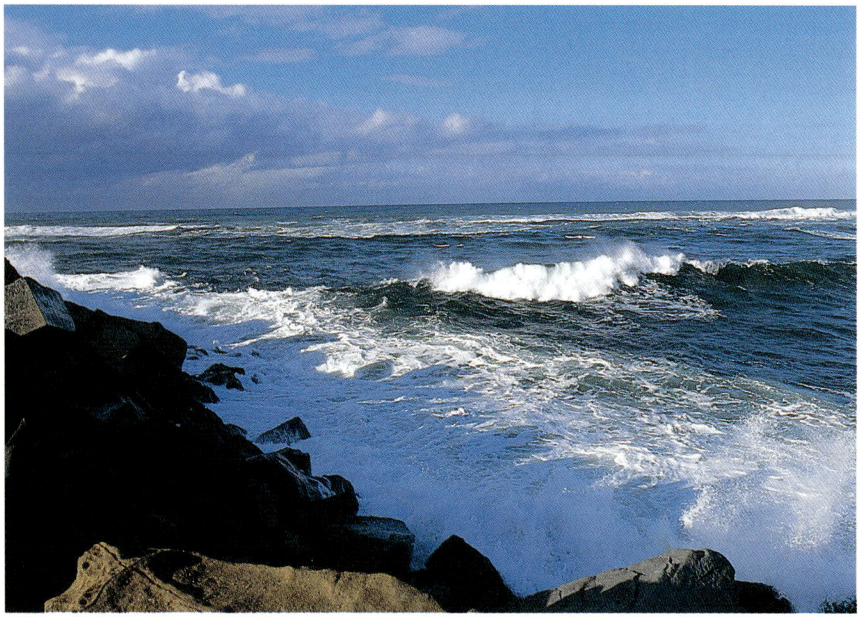

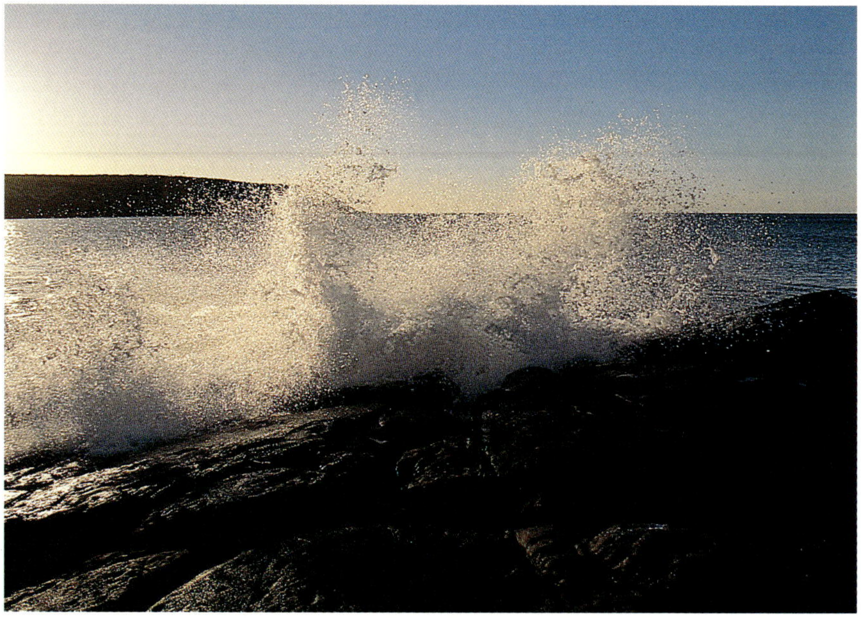

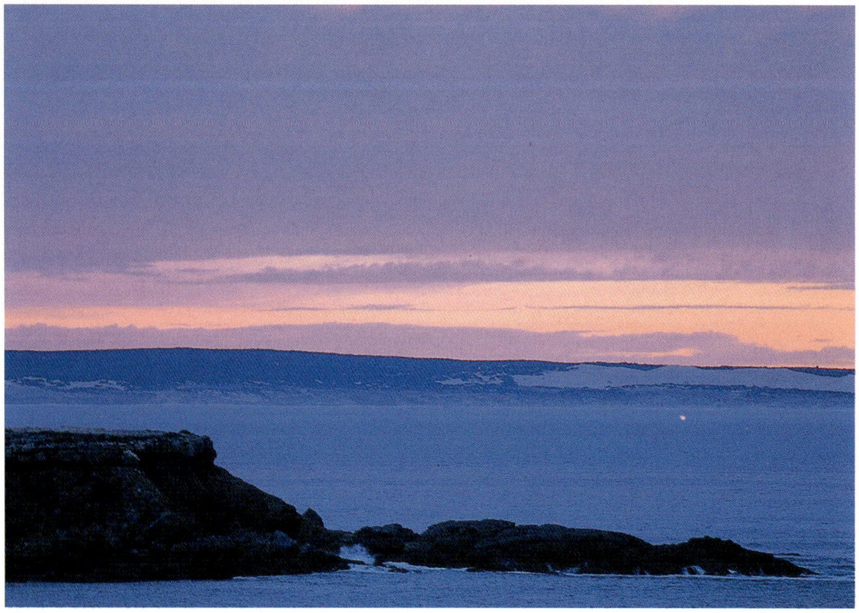

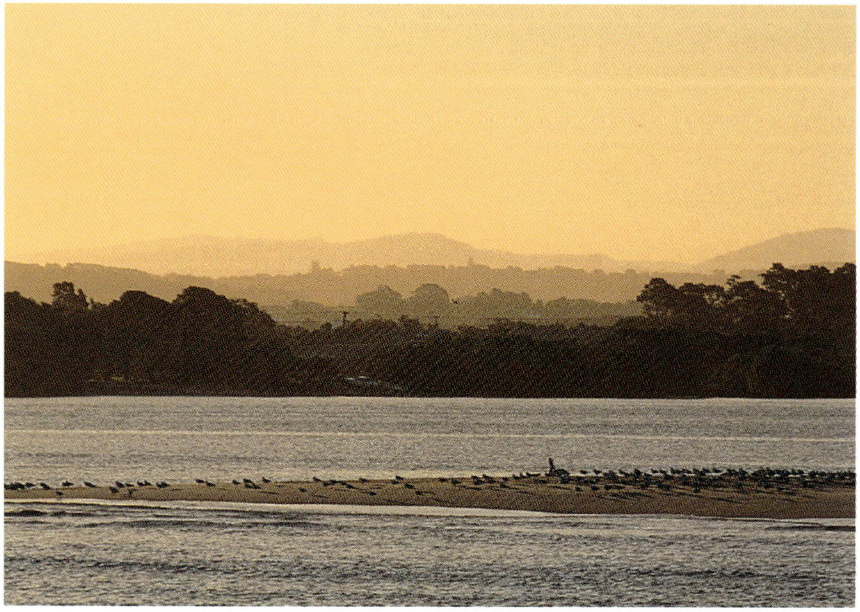

Opposite top left: Rolling, white-capped breakers crash onto a beach in northern New South Wales. Australia's pounding oceans make its shorelines popular with surfers.

Opposite top right: The waves that wash the rocks at Stokes Bay on Kangaroo Island create sprays that send flecks of gold over the deep colours of the sea and sky.

Opposite bottom left: The first light of day washes Fishermans Bay at Port Lincoln in South Australia in luscious hues of blue, pink and purple silhouetting a sleepy coastline.

Opposite bottom right: Magical evening light bathes the Richmond River estuary, near Ballina on New South Wales' northern coast in many shades of pale gold.

Right: The dark, jagged rocks and cliffs at Fitzgerald River National Park in southern Western Australian are beautifully complemented by an azure sea tinged with milky-white foam while pastel clouds sweep across the sky.

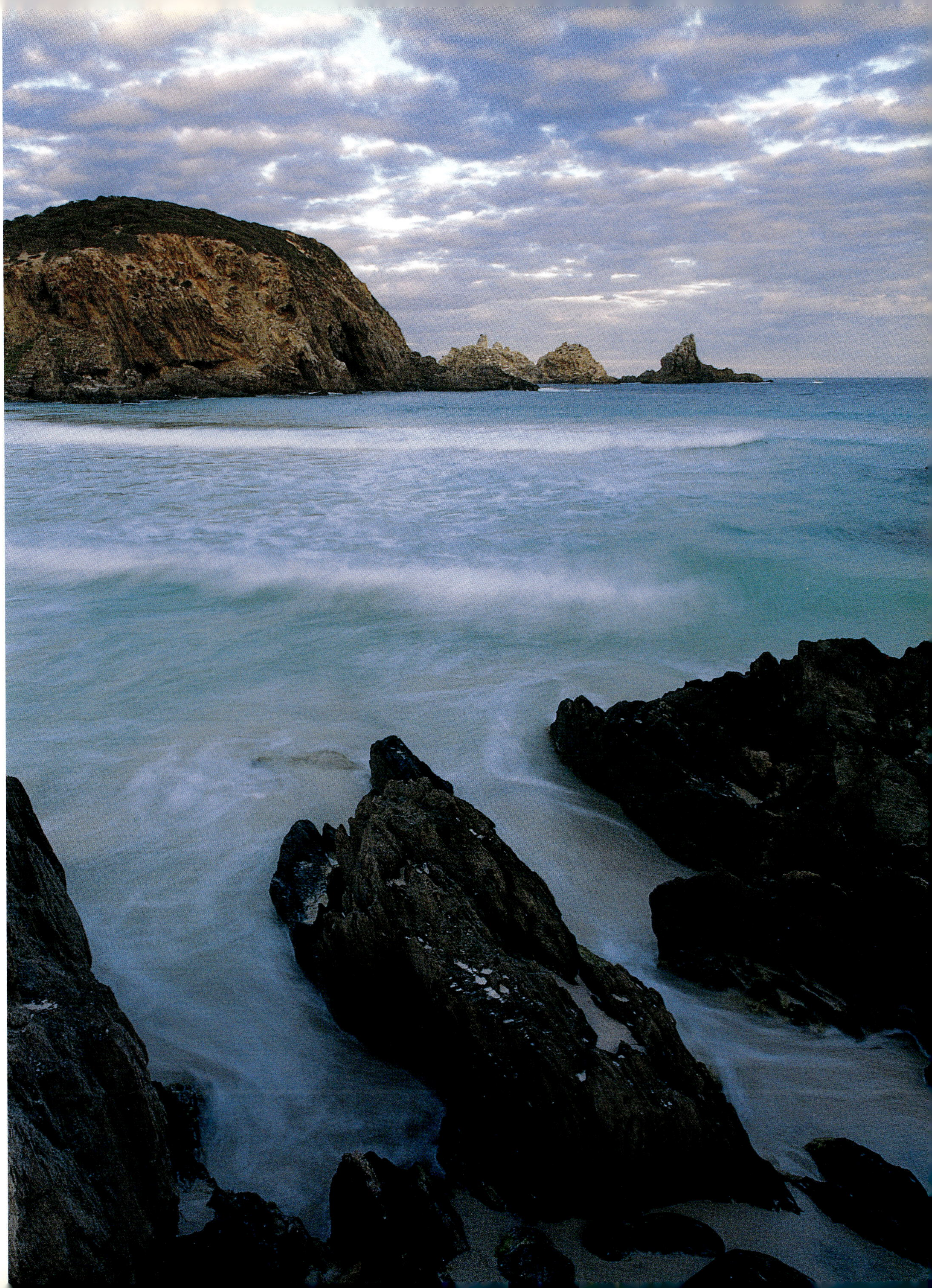

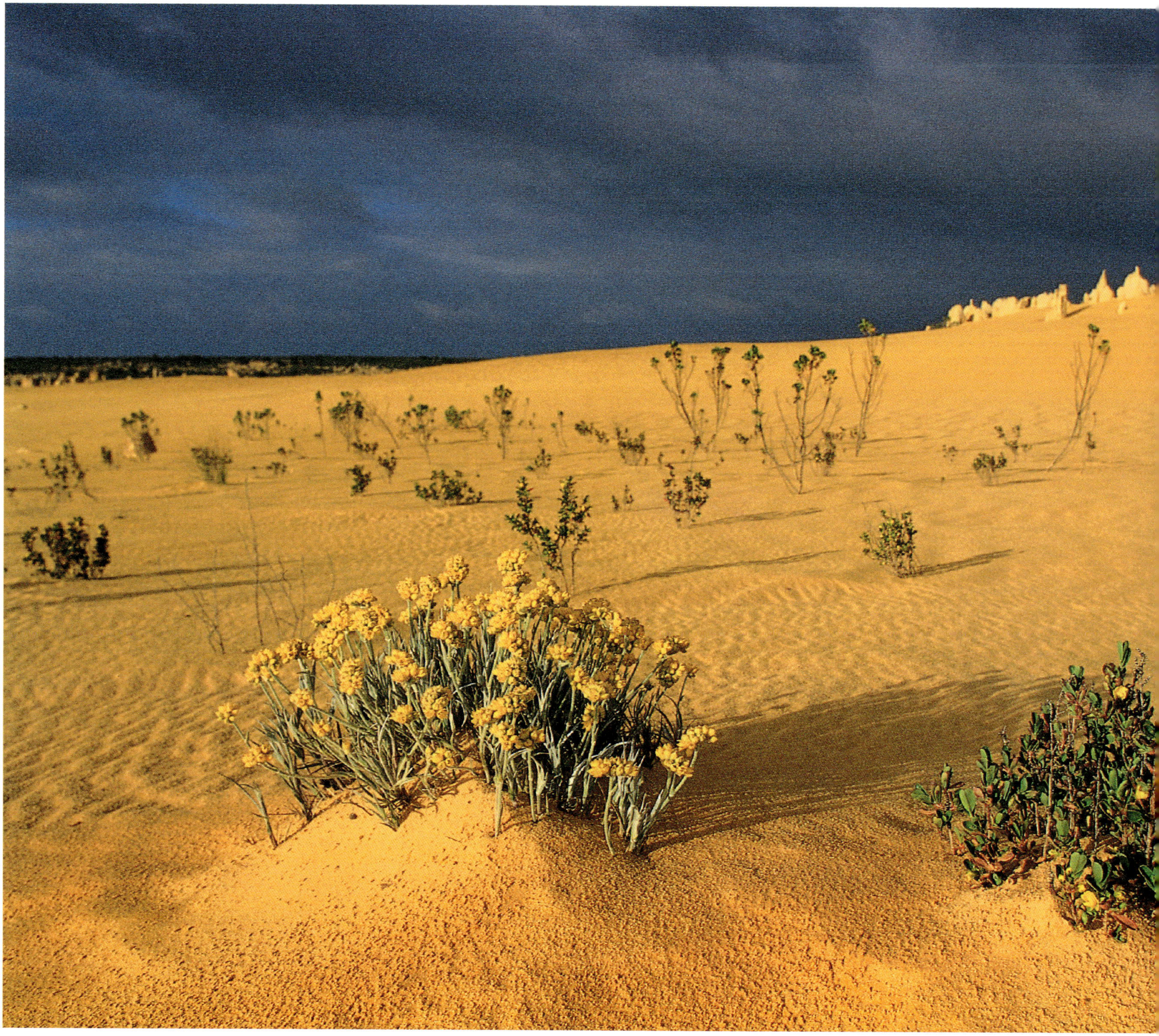

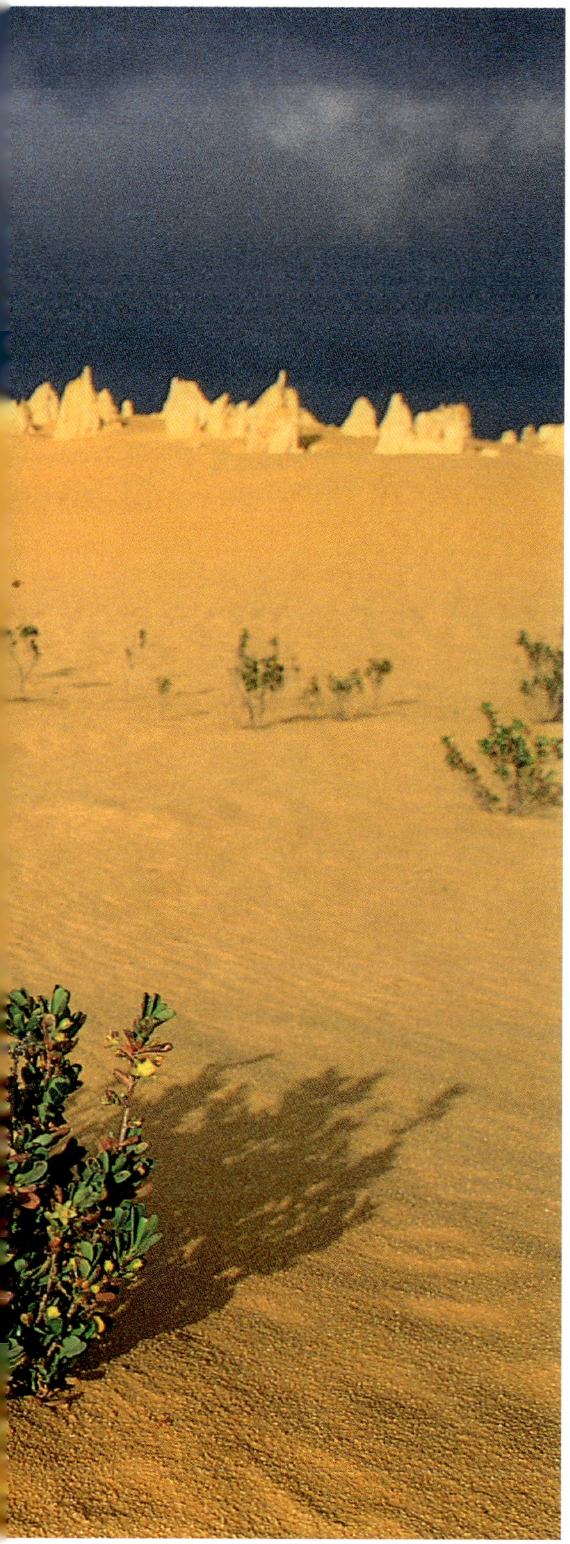

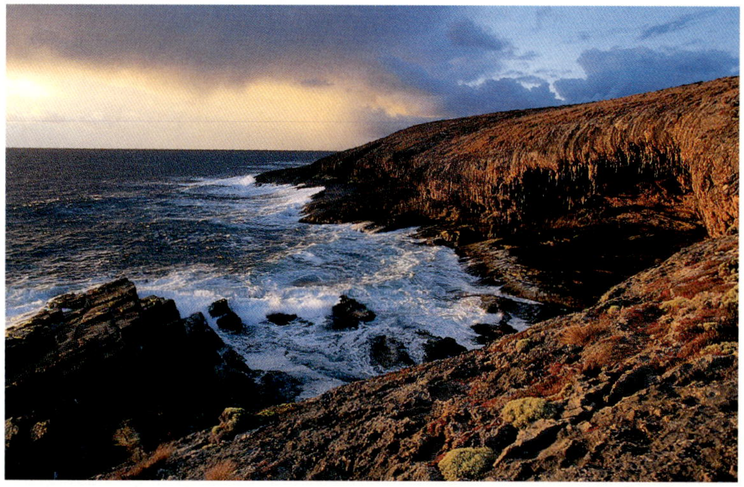

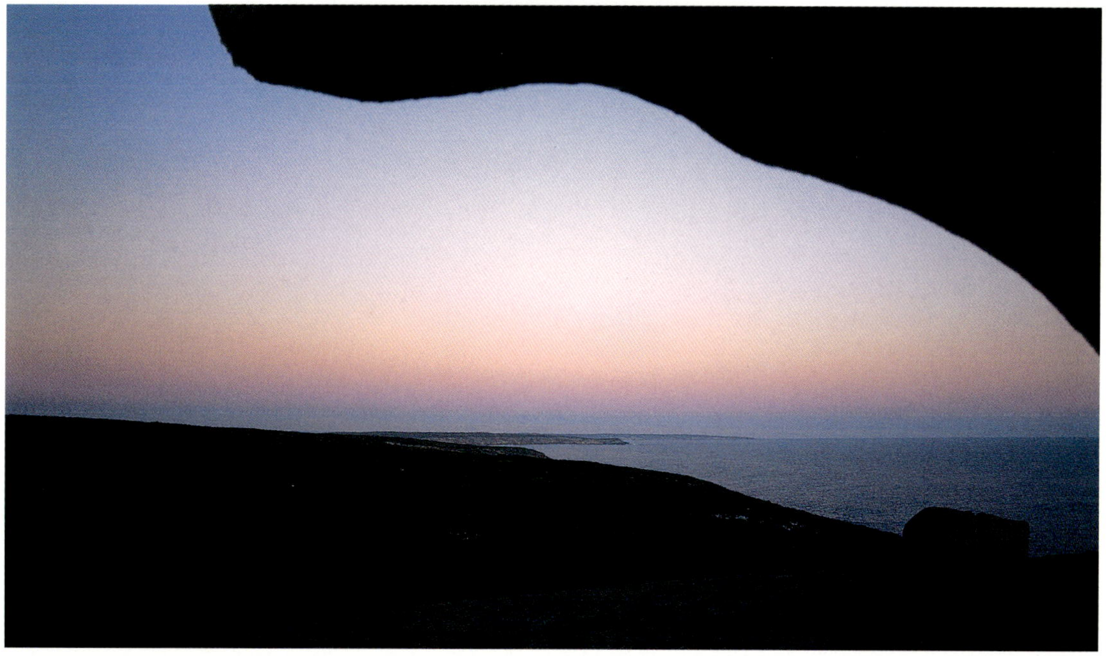

Left: The Pinnacles in Western Australia stand like pillars of a ruined building. Indeed, the golden forms were believed to be an old city by 17th-century maritime explorers.

Top: The richly coloured and heavily eroded granite cliffs of Cape du Couedic display a passionate mood. The island's most south-westerly point is frequently battered by rough seas.

Above: Kangaroo Island's coastal scenery is dramatic. The dark, curvaceous contours of the Remarkable Rocks envelope the coastline and the pink streaked horizon.

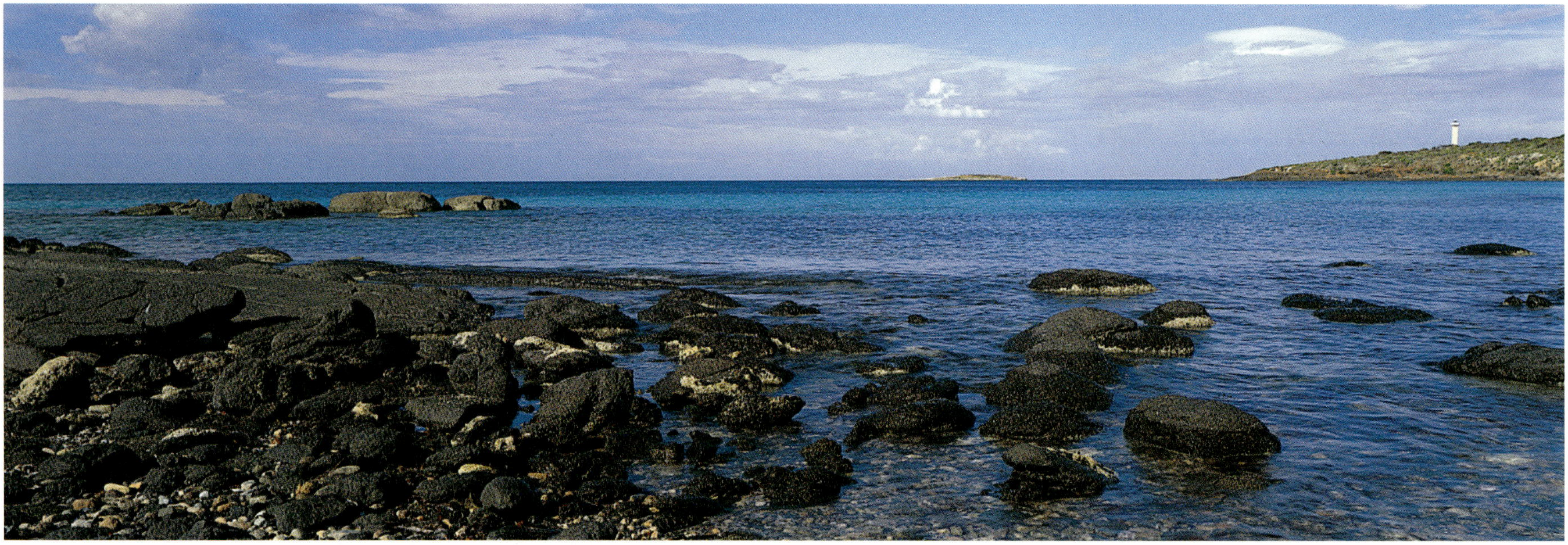

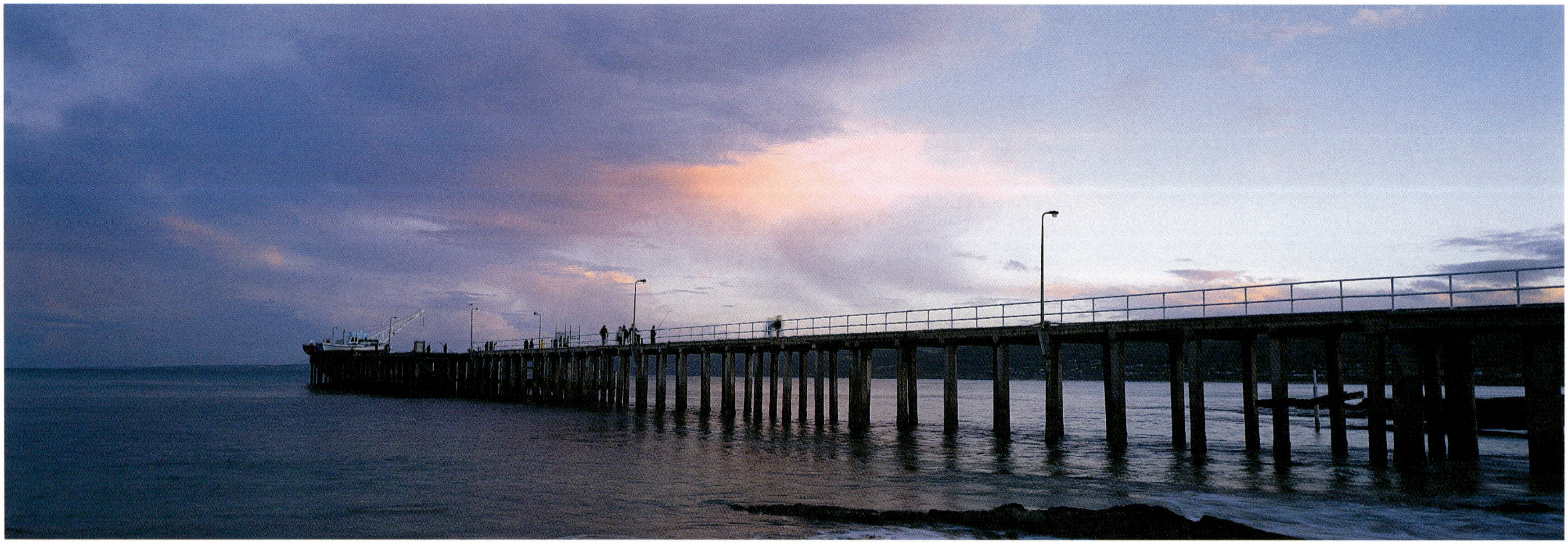

Top: The waters lapping remote Cape Donnington at Port Lincoln at South Australia's Eyre Peninsula provide a bounty of marine life, including tuna, prawns and abalone.

Above: The charming town of Lorne on the southern Victorian coast is an established fishing centre and also a popular holiday resort.

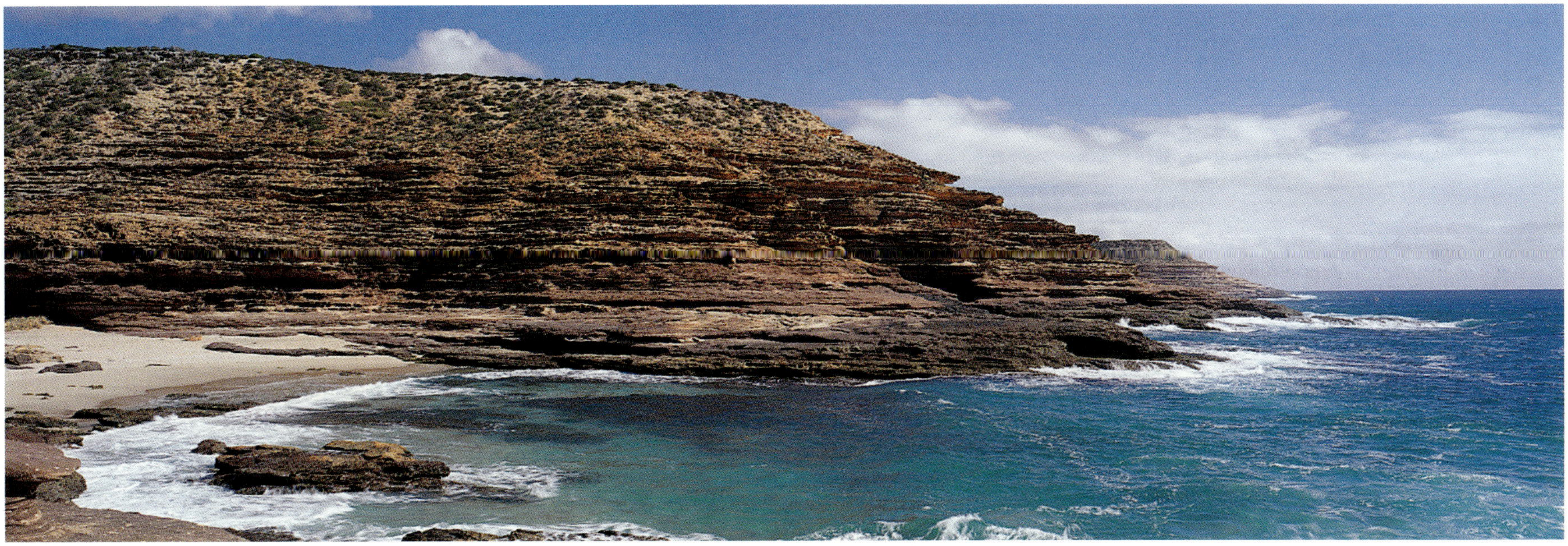

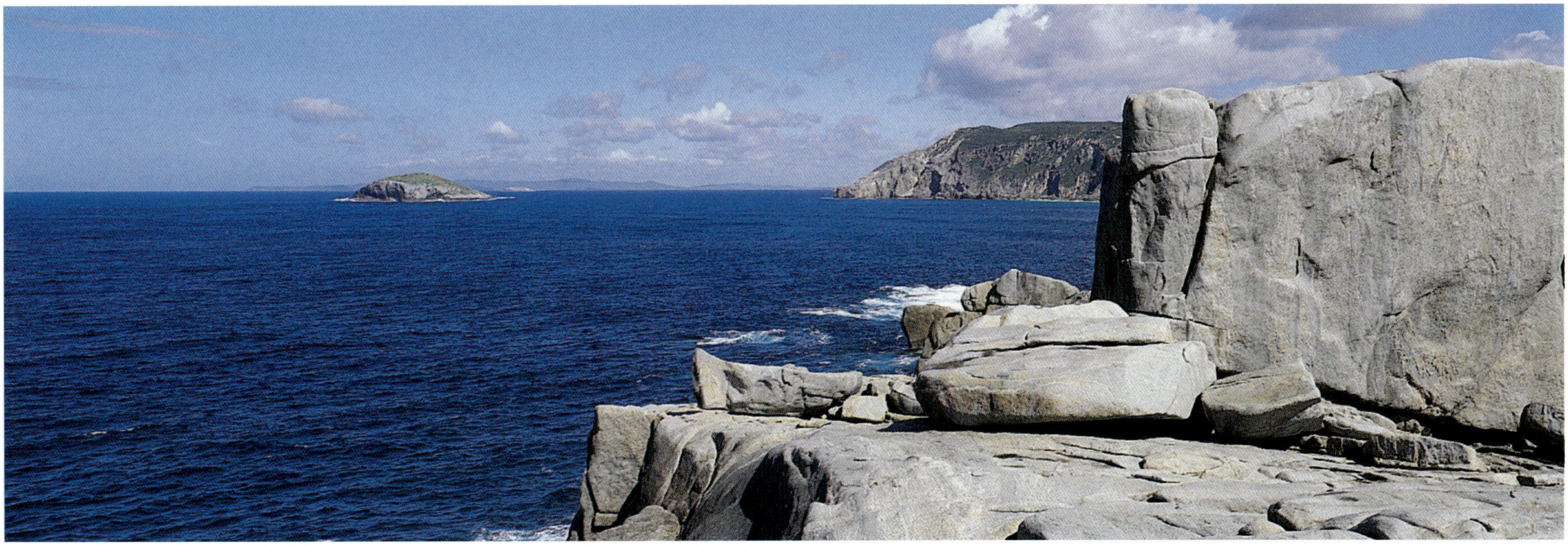

TOP: The tawny sandstone of Pot Alley at the Kalbarri National Park is grooved with horizontal bands. Geological forms play a crucial role in Australia's coastal landscape.

ABOVE: The coast around Albany in Western Australia is composed of granite. These massive slabs and boulders are very robust against the effects of erosion.

RIGHT: The low-growing heathland plants of the Fitzgerald National Park on Western Australia's wind and wave battered southern coast present the ocean with quite a different picture than the usual bare rocky headlands.

RIGHT BELOW: Fishermans Bay at Port Lincoln in South Australia is an untrodden coastal paradise. Beyond the cities and popular tourist resorts, the Australian coastline contains thousands of sandy beaches that are more often than not deserted.

FAR RIGHT: The dense woodland that covers Queensland's Whitsunday Island seems to stretch out longingly to an incredibly inviting turquoise-blue water. It is scenes like this that tempt innumerable tourists to the region each year.

FOLLOWING PAGES: Four Mile Beach at Port Douglas shows a very different face to its normal vivid tropical colours on this moody day. Remarkably subdued greys and greens settle on a landscape that is customarily turquoise-blue, lush green and gold.

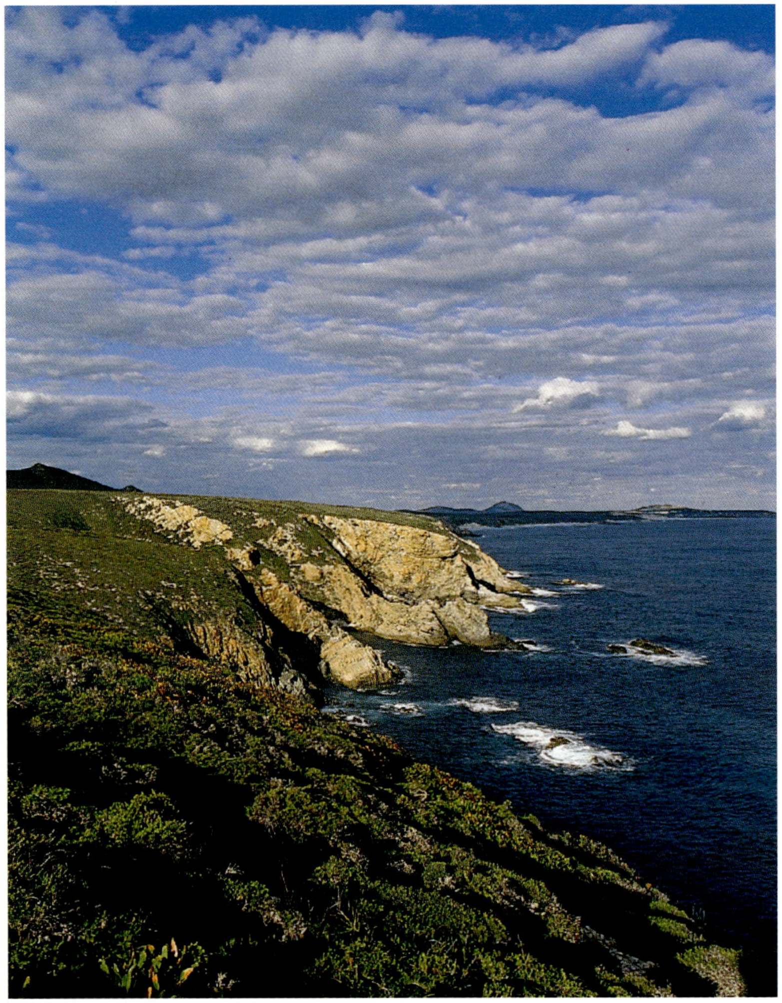

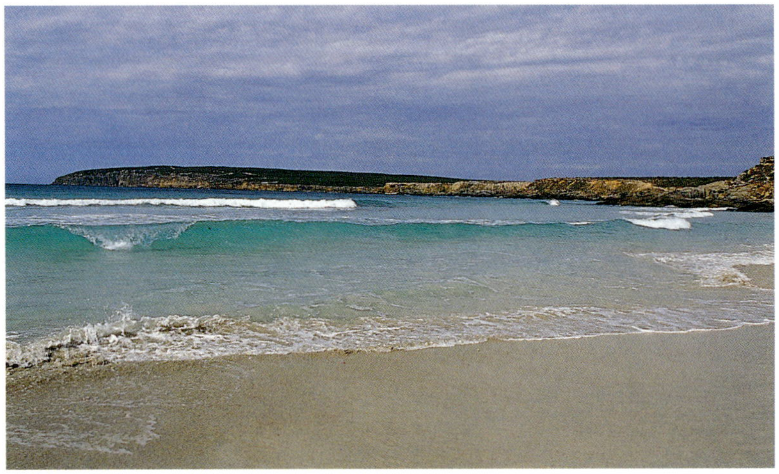

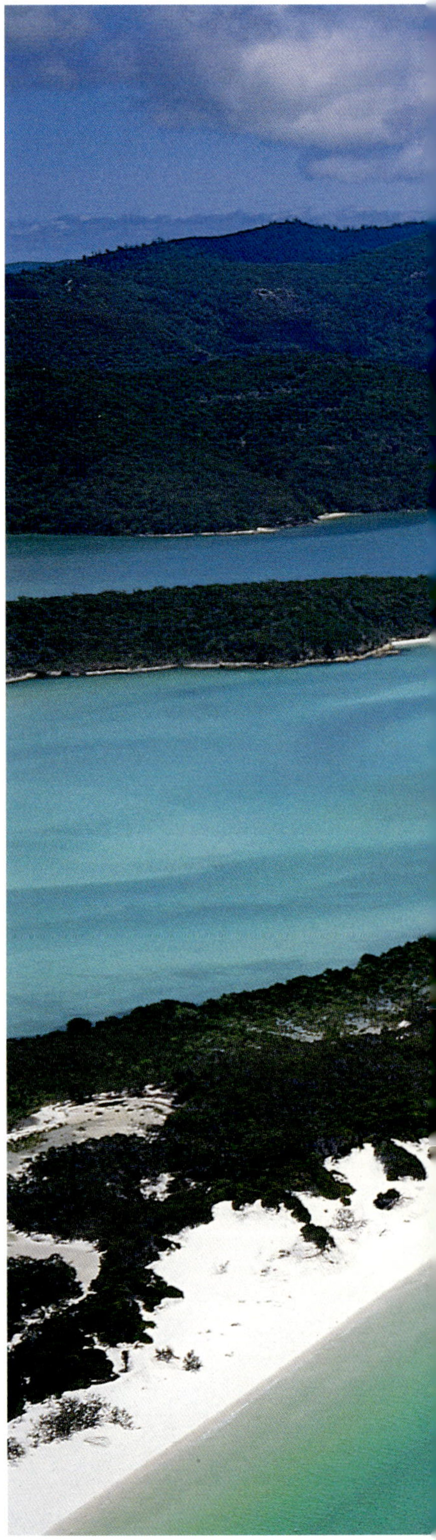

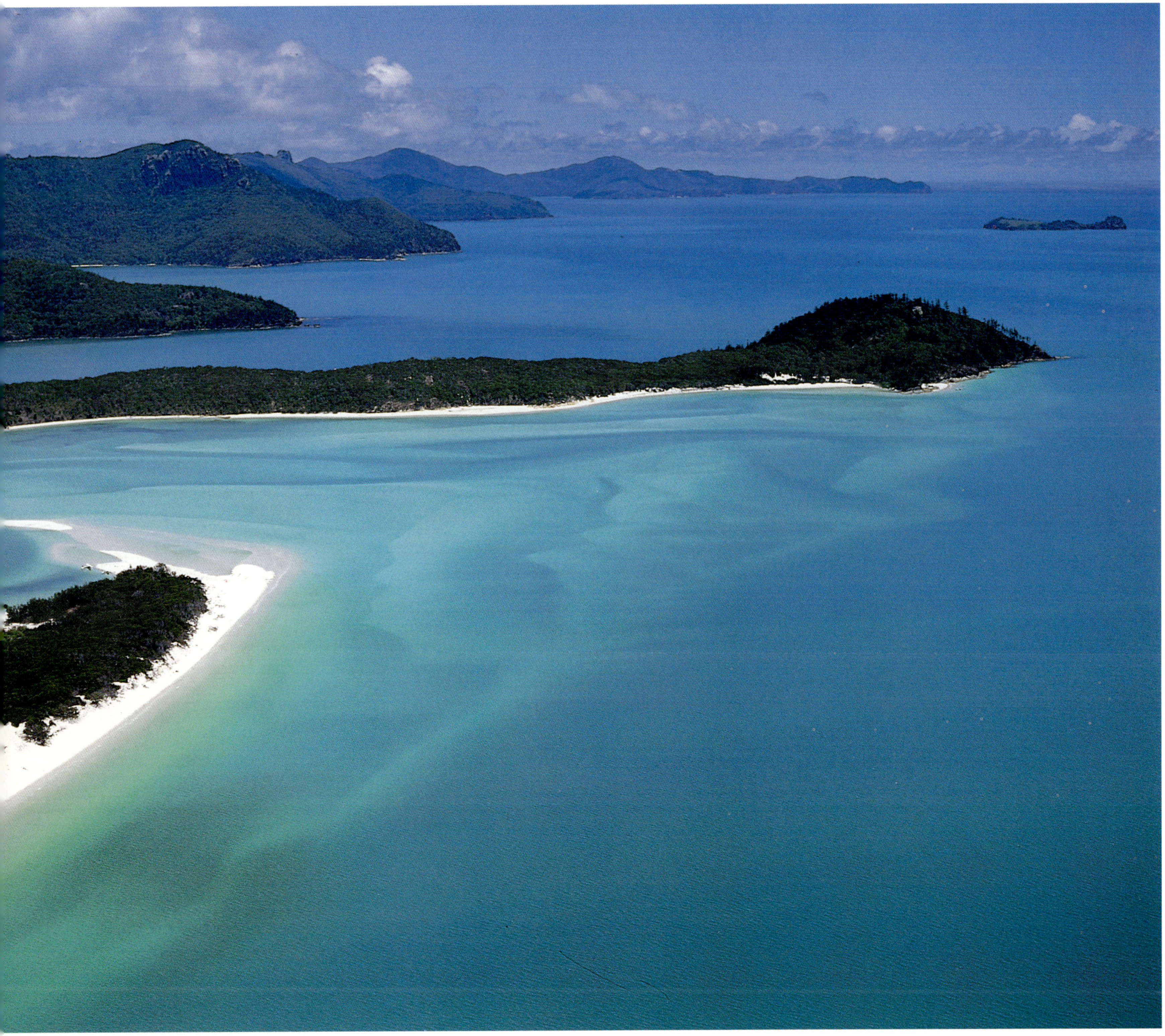

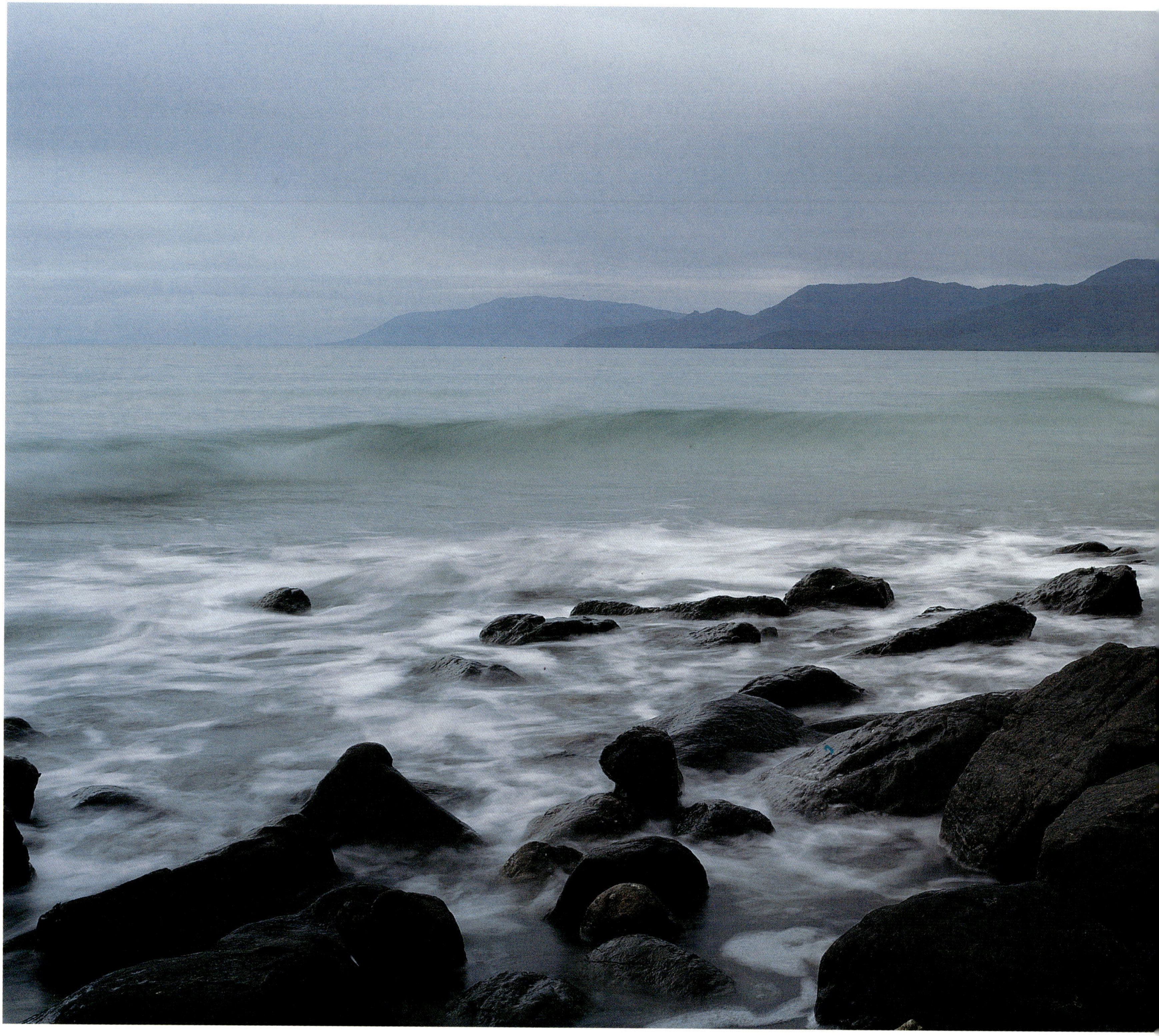

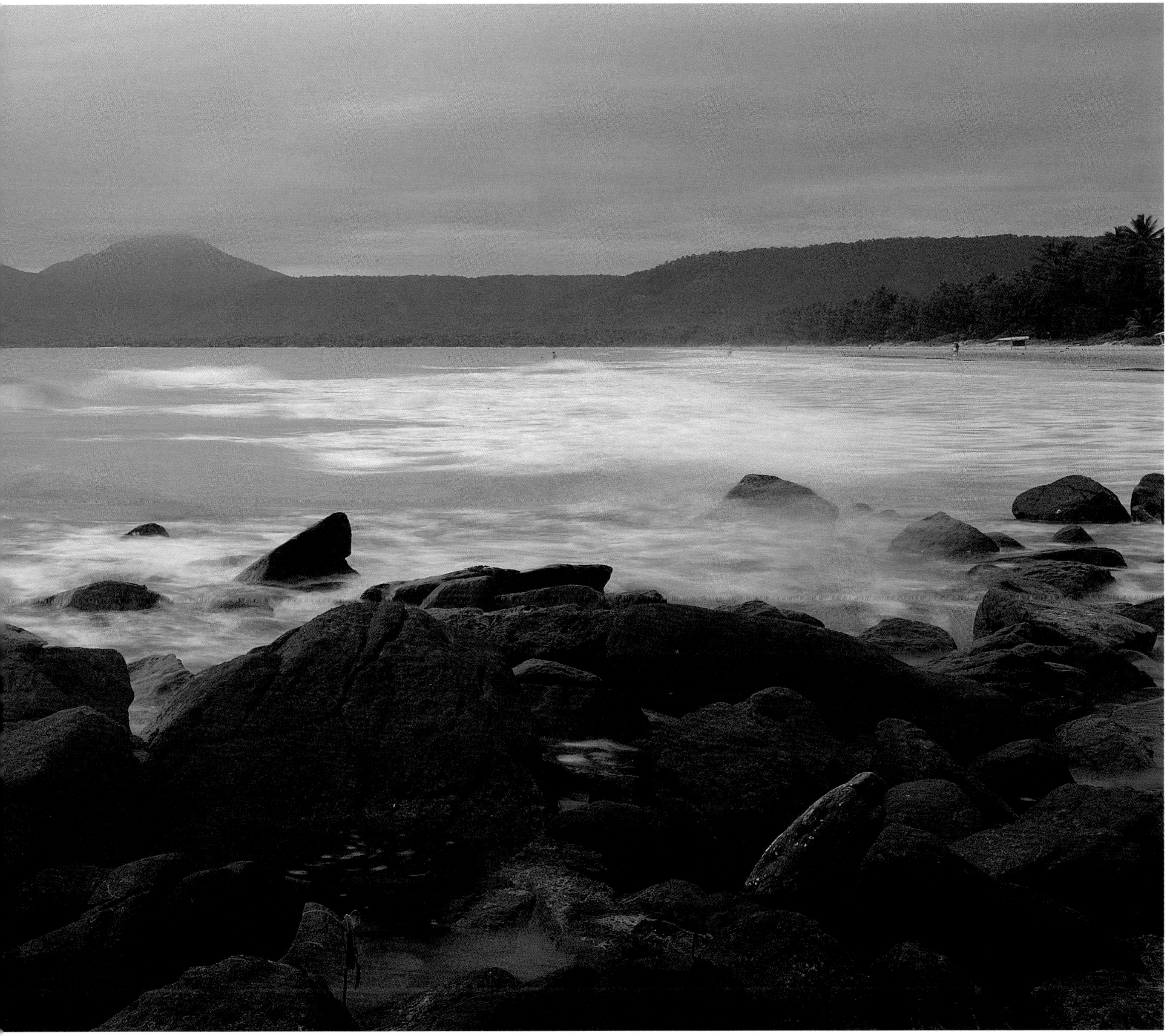

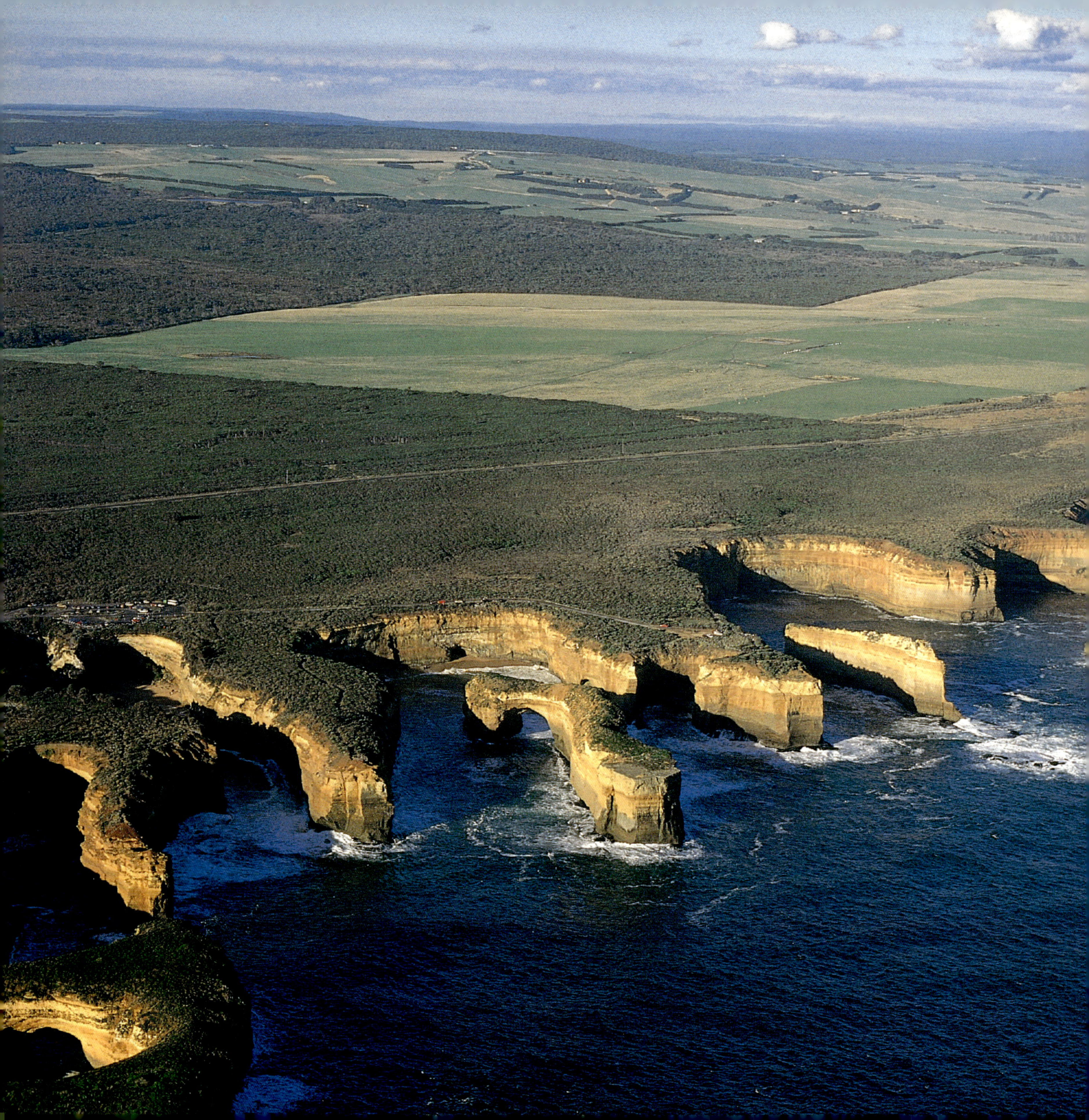

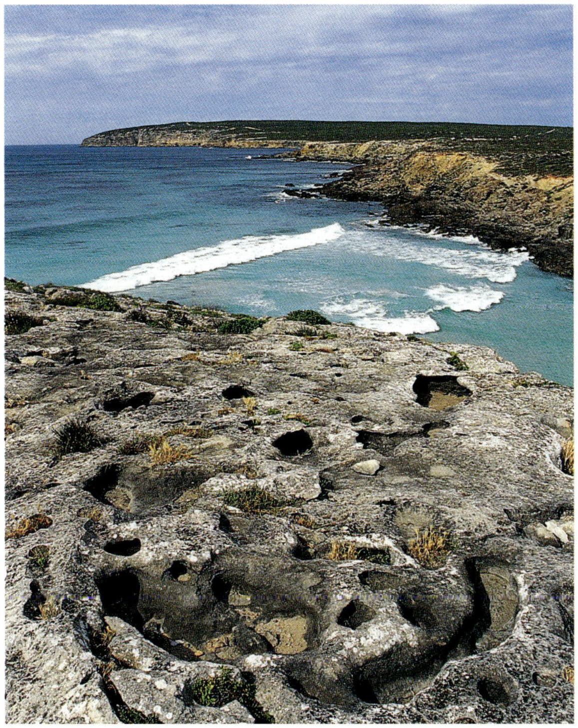

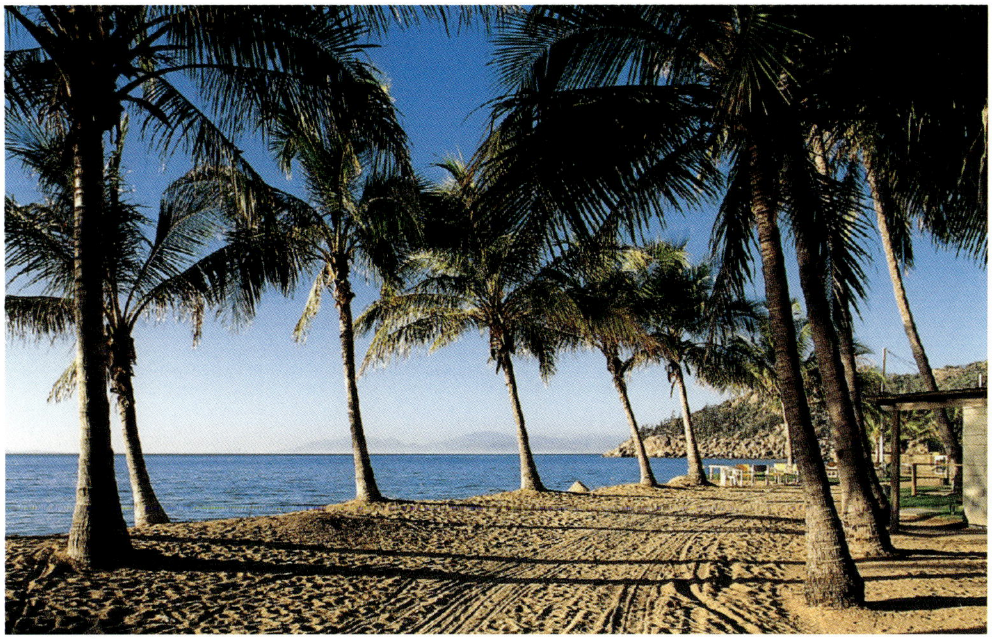

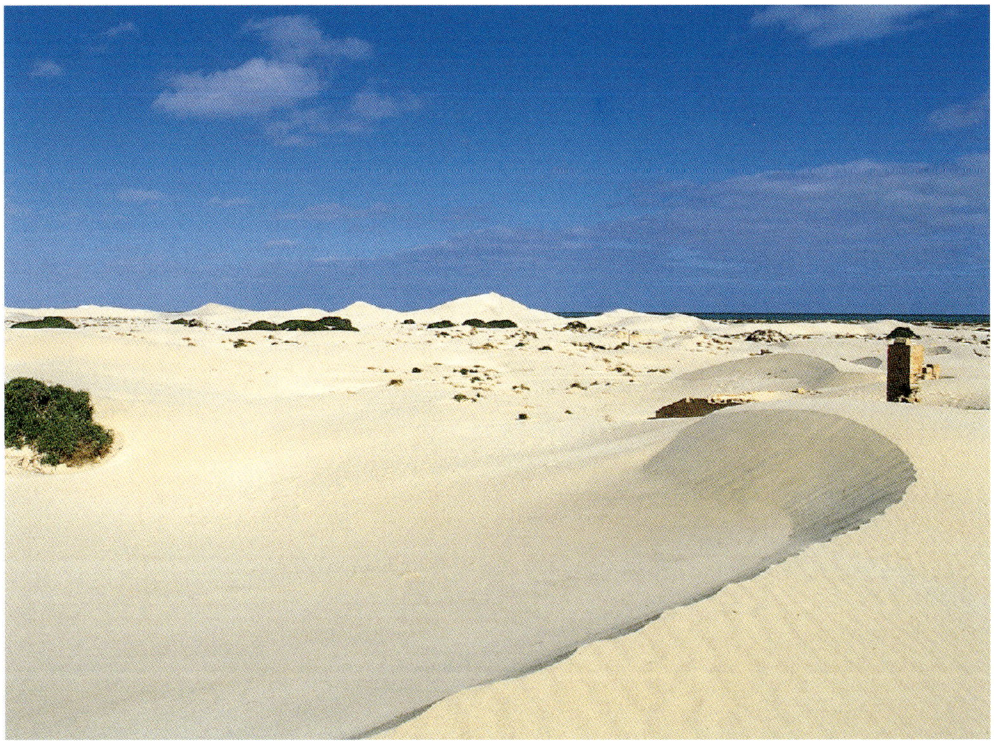

Opposite: Victoria's sliced coastline reveals how the massive stacks of rock, known as the Twelve Apostles, have been separated from the mainlands by the mighty force of the deep blue sea.

Above left: The Eyre Peninsula in South Australia is an undisturbed landscape of rocky headlands, small coves, clear waters and rolling surf. It has withstood the march of progress and, even today despite its idyllic conditions, remains sparsely populated.

Above right: The popular holiday destination of Magnetic Island off the north Queensland coast possesses all the makings of a tropical paradise—brilliant sky, golden sand, invitingly blue ocean, and swaying palm trees.

Left: The shifting coastal dunes of the Nullarbor Plain in Western Australia have gradually stretched further inland and all but engulfed an historic 1870s telegraph station at Eucla.

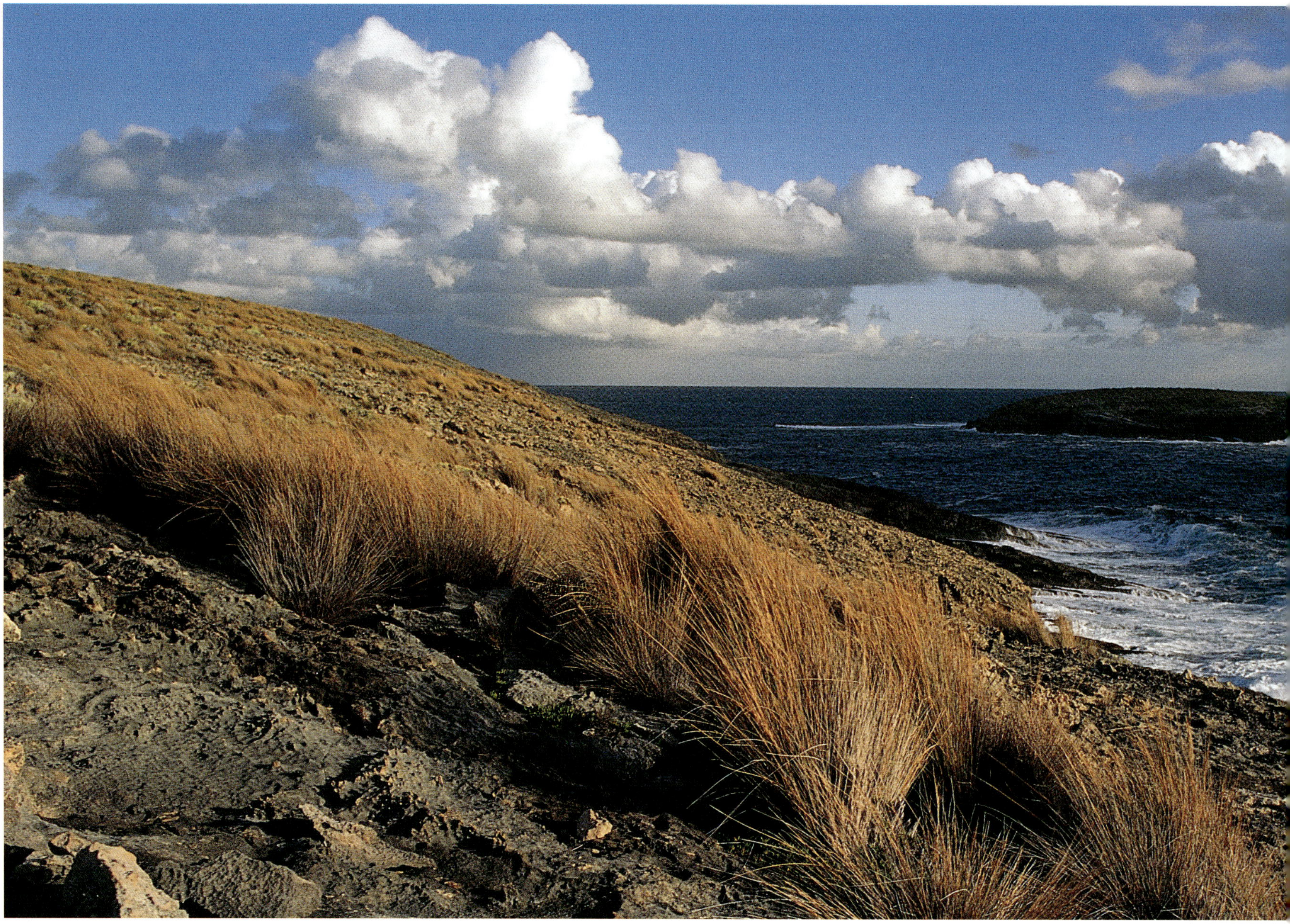

ABOVE: The elements have left their mark on Cape du Couedic at Kangaroo Island. The headland bears the brunt of winds and waves from the Southern Ocean that roll north from Antarctica.

OPPOSITE TOP: The powerful effect of wind is seen in the sand of the aptly-named Little Sahara on Kangaroo Island. The golden dunes change pattern shape and direction in the shifting breeze.

OPPOSITE BOTTOM: The sun beams through the Island Archway at Port Campbell National Park.

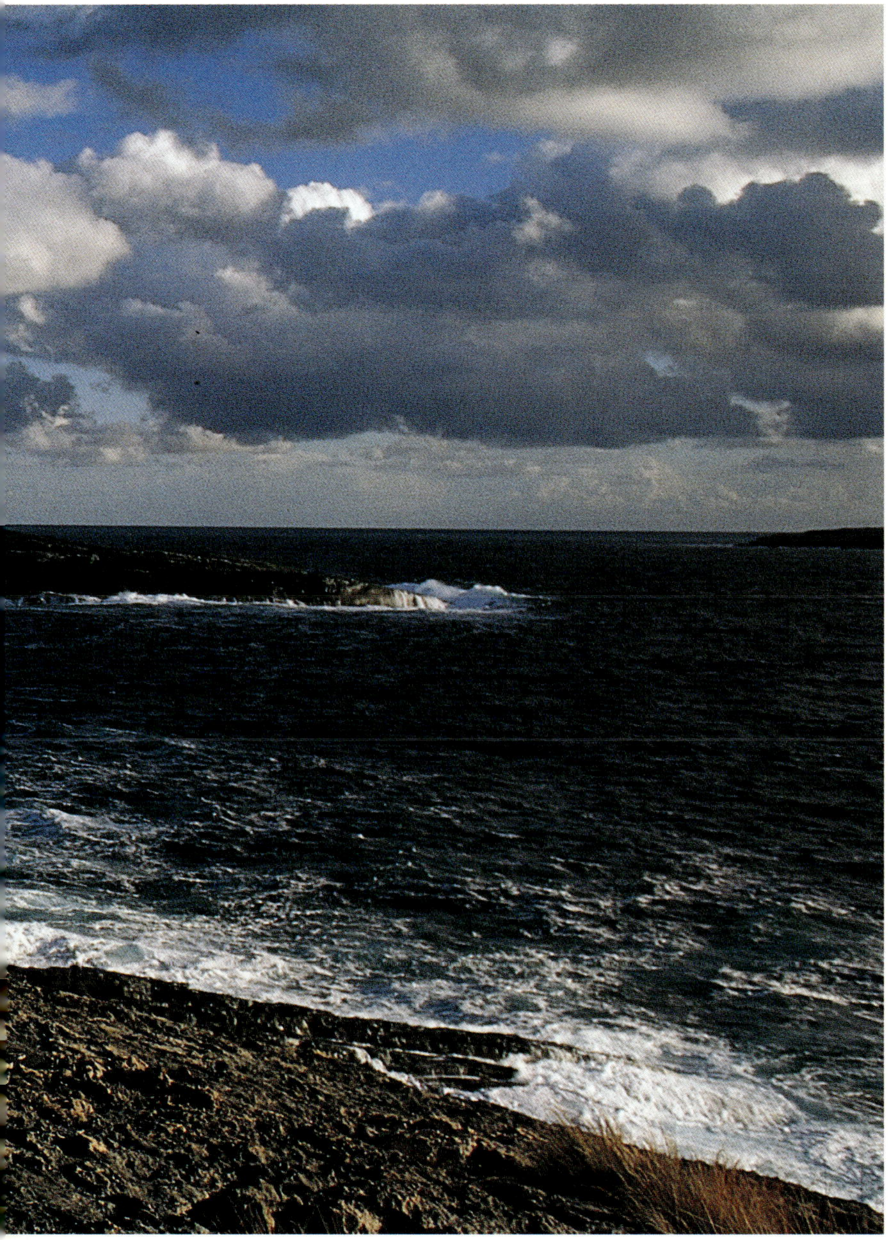

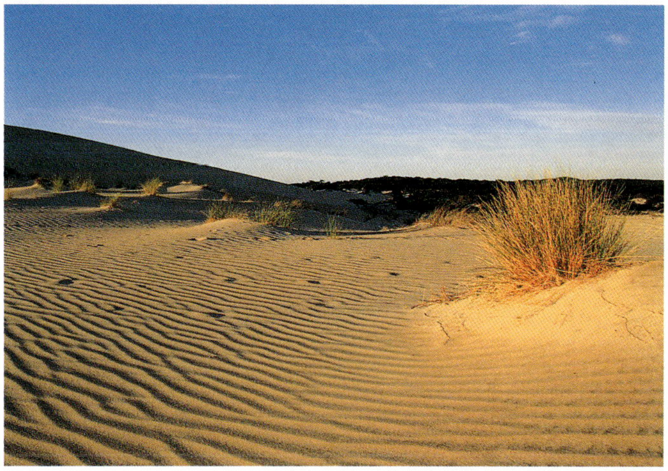

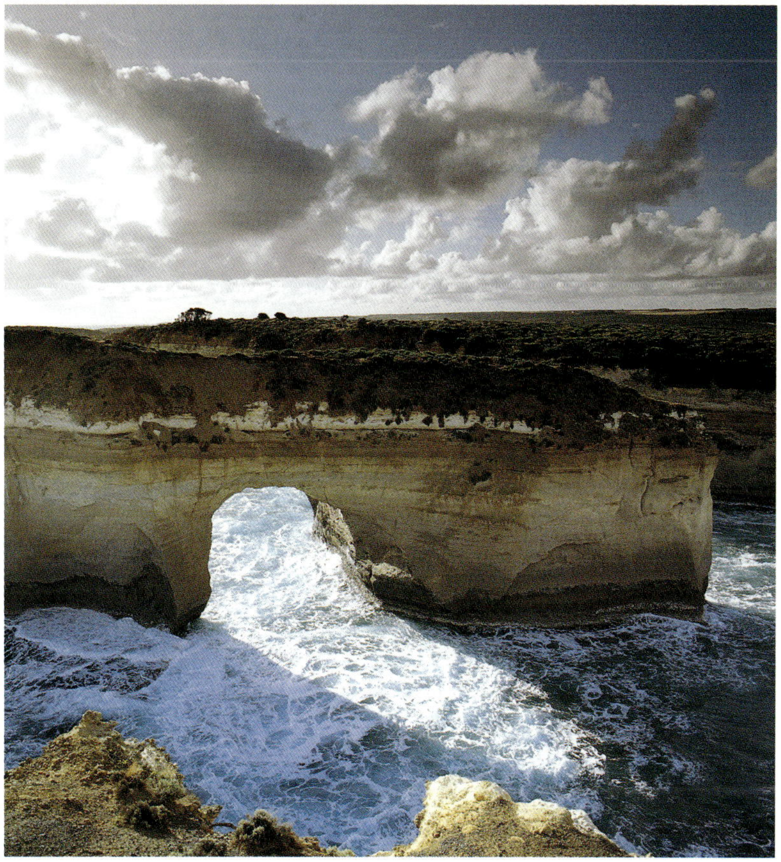

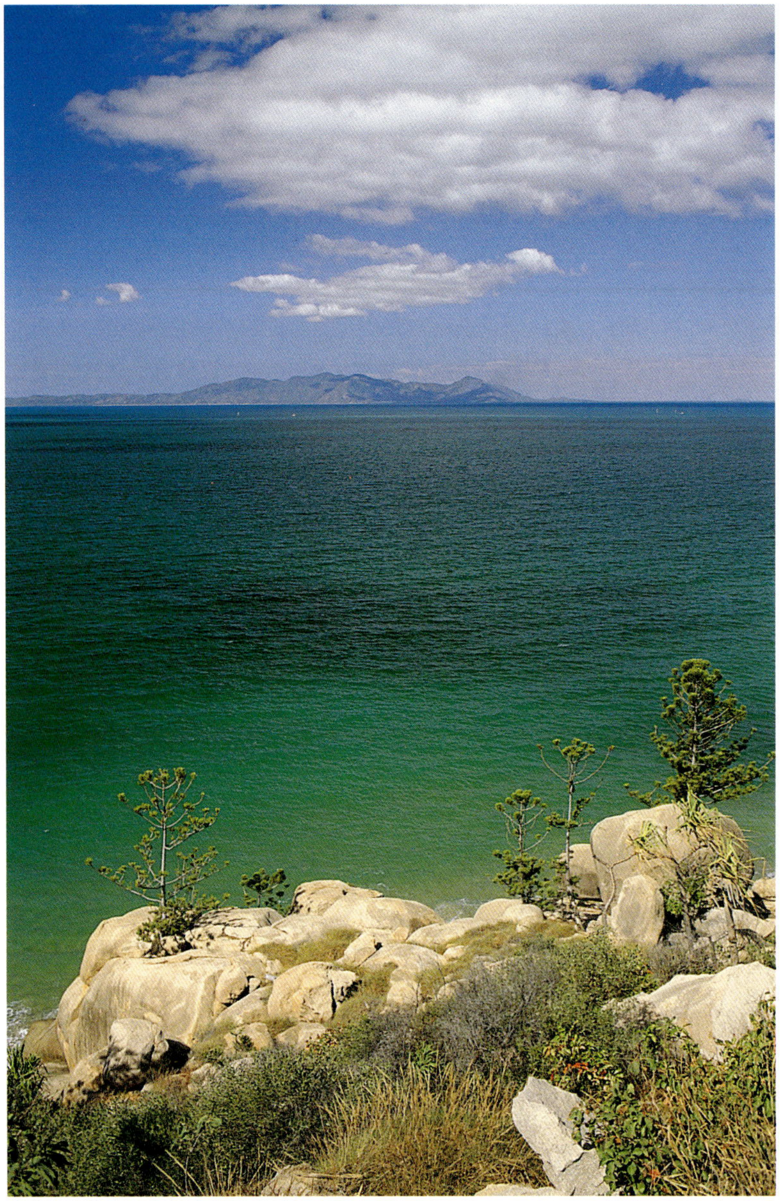

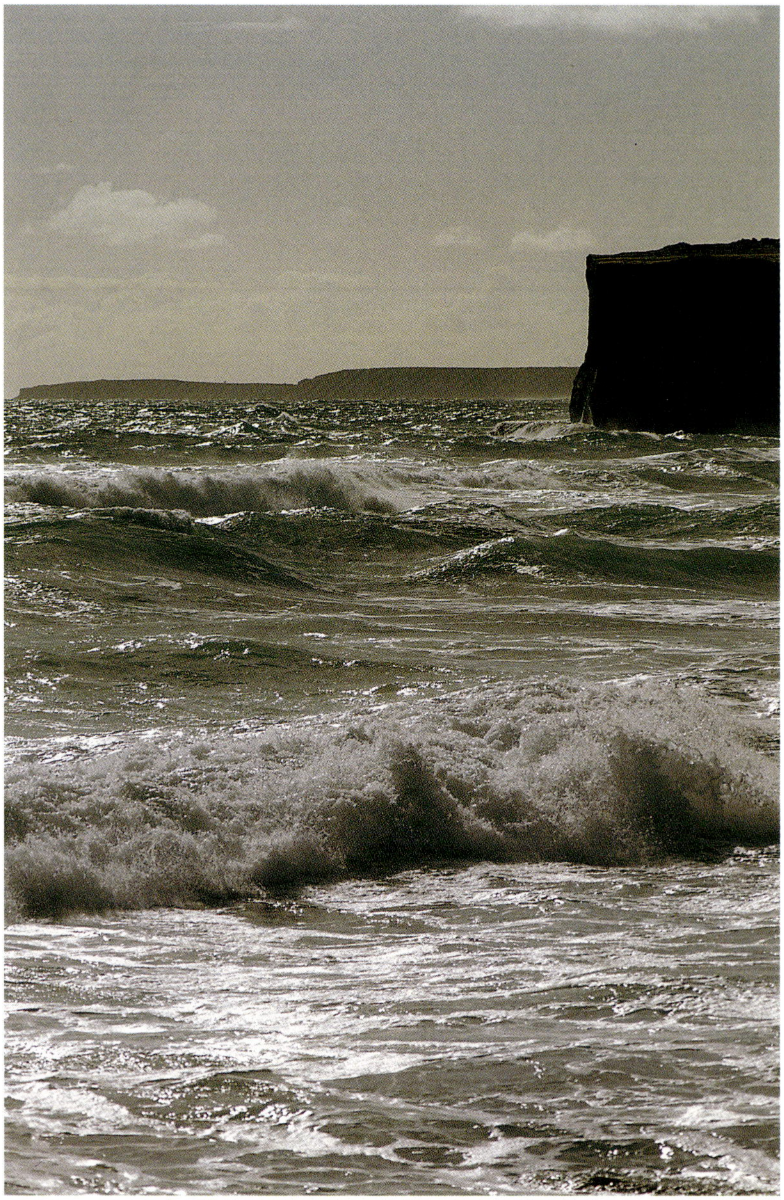

Above left: The turquoise water at Magnetic Island in Queensland is inviting under a typical idyllic sunny sky with only wispy cloud floating overhead.

Above right: The powerful southern sea near Port Campbell washes towards the sheer cliffs, which seem to belong to another, far more chilly continent. In a stormy grey light, the ocean appears even more threatening and forbidding.

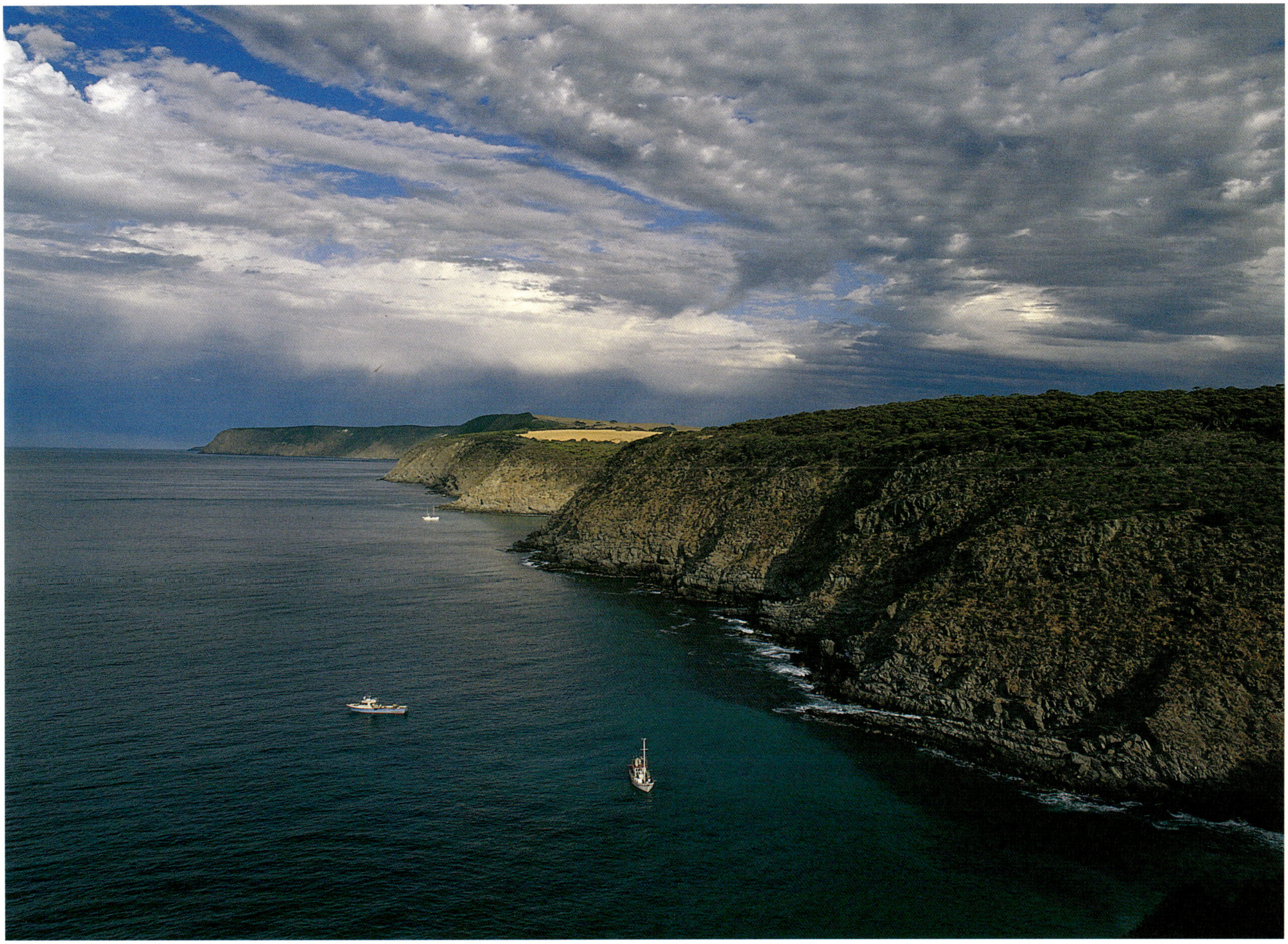

Above: As it stretches far into the distance, the southern coastline's panorama well illustrates the fact that *Scenic Australia* is an island continent washed by seas that range from wispy white through turquoise to the deepest slate blue.

Produced and published in Australia by
New Holland Publishers
3/2 Aquatic Drive, Frenchs Forest
NSW 2086 Australia

ISBN: 1-86436-268-5

Publishing General Manager: Jane Hazell
Publishing Manager: Averill Chase
Designer & Typesetter: Arne Falkenmire
Editor: Joanne Holliman
Production Controller: Paula Leavy
Picture Researchers: Karen Adler, Vicki Hastrich

Reproduced, printed and bound by Toppan Printing Co (S) Pte. Ltd.

Title page: In winter snow covers the alpine area of south-east Australia, and challenges the usual arid-climate image.
Contents page: Inland Australia appears to roll on red forever, like the terrain around the Calder Highway in Victoria.

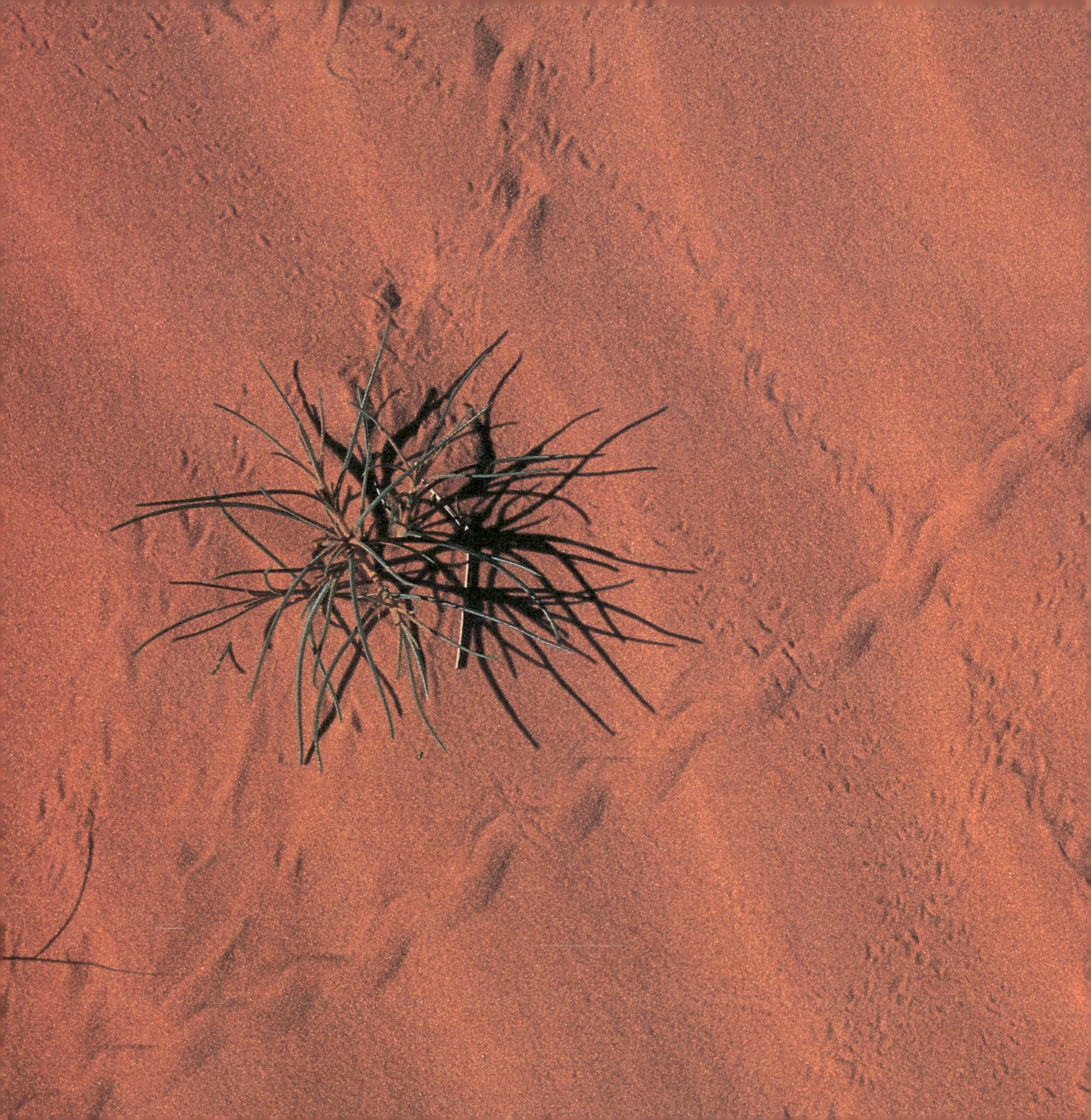